RVing

in Mexico, Central America, and Panamá

Faraway Facts and Feelings

by

Plaxton & Plaxton

Canadian Cataloguing in Publication Data

Plaxton, John, 1941 -
RVing in Mexico, Central America and Panamá

Includes index.

1. Plaxton, John, 1941- --Journeys--Mexico. 2. Plaxton, Elizabeth--Journeys--Mexico. 3.Plaxton, John, 1941- --Journeys--Central America. 4.Plaxton, Elizabeth--Journeys--Central America. 5.Mexico--Description and travel. 6.Central America--Description and travel. 7.Recreational vehicle living--Mexico. 8.Recreational vehicle living--Central America. I.Plaxton, Elizabeth. II.Title.

F1409.3.P62 1996 917.204'835 C95-911191-3

ISBN 0-9680314-0-4

Distributed by **Gordon Soules Book Publishers Ltd.** • 1354-B Marine Drive, West Vancouver BC Canada V7T 1B5
• 620-1916 Pike Place, Seattle WA 98101 US
E-mail: books@gordonsoules.com
Web site: http://www.gordonsoules.com
(604) 922 6588 Fax: (604) 688 5442

Edited by Elizabeth Plaxton & Anne Cabatoff

Photographs by Elizabeth Plaxton

PRINTED IN CANADA

Travel 'N Write

1996

"I sure as H--- wouldn't drive a Class C motorhome through Central America. You've got to be crazy."

Neighbourly Advice

"Mom, Dad, don't leave us . . . At least phone once in a while."

Our Two Youngest Sons

"You should write a book."

Bea Pritchard

"That sounds like just what a traveller needs!"

Leo Roy

"The human side of travelling, not just important facts."

Anonymous

"Whenever I got a letter from John and Liz, everything else was put on hold, immediately."

Pat Regan

"Your articles are so interesting. It's almost as if I were right there with you."

Mia Schaefer

"When you finish your book, write me. I want a copy."

Other RVers

To our children
- Christine, Larry, Bruce and Robert -
whom we missed a lot.
Sometimes.

And
especially
to my loving wife
whose daily diary was a godsend,
whose memories are different from mine,
and who is a good loser and a much better winner.

FOREWORD

We travelled by ourselves, living our mottos "Take a risk, it's more fun." and "We'll go where no RV has gone before." This book, a series of short articles, discusses faraway cities and places Liz and I visited in our Class C motorhome and on my 305cc motorcycle in 1994/95. They include personal incidents—our joys, our frustrations, our accidents—and a few suggestions and directions to important locations such as propane plants, Canadian Consulates, and RV parks.

We began our travels with twenty hours of nighttime Spanish lessons, two text books which we were too lazy to use, and absolutely no understanding of the phonetic basis of Spanish. We could barely understand each other when saying the simplest things. Obviously, during those many months down south, we have learned some español; but even now I doubt we could pass a grade 11 final exam.

We travelled on a monthly budget which was limited by a small annuity, but we soon discovered that having lots of time was much more important than having lots of money, as long as we had *some* money. Whenever we travelled too far and gasoline used up too much of our budget, or we had unusually high repair bills, we would just camp somewhere until we could afford to move on. One back-packer was surprised to discover that it cost us less to travel than it cost him.

Other than our first time in Mexico and Costa Rica, we bought no vehicle or medical insurance. We reasoned that because we had to travel into the middle of each country, while using up half of our allotted visa time before we would be able to buy any insurance, why bother? Fortunately we didn't need any.

Liz and I enjoyed ourselves most of the time. We enjoyed writing this book, and we believe you and your travelling friends will enjoy it too. Maybe one day we'll meet in a highway pullout or in a camping area, and we can listen to your stories about your travels. Hopefully, some of them will have been in the exotic and friendly countries of Mexico, Central America and Panamá.

Hasta Luego.

TABLE OF CONTENTS

Note. The letters in front of the page numbers are the first letter of a section; for example, **H** for **H**onduras.

Letters to an Editor

Mexico

Before you begin . . .

There is a table of contents and an index of city names and interesting places. The index has page numbers that indicate the section or country where a city name appears. You might want to use them when you think to yourself "What did they write about . . . ?", "What will we see if we go to . . . ?", or "Where did I read about that?"

The first article in the first section summarizes our expenses for the eighteen months we were travelling. We travelled cheaply because we had to, but at least we travelled. Other articles discuss some of the things that we would do differently, now that we've been there. Considering how ignorant we were when we started, Liz and I did very well.

The second section contains letters to the editor of "*The* RV Times", a Canadian magazine printed in British Columbia. It is freely available at many Recreational Vehicle (RV) dealerships, as well as several other stores. The first four letters explain how we got started; the others provide a dated, encapsulated overview of our travels. Deletions and editorial changes were made to limit repetition later on in this book.

Each remaining section discusses what we did and what we saw in a specific country. Countries follow in geographical order from North to South. Details for each country are in similar categories, as can be seen in the table of contents.

The articles in each country are in chronological order. Therefore so are our impressions, from initial exuberance to complacent acceptance to ho-hum to UNbeLIEVable! Because we travelled through most countries twice, attitudinal changes might be noticeable.

We've included basic maps, with the hope that some of you will refer to a more detailed atlas, or to the maps you have with you as you travel in these marvellous countries.

If you want to comment on some of the information or misinformation (time changes all things) in this book, your letters will be readdressed to wherever we happen to be. Having driven as far south as we could go on land, in the warm months of 1996 Liz and I are going to drive on land as far north as we can, to

Inuvik, North West Territories. After that, we'll be somewhere else in this old and new and exciting and frustrating and beautiful and interesting world of ours. Full-time RVing is a wonderful lifestyle. Please write to:

John or Elizabeth Plaxton
postal Travel 'N Write
PO Box 21104
Orchard Park Post Office
Kelowna, BC
Canada V1Y 9N8

e-mail: jplaxton@awinc.com
rving@ogopogo.com

Time passes and things change. Exchange rates for local currencies will be different, as will be costs of food, fuel and entertainment. When you visit where we visited, it will not be the same. And your reactions certainly won't be the same as ours; our friends think Liz and I are crazy. They might be right.

But we swam in warm tropical oceans, devoured delicious food not available in Canada, ate juicy fruit that we couldn't even name, climbed Mayan and Olmec pyramids, watched a mother turtle lay her eggs, swam in the Panamá Canal, and sailed the Caribbean in our motorhome. And we wrote and published our first book.

Join us. Hasta Luego.

Getting Ready and Being Prepared

The Bottom Line

Before going into detail about the attractions of each country, Liz and I thought it might be interesting to summarize what this trip cost us. We were having fun and we didn't record every cent or centavo spent. If and when you travel a similar route, your figures will be considerably different because you will have different attitudes, different lifestyles and different equipment than we did.

We estimated that we would need Can$ 1,500 per month, with gasoline being our greatest expense. We also set aside $5,000 for repairs and unknown but expected additional costs. We planned on being away a year, if we came back.

Our total time spent travelling from Kelowna, BC, Canada to Portebelo, Panamá and return was 541 days, or one year, six months and two weeks. Almost half of that time was spent in Mexico.

We travelled 43,255 kilometres; travelling in Mexico and the USA accounted for more than half that distance. There was no relationship between days and kilometres spent in any one country; driving conditions were just too variable. We used a motorcycle (without a speedometer) and shanks-mare and public transportation to get around and sightsee whenever we parked for more than a couple of days.

Even now Liz and I still think that Panamá is so very far away. And yet there are many people in Victoria, Winnipeg, Toronto, Montréal, Halifax and other cities who travel much more than that distance in a year and a half, and they never leave their own province. We travelled a mere 28,835 km or 17,690 miles per year.

Our vehicle consumed approximately 15,863 litres of gasoline which cost $9,238.94, for an average of $0.58/L. Our average gas consumption was 2.73 km/L. Each kilometre cost $0.21 for gasoline, plus a little more for oil, brakes, spark plugs, etc. Gasoline was our absolutely greatest recurring expense. Next time we go we'll have a diesel engine and cut our costs to about half of that!

We bought a Can$ 625.00 awning for our motorhome so we could be outside during the rainy season. It was used almost exclusively as a parasol, or sunshade.

Oh yes indeed, we did have mechanical problems. A blocked transmission cooler forced us to buy a $1100 reconditioned transmission. A two-cent clip slipped off its shaft and we had to replace a $1200 refrigerator. A hydraulic hose wore through and a Ford dealer was $125 richer. On good highway, blacktop with potholes, dirt roads, and cobblestone paths we wore out and tore up seven Load Range D tires which cost more than $100 each to replace. One good looking but defective part caused five brake failures and reduced our bank balance by at least $450 while raising our blood pressure by a fifth of that amount.

Minor repairs to our living area were just that, minor. Fortunately, I had brought my tools and could fix all those problems myself. Almost anything I needed I could get, eventually. Screws and bolts and wire and duct tape and scraps of wood and metal probably came to less than $100.

We had medical expenses as well, mainly as a result of three motorcycle accidents. Total cost for surgery, anti-inflammatory pills and antibiotic prescriptions was $489.77. We recovered $48.60 from our out-of-country insurance, which cost an additional $680 above and beyond the $384 provincial medicare payments. Insurance companies won that round.

The insurer of our motorhome and motorcycle in Mexico took $835 and kept it all. We chose to have no insurance in Central America, and didn't need it.

Food costs were $5,260 for groceries and snacks plus $1,970 for restaurant meals. In other words, for $400 per month Liz and I ate well but not luxuriously.

Entertainment—live theatre, park fees, museums, etc.—was a mere $760. There were many free activities well worth seeing. In Mexico, almost all government-sponsored tourist attractions are free on Sundays.

Cost of souvenirs was less than $700. We would have spent much more if we could have foreseen the significant increase in Canadian Customs and Duty allowances. Ah well.

Clothing replacements, T-shirts, swimming suits, shorts, purses, shoe and sandal repairs, new sun glasses, watch batteriesand I don't know what else came to $1192.

I lost US $20 when my wallet disappeared in Guatemala. A thief grabbed a gold chain from around Liz's neck; fortunately she found a more expensive one in Huatulco beach sand. I foolishly left a pair of wet running shoes and shorts outside overnight and, naturally, they disappeared. $90 would more than replace anything we lost, except a pair of prescription glasses I left behind in a phone booth.

We think the real thieves were those persons who bilked tourists and non-tourists whenever they crossed into their country. Only twice did I get receipts for more than one half of what I had to pay to go from one country to another. Border crossings were the only frustration that would deter me from going back to Central America.

Two South Americans we met were disgusted; they thought European border crossing and customs were bad, until they travelled through Central America. Mexican border crossings are straight forward, honest and quick.

Except for El Salvador we entered and left each country twice. Not once were the costs the same. With our two vehicles, and including costs for necessary visas, all border crossings came to a total of $773.16, or a meaningless average of approximately Can$ 65.00 each. Arguing politely saves money.

One or two policemen in every country tried to put the bite on us, but only two succeeded because we had definitely screwed up. Total cost was $38.50, which was much less than the fines would have been. However, most policemen and policewomen were extremely helpful and courteous!

Finally, we spent a few hundred on odds and sods, this and that, and a few things like telephone calls, faxes, postage, photocopying, a short wave radio, sidewalk vendors, gifts to locals, and surprises to each other. And other things we have simply forgotten about.

In a year and a half, Liz and I spent between $30,000 - $31,000, or about $1,650 per month. We were slightly over budget but we enjoyed every extra penny. And with naturally selective hindsight, we enjoyed every minute as well.

Things we would do differently

Because we often would be driving in mountainous valleys on twisting roads, I thought a powerful 7.5L engine would be ideal. However, now I'd prefer to have a five-litre diesel engine. It would provide sufficient power while using less fuel. Diesel fuel costs about two-thirds that of gasoline. I seldom drove over 80 km/hr, even on level highways.

Liz and I hate driving into cities, and we always left refilling our permanent propane tank until the last possible moment. We ran out once. A spare ten-litre bottle would have been useful, and small enough to store. In addition, we would've needed an adaptor hose to connect to our system.

An outdoor propane stove would also have been a blessing on hot, calm days, as most were. Cooking inside made our over-the-cab bedroom scorching hot. Sometimes we sweat so much that we had to wash sheets every second day.

If in Texas, and possibly other states, I'll make sure to keep receipts for everything we buy. Then just before we leave for Mexico, I'll go back to those stores and fill in State forms that give me an exporter's discount.

Because trailer parks were almost nonexistent in Central America, there were times when we had to dump on the side of a side road, near or in a garbage heap when possible. Dumping grey water was never a problem, the locals do that all the time in front of their homes. Dumping black water always bothered me, but amazingly, within minutes of dumping black water on the ground, the smell is gone. Nevertheless, I would go out of our way to use baños or servicios or public bathrooms in tourist centres whenever possible. I had to dump into a bucket then carry the bucket to a toilet. Next time I'll have an airtight bucket; the smell was awful. We'll also buy some air freshener.

I'm going to weld or bolt a small metal vice onto the steel back bumper. I used a pair of vice grips to clamp small items tightly, but bigger items were impossible. There always seems to be something that needs to be drilled or filed.

Things we wished we had taken along.

Even though Liz and I had three or four months to prepare for our trip to Mexico and Central America, and even though we talked with RVers, there are several additional items that we should have brought with us.

We should have brought several maps and postcards and pictures of Canada to give away.

We should have brought along one or two handfuls of wire or plastic bag ties. Production of plastic bags seems to be a primary industry in Central America, but there are no reusable ties.

We had several well-sealed plastic containers. We bought more to keep ants and weevils out of foods such as porridge, sugar, flour, crackers and pasta.

We finally purchased a 19L container of purified water for drinking. Even though it's light plastic, a full jug is a heavy, awkward container to lift and tip without spills. An electric pump or a hand pump is a necessity.

Central American grapefruit are very juicy. Without a simple little curved knife that cuts around the edges and lops off the stem, that juice often ends up on the table, my clothes and my glasses. We should have had a grapefruit knife.

Before crossing into Mexico again, we'll also stock up with as much beef as possible. Mexican beef is very lean and tough, unless you can find beef for export. However, Mexico provides great pork products such as bacon, smoked pork chops and sliced ham for sandwiches.

Although Mexico makes several excellent cheeses, we'd take along a lot of Canadian cheddar cheese, and a few bottles of soft, spreadable cheese.

We'll take lots of canned goods too. Many selections are available, but they're priced at about double what they cost in Canada.

I'm going to buy lots of peanuts and chocolate bars and raisins. Liz is going to store away a ton of potato chips and dip for her occasional junk food attacks.

Locked into the chuck of my rechargeable battery-powered drill and placed inside a two-litre plastic jug, a paint mixer attachment makes a great substitute for a blender.

I brought the tools and duct tape but forgot the nails, screws and bolts. Minor repairs are an annoying reality. Even more so, is the fact that hundreds of those cheap but useful pieces were stored back home.

Long hoses and electrical cords are essential. Several times I had to use two of each to stretch out to 33 m (100'). I'd change to the heaviest gauge (smallest number) possible for longer electrical cords.

It would have been nice to use a small, powerful 12V vacuum to clean cab seats and motorhome cushions, as well as being able to suck up the dust in those hidden corners at the back of cupboards.

A windshield cover was great for keeping solar rays from damaging or fading the dash and seat covers. More important, it kept the motorhome cooler. We were forced to make our own.

Picnic tables are few and far between. We should have brought a fold-down or take-apart plastic table. Salt from the oceans wouldn't rust it.

Extra folding stools were great for unexpected company. They're better than chairs because boring guests soon tire and leave. Stools can also be used as small side tables.

A solid garden rake is handy for removing buried glass and metal from beach sand around a trailer.

A toilet plunger is a useful tool to help with washing clothes because it pushes the water about marvellously inside a large bucket. Of course, if I had a built-in washer I wouldn't have to reinvent the machinery of my grandmother.

We brought a Coleman lamp with us, and used it several times. I should have brought along four litres of white gas; lamps there use kerosene. Mixing equal parts of white gas and unleaded gasoline worked well. Using only unleaded gasoline worked too, but the light is yellowish.

Computer paper and many other computer accessories are available, but expensive. If you have a computer, bring everything you might need.

Letters to an Editor

Kelowna, BC, Canada
June 1993

Dear Sheila;

My wife and I are going to buy our first 23-26 foot motorhome. We will live in it for about a year as we meander to Costa Rica, stay for several months, and return to Beautiful BC.

But there are so many questions! What do we look for when buying?

Should we buy a used vehicle from a dealer, or from an individual and save GST? Should we buy a vehicle that is 5, 10 or 15 years old? At what mileage can we expect to start having troubles with used engines and power trains? Which vehicles are better than others? Are Class A's really worth the extra money when compared to Class C's of the same length? Is it difficult to attach a mount or rail for a 305-cc motorcycle? Which are the best engines (long lasting, efficient, or both): GMC, Ford, Chrysler, Gas, Diesel, Propane? Realistically, what kind of mileage costs can we expect? How much insurance is enough, and how much extra will be needed in Mexico and Central America?

We think you get the idea. Two more questions, which may be much more practical, are: (1) How do we get a Buyer's Book on Motorhomes, much like the annual Consumer's Report on cars? and (2) Where do we get a checklist for things to look for, and lookout for, when buying a motorhome?

John & Liz Plaxton

Kelowna, BC
August 1993

Dear Sheila,

Liz and I were pleasantly surprised to receive a phone call and two letters offering advice on buying a motorhome. We had no idea our letter would be published.

First came the phone call from George, ex-RV Times editor, and we have set up a chat luncheon. Then came an informative letter from Debbie Paulin of the RV Dealers Association of BC which included issues of two magazines and a list of available publications. On the fourth day, Denys Prosser sent along a very informative letter and a photocopy of some of his lecture material. Many thanks to all of them.

While trying to get a Costa Rica video from our local library, we met a woman whose parents have travelled to Central America every year for eleven years. Sadly, we never managed to meet with them.

RVers must be something special, and we think we'll be glad to become one of them. Once again, thanks for all the help and kind words of encouragement.

Kelowna, BC
August 1993

Being prepared is hard work!
(Are we Having Fun Yet?)

WE DID IT! We made the decision to travel through Central America for a year. And we bought our first motorhome. But did we do the right thing, did we make the right decisions?

Before we bought, we set a maximum price and stuck to it. That was hard because there are so many features that cost only a couple of hundred dollars more.

We looked at trailers for six weeks, starting off with Class Cs, then As, then fifth-wheels or fivers, then back to Cs. Although it was a hectic and pressured six weeks, we're glad we took the time. We almost bought on the second day and that would have been a mistake. Later, we saw two trailers dealer-listed at $20,000 which we had looked at privately when they were $15,000; obviously that's how they get their bargaining power. We asked a lot of questions, which got better and more pointed, and listened to several dealers, most of whom were very helpful.

When we finally saw a motorhome that we liked that was in our price range, we took it on the highway and gravelled roads to test for squeaks. We even drove it onto federal weigh scales to check its weight and balance, at no cost.

The trailer we have now is not overweight, but almost so when liquid-filled and closet-filled and food-loaded and motorcycle-mounted. Our motorcycle had to go on front in order to maintain a proper weight and balance ratio.

There is no cab air conditioning so airflow past our motorcycle shouldn't be a problem.

I crawled over and under every part of the vehicle. Then I had the top of the motorhome inspected by an RV parts and repair business. The lower part was inspected in a garage where mechanics could raise it off the floor to check brakes and bearings. It was $170 well spent (because we then knew what additional costs we could expect), cheap insurance (our first choice didn't pass the test), and more than recovered (our RV dealer didn't have to make any checks or do propane certification).

We bought a clean 1979 Security 23' Class C with (1) a permanently made-up, extra-long, queen-sized foam bed over the cab, (2) one large, airy, three-windowed living/dining room+kitchen over the dual wheels and (3) a large washroom in the rear. I had a dry shower without hitting my head or arms; Liz "made" our bed and we "slept" in it. The RV-body sits on a chassis that seems longer than most, and which rests on extra-wide 16.5" tires. The whole thing is powered by a Ford 7.5L (460 cubic inches) gas-guzzler. It would be cheaper to fly to Costa Rica, but we would miss the adventure and those terrifying drivers.

Many minor repairs were completed in one weekend. Whoever wired those extra lights and CB did not know what he/she was doing. I refused to work on the propane system because that is a job for those who are qualified. None was needed.

To be on the safer side, we also bought a duplicate set of keys (one mounted in the motorcycle), a complete set of belts, filters, lights, fuses, and a long pressure gauge to test those inner tires. We scraped and resealed the roof and several windows in preparation for tropical rains. We replaced locks on external storage areas, and we will be carrying levelling blocks, jumper cables, an extra jack, tow cable and a "come-along". In case we get contaminated fuel, we bought an additional propane regulator and even installed a second gas-line filter with manual bypass.

Being proud of our country, we also bought a Canadian flag to hang from our awning, got a Canada wheel cover for the spare tire, and painted a Maple Leaf on our roof so that airborne traffic police would know we were tourists. We also got a lot of Canadian Flag pins to hand out.

We agree when we hear "buy longer than you think you need" but nevertheless we settled on 23' because we want maneuverability to travel winding narrow back roads without swinging our rear end into oncoming traffic. (How else do we get to see those really spectacular vistas, and maybe even some Bandidos or Contras?) My major concern is having to get up in the middle of the night to let Liz visit the loo; she won't sleep on the outside in case she falls out of the over-cab bed.

The quiet 7.5L engine provides ample power for climbing mountains; there are a lot of them en route. Because it was built before all that computerized, fuel-saving, antipollution gear was invented, even I and a backwoods mechanic can work on the engine if need be.

The dual traction tires (snow tires) will help in the mud of rain forests. Because 16.5" rims were once used on older military vehicles, they might be readily available down south [Note: They weren't.] We've had all six wheels balanced, and what a pleasure it is to float over blacktop. Now we'll have to buy a vibrating recliner chair in which to relax.

We got a phone call on August 25 from a pleasant fellow in Langley, who mentioned that he had read our first letter and that he had a motorcycle mount with headlights, built for a Ford 250/350. Would I be interested? I was (just how lucky can one couple be, the exact vehicle we bought) so we arranged to meet in Merritt. It was an ingenious work of art and engineering at a fair price, so we bought it.

We insured our rig until the end of November. Thereafter we should be in Mexico where Canadian insurance is invalid. BC provincial insurance will accept a fax renewal and credit-card payment upon our return to the USA next year. Hmm . . . what will be our forwarding address for those new tags?

BCAA has some affiliations in Mexico [Note: When in Mexico we couldn't find any, but we didn't need them anyway.] BCAA Travel Gold coverage was recommended by a well-travelled RVer. Supplemental medical coverage is good for a maximum of 365 days, and can be renewed only in Canada. Once only (perhaps more, each situation is reviewed) BC Medical Services Plan will provide reduced out-of-country coverage for a year, provided premiums are paid.

We decided to sell our house rather than rent it. After all, we might need money to pay off medical bills or hostage ransom, or to buy land near the Equator. But that has created an interesting dilemma. What is our Canadian residence for income tax purposes, and our address for forms at international borders? At least our passports and birth certificates will prove we are Canadians.

Before we were even sure we were going to buy a motorhome, we joined an international RV club and got membership cards, etc. the week after we bought our rig.

It's been six weeks since our international phone call, and still we've not received a parcel from the Canadian Embassy in San José; we were warned that mail would be slow. We're just now getting in contact with the various foreign embassies and consulates located here in Canada. Nothing to report yet, but we are looking forward to some good information and suggestions.

On a different note, like several other travellers, I too will be taking along a portable computer. It will be used to keep a diary for our book, and to send letters and disks to family and friends, and to The RV Times.

The portable runs on 12V batteries because there will be many days when 110V AC is not available. We don't have a generator, but we do have more storage space. The computer must be small enough to fit in one cupboard, along with printer, paper, disks and references.

Because I already have a small dot matrix printer, printing must be done when 110V is available.

Having to go back to DOS programs is a severe sacrifice, much more so than our moving from a five-bedroom house into a motorhome that is smaller than our kitchen. But at least my big computer will be there when we get back. Oh me, oh my, the challenges we computer-holics have to face.

Well . . . We did our homework, made some tough choices, and fixed up our new-to-us motorhome. We've agreed to expect the unexpected, have agreed to not hear the occasional four letter word and prayers to a loving or vengeful deity. We'll study Spanish mañana.

Liz and I are ready, nervous, excited, impatient. Look out USA, Mexico, Belize, Guatemala, Nicaragua, El Salvador, Honduras, Costa Rica and Panama. The Plaxton's are loose and running amuck. Let the fun begin.

Kelowna, BC
November 1993

Dear Sheila;

I'm almost embarrassed to write this letter. "The best laid plans of mice and men gang oft aglay." We are still in Canada because our house hasn't sold. The market came to a sudden halt the day after we listed, which was the day that national television broadcast that our city has the fourth highest housing costs in Canada. Departure for Central America is now scheduled for Spring 1994. Ah well. Now there's time to receive letters from embassies and consulates that have yet to respond.

What a let down to have to unload the tiny, artificial Christmas tree, the miniature lights, the Santa Claus napkins, and couple of seasonal tapes and store them back in our home.

Kelowna, BC
December 1993

Dear Sheila;

We have sold our house and home, following an offer that couldn't be refused. It was made nine days after taking our house off the market, and two days after beginning a new job.

While in BCAA offices in Kelowna, I bought an interesting book entitled "Central America by Chicken Bus" by Vivien Lougheed. It tells us a lot more than the consulates and embassies did. Maybe we should write a book too. For example, having extra passport photos and photocopies of one's passport can speed up some border crossings. Practising for those southern market places, I managed to barter them down a couple of bucks, which paid for the GST. Yea, soon no more GST!

Because of the probability of not having 110V easily accessible in many places we are going to visit, Liz bought a 12V DC curling iron and I got a 12V soldering iron. I couldn't find a 12V or Butane clothes iron, so we'll have to travel in wrinkled cotton.

Recently I learned that Canadians should not send stamped letters to Central America. It seems that many letters are stolen for our beautiful stamps. If you want to improve the probability of your letters getting through, use a postal meter.

An important reminder. When you are going to leave your homeland for a long time, make sure your driver's licence doesn't expire while you're travelling. You could end up marooned behind a dilapidated old garage in the middle of nowhere, hiding from State Police or Federales, and living on 110V stolen via an illegal screw-in light bulb extender with a built-in socket.

In January, I'll remove that handcuff of time; the watch battery can go dead for all I care. Then we'll rush through the USA and zip into those warm countries to the South.

Our dream of travelling to Latin America has come true.

Washington, USA
January 1994

Dear Sheila;

When we sold the house, we had to move out in mid-December. Christmas wasn't so bad because our kids had to host us for a change. Liz prepared the big meal, using pots and pans and dishes she was used to. Somehow they all showed up in the kids' apartments.

We sold our car on the night before the morning we left. With events happening right down to the wire, I should have an ulcer.

We crossed into the USA a day later than planned. Mi God, two days on the road and we're a day behind already. Sheesh. We couldn't get our passports stamped because customs agent, P.T. "Jerk" refused, even though we needed dated proof for medical coverage.

We are on our way. Southward Ho.

Northern Mexico
11 marzo 1994

Dear Sheila;

I hope that RVers who travel through Chihuahua will consider setting aside at least a week to visit Creel, Batopilas and the Copper Canyon. We saw it when it was dry and dusty, but we were still impressed. Imagine what it would be like just a couple of weeks after a rainy season.

Our trailer and motorcycle are working well, thanks to several ideas forwarded by the readers and contributors to your magazine.

Because a rusted old hydraulic line suffered an aneurysm, we suddenly lost our brakes in the midst of morning traffic in Culiacán. It was hard to breathe when my thumping heart was high up in my throat. But four hours and Can$ 37.00 later they were fixed and we were on our way. The Mexicans were most helpful. One young man spent an hour with us, even accompanying us to a garage. It's nice to see a reality that poo-poos horror stories. Also, in Batopilas I went back to a grocery store and was handed change as I walked in; it seems that I had overpaid the day before with the wrong coins.

That's all for now. It looks like we'll spend about three or four months in Mexico; we can't afford the gasoline needed to travel those many miles to the Guatemala border in a hurry. Time is free but the monthly budget is fixed, so we'll drive a little and park a lot.

Acapulco, Mexico
20 mayo 1994

Dear Sheila;

Our old refrigerator failed about four weeks ago. Overheated, it vented ammonia gas and liquid from the pressure relief valve and it doesn't work anymore, cause unknown.

Acapulco was the last of four cities—Manzanillo, Guadalajara, and Colima being the others—where we tried to repair our fridge. Once again, Liz and I hopped on our Kawasaki 305 and drove around the centre of a city, checking out addresses we got from a phone book. We've discovered that phoning just doesn't work when we have a problem. Because we can't speak the language, we have to go and talk face to face.

Eventually we visited Refrigeración Nieto de Acapulco where the staff spent a full hour phoning around to various stores and businesses asking if anyone could help two Canadian tourists. Finally, success. We needed an hour to drive across town to a milk pasteurization and packaging plant—Leche LaLa—where they spent almost two more hours trying to help us. Unfortunately, they just didn't have the equipment to install ammonia into a small refrigerator. Everyone tried hard, and we really appreciated their efforts.

So, if you get tired of hearing horror stories about Mexicans, remember this one. Or mention that a young Mexican man gave us a prepaid Latadel card so we could use a phone that wouldn't take coins, and that he seemed insulted when I offered to give it back or pay him.

But now for the rest of the story.

My beautiful beloved will not travel for a year without being able to keep food refrigerated or frozen. Besides, our Styrofoam box just hasn't done a good job of keeping beer cool in this tropical heat, which forces me to agree with her. So much for our pioneer spirit.

We are now heading back to Texas, USA to get our fridge fixed or replaced. Because our journey is our destination, we will be travelling where neither of us has gone before. Spending an extra two months in Mexico is certainly not a hardship, but we do regret the delay in taking Spanish lessons in Antigua, Guatemala.

Oh, we'll get to Guatemala and Central America yet. We just don't know when, and we don't care.

Guatemala
26 agosto 1994

Dear Sheila;

"I'll kick when I've had enough." Liz meant it too, because half an hour later a sharp rap on my shins and a "You can play Boggle with me now!" reminded me I do have a very understanding wife, up to a point. This particular point occurred as I was nonstop halfway through the fifth back issue of your magazine.

Thanks for sending them to the consulate in Guatemala City. Not having a short wave radio (dumb, dumb) I was feeling the need for some Canadian news. Who did win the Stanley Cup? What federal budget?

I particularly enjoyed the article and comments about converting or inverting 110V AC to 12V DC or vice versa. But as you know, Liz and I use 12V for everything electrical, which suits us fine because many times 110 VAC isn't available.

An article about battery water level was timely. Although I often check both batteries under the hood, I had forgotten about the extra RV battery in a storage compartment. Yep, it needed water. Not the local hard water which will kill a battery quicker than a Fer de Lance, but distilled battery water.

For our type of travelling, water for drinking and washing is more important than electricity. I'm glad we decided to use our large compartment for storage and not to buy an expensive and heavy generator.

Is there a company that produces an electrically-powered air conditioner that can double as a heater? Often a short burst of warmth is all that is required to get rid of the morning chill, and to convince me that I really should get out from under my warm comforter. It can be cool up here at 1750 m (5500') above sea level, even in the tropics.

Wheeling Safely into the Outback" struck a responsive nerve. Mexicans and Central Americans have expressed so much concern about our safety that I have become paranoic, even though nothing has happened to us. I've crisscrossed the rear window (easily accessible via bumper and ladder) with barbed wire, put screws into the sills to prevent sliding windows from being opened any more than four inches, put interior sliding locks on the cab doors, slipped pieces of drinking straw around the push-in buttons on the no-draft windows, and mounted pins to prevent the door locks from moving upward. The side door already has a two-inch dead-bolt, as well as the usual handle lock. I feel better but, in truth, locks only keep honest people honest. If someone wants in badly enough, he or she will get in somehow.

Which is why I've rigged up two switches to the horn. One is by my foot when I'm driving. When I get stopped by the police I can always turn on the horn (accidently) and maybe they'll go away. The other is beside our over-the-cab bed and can be flicked on while we are in bed or sitting at the dining room table.

Fortunately, violent crime against tourists is quite rare in this part of the world, mordida or "the bite" has been the only attempt at taking what belongs to us. We feel safer here than in Canada or the United States!

I truly enjoyed your venture into the Yucatan: it brought back some fond memories. Palenque is great, but you really should have bluffed the border guards and gone to Tikal, which is fabulous.

Sheila, maybe in another six months or so, you can send the latest back issues to the consulate in Panamá. We should be there by then, unless we get sidetracked by golden beaches, zoological jungle preserves, lush rain forests, flaming volcanoes, teak plantations, or just friendly people who ask us to stay for another day or two.

El Salvador
07 noviembre 1994

Dear Sheila;

Liz is fine.

In fact, as the first anniversary of our departure for Mexico and Central America draws nigh, I find it difficult to imagine my enjoying this trip as much with anyone else.

Two weeks ago, we were camping in a real trailer park next to a burnished-pewter Pacific beach near El Cuco in southeast El Salvador. I was practising stops and turns on the moist, hard-packed sands when our motorcycle decided to get even for all the mistreatment I've given it.

I write this with my knee on a footstool and my foot up on the opposite dinette seat, keeping the blood pressure as low as practical because of a sliced artery and a swollen, motorcycle induced 3 1/2" gash above my left ankle. It required 15 stitches as well as several anti-inflammatory and penicillin pills. The other cuts and burns were minor. I received excellent medical service out there in the boondocks.

But I refused to sit still and infection set in. We had to get some very powerful pills from a doctor in San Salvador, and now I am sitting still.

We're drycamped in a paved parking lot in Turicentro Apulo, only a few kilometres from the capital San Salvador. We've just finished enjoying an excellent El Salvadorean national dish called Pupusas, which must be prepared by hand and cooked on a wood stove. They are small but thick tortillas, stuffed with cheese and meat or beans, and topped with delicious, home-made pickled coleslaw. We sometimes smother them in a thick, barely-sour cream.

This will be a different holiday season for us, and it would sure be nice to have our kids tenting beside us. However, alone together among green trees and palms, Liz and I wouldn't change a thing. We can't have and do everything, so we have chosen to fulfill a decade of dreams. Maybe someone will make a snow-man for us, and dress him in a bathing suit, sunglasses and a straw hat.

Merry Christmas and a Happy New Year.

Muy Feliz Navidad y Feliz Año Nuevo!

Are we having fun yet? You'd better believe it!

Nicaragua
04 enero1995

Dear Sheila;

Christmas and New Year's Day were spent parked in front of, and in, the home of a Canadian couple who are working for CIDA for the re-electrification of Nicaragua.

Say hi to all your readers for us. When are some of those full timers going to drive on down to Central America? It is a worthy and worthwhile challenge, and a lot more exciting than Mexico.

All countries have several special places. Honduras is my favourite; Liz prefers Guatemala.

My brother retired last August, and he and his wife completed an Alberta to Prince Edward Island to Alberta trip by camper-van. He travelled 18,000 km in 2 months; we've travelled a mere 22,000 km in 11 months. I have to laugh because he thinks we're great travellers.

Costa Rica
16 febrero 1995

Dear Sheila;

Sorry for the delay, but it has been very difficult to find a place where I can plug into 110 V AC, which I need for my printer. I would never inflict my hand scratching on you.

Honduras, Nicaragua and Costa Rica have necessitated lots of drycamping. A couple of trailer parks we did find weren't worth the money.

January 12 was the first anniversary of our travels to and through Central America. Liz and I spent that sunny day reading in lovely, quiet San Juan del Sur, Nicaragua while being covered by small, non-biting bugs from the branches above. We had our laundry done by someone else, telephoned Canadá, and strolled along another clean Pacific beach to restaurant Playa Azul for a lobster supper. It was just another casual day.

How quickly time travels when we're having fun. A year and three weeks have gone by and we still haven't seen everything we want to. I guess we'll just have to drive through all those countries again.

Bad news. Because we entered and will return to Costa Rica within three months with a vehicle, any vehicle, we will be allowed only a 3-day transit visa for the second visit. And because of many curves, high hills and deep dales (thank you, 7.5L engine), it will take us most of those three days.

There is a small probability of our trying a Caribbean ferry from Panamá to Costa Rica, which could be interesting.

Good News. A ferry service from Colón, Panamá to Cartagena, Columbia was inaugurated in November 1994. Now drivers can stay with their vehicle when it's shipped around the impassable Darian Gap. Bad News. Vehicles cannot return to Panamá by ferry. Motorhomes must make a one-way trip to South America, or return home by other means or destinations.

Panamá
3 marzo 1995

Dear Sheila;

WE DID IT! We drove over the Bridge of the Americas and the Panamá Canal.

Then we continued on to fabulous Portobelo, signed on as line handlers for a 43-foot sloop, and sailed through the Canal, stopping overnight for a refreshing swim with the crocodiles in Gatun Lake. Travelling south EAST to get from the Atlantic to the Pacific Ocean is an unnerving experience for an ex-air-navigator.

Then we sailed the dark blue Caribbean atop of our motorhome, spending four exploratory hours meandering through mangrove swamps and isolated fishing hamlets.

Leaving the ferry behind, we crossed the Panamá-Costa Rica border by straddling the rails of a noisy, old, single-track railroad bridge. In response to our questions, we were only the second rig to struggle through Sixaola in the last few years.

After a quick three days transit through Costa Rica—a stupid and expensive rule—we are now resting at Playa Pochomil on the Pacific side of Nicaragua. We're loaded down with two miniature oxcarts, several hammocks, a massive rocking chair, a few T-shirts, miscellaneous knickknacks, and 13 envelopes of pictures. Of course, there will be more souvenirs; we know what we want from each country we are going to revisit.

Although we had been planning to return in late fall we'll have to travel faster than expected—double time, hup, hup—because our son is getting married in August. But that's okay. Although we left sites and sights unseen in each country, we are beginning to get the feeling that we'd like to be back in Canada right now. Of course, after a week or two of seeing family and friends, we'll probably want to be back on the road.

During the last nine months we've seen a Class A and C from Ontario, another A from Alaska, a fiver from Ohio, and a Westfalia from Saskatchewan. For several weeks we travelled with a Swiss lad in his Mercedes Benz (MB) van and storage-trailer. We also spent a couple of days with a German couple who have this unstoppable "MB-tank" they are planning to take to South America, Eastern Europe, Africa, India and other exotic places. In Costa Rica, one caravan zipped past before we realized it wasn't a mirage. This area is getting crowded!

Mexico, Central America and Panamá are fabulous places to visit, if you like to drycamp. We've had some interesting experiences and we've recorded tremendous memories! Best of all, we'll have them until we go senile, which is a very long time away.

Guatemala
24 abril 1995

Dear Sheila;

We're heading back to Canadá in a hurry. Our son is getting married this summer.

I am writing this letter with two thumbs, seven fingers, bruised muscles, and numerous cuts and abrasions.

Earlier I wrote about the time in El Salvador when I suffered a 3 1/2" gash above my left ankle. Emergency treatment and fifteen stitches in a local clinic, antibiotics and anti-inflammatory drugs for ten days, and a next day inspection cost Can$ 0.67. Because of my stupidity, infection set in a week later, and treatment by a specialist and truly powerful antibiotics cost about Can$ 65.00.

Two weeks ago in Nicaragua, while our rig's rear brakes were once again being fixed, I decided to work on my motorcycle. I was having trouble getting heavy oil onto all parts of a moving chain, so I was guiding it with my finger. My finger slipped between the chain and sprocket and, presto, my left index fingertip was gone. Immediately, I was taken to a hospital where, after waiting fifteen minutes, two doctors fixed me up as best they could. They chose to remove the fingernail and a bit more flesh and bone, but left the knuckle. There was no cost; and it was impossible to give a gift or anything to the hospital.

I had to buy some antibiotics and anti-inflammatory pills, which cost Can$ 12.00.

Friends have said that I am not all there. Now I have to agree.

A week ago I had to visit a church-sponsored hospital in Valle de Angeles, Honduras to have the stitches removed. It cost L.30, or Can$ 4.80. I bought more powerful antibiotics which, at Can$ 47.00, were very overpriced; I hope the extra money goes to help the locals.

During Semana Santa (Holy Week, or the Easter holidays, which everyone takes) we were returning from a balneario, or swimming complex, on our motorcycle. Outside of Gracias, Honduras, Liz and I were hit from behind by a speeding drunk driver who tried to pass us on our right. He almost missed us, but his rear truck fender hit the handlebars. He kept on going.

Fortunately we had our motorcycle helmets on, and the dirt road was rough and rutted so we were going slowly. Liz needed several bandages for a two-inch gash on her elbow and many additional scrapes on her right arm and leg. I had fewer cuts and less road rash because I landed and skidded on my back. But my right calf was badly bruised, as was the large muscle below my right shoulder blade. Neither of us had any broken bones. Emergency treatment cost nothing, but we had to buy more antibiotics for Can$ 12.00.

That afternoon I couldn't get off a restaurant stool because my back was in constant spasms, and we had to get a doctor to come by and shoot me full of muscle relaxants. Then I stopped crying. (I couldn't walk for two days without my back going into spasms that were severe enough to bring me to my knees.) Liz consulted with the doctor and he put three stitches in her elbow in order to close the open wound. The doctor's services and more pills cost Can$ 27.00.

When travelling in Central America, you don't have to buy expensive medical insurance. Small town emergency medical treatment is just as good as Canadian small town treatment. Prescription drugs usually cost less.

I mention these incidents only because I want to stress that Liz and I have received good emergency medical treatment in Central America when we needed it, and for very little cost. This is just another reason that RVers should visit this beautiful area.

Canada
September 1995

Dear Sheila;

We're back. We rented a one-bedroom apartment and will stay in Kelowna until the end of April. This accomplishes two objectives: (1) we have a place to stay for at least six months and thus re-establish residency for BC Medical Services Plan coverage; and (2) we have a place which will keep us warm until we begin next summer's travels to Inuvik, north of the Arctic Circle.

Our trip down South was interesting, fascinating, frustrating, challenging, wonderful, great, and worth every penny, peso and centavo. But the moment we crossed the 49th parallel into Canada – our home and native land – the skies glowed bluer, the sun shone golden, the grass grew greener, and the money was multicolored. We experienced quite a kaleidoscope of emotions, but the predominant one was "We're Home!"

But we were almost sick to see hundreds, nay thousands, of items available in grocery, hardware and department stores. Canada and USA really are lands of plenty. Nevertheless we are getting over our culture shock and quickly readapting to extravagance.

We're also cold. What happened to August?

We border-crossed into Alberta then drove through the Rockies. They are absolutely majestic, and are better than anything we saw in Central America. But we have learned a few things while we were gone; we took lots of time to travel Highway 1A. It hurts to realize that we missed such beauty during all those times that we sped to and from Calgary.

We arrived in Kelowna two weeks before our son and daughter-in-law's wedding, and immediately had to buy a watch and a scheduler. We were hardly involved, but after our eighteen months of laid-back, no-deadline living this was a busy and stressful time for us.

Two days after the wedding, Liz and I were on the road again, this time to see more of Beautiful BC. We spent a few days recuperating at a quiet spot on the west side of Okanagan Lake, then ventured back into Kelowna to dump the tanks, to fill up with water, and to restock the fridge. We said "Hi-Bye" to our young adult progeny, then took off to visit the Kootenays.

A last minute change necessitated acquisition of Forestry Maps because we decided to visit the Boundary Area. Those historic and picturesque towns of Beaverdell, Midway, Greenwood, and Grand Forks and such quiet, clean, uncrowded and minimally-serviced areas of Conkle Lake, Howe Creek, Phoenix ex-mining area, and Jewel Lake make us wonder why we hadn't done this sooner.

Grand Forks has the GF Hotel, and its famous Russian Borscht. It also has several campsites—dry, or with electrical and water—next to its central City Park and Farmers' Market. And at the west end of town, a block from a Chevron station, the town provides drinking water and a sewage dump facility. (Thank You.)

Unknown to us, we got to Howe Creek just as the hunting season opened, which explained why there were so many vehicles on that 16 Km of dusty wilderness road. Three days later, all those unsuccessful hunters were gone. Then, at early dusk a doe came out of the woods and helped us eat salted peanuts, sunflower seeds, and celery. We didn't even shoot a picture.

During our BC travels, Liz and I have seen several squirrels and chipmunks, five deer, a coyote, half a dozen grouse, four peacocks and peahens, dozens of fingerlings feeding on flies, two fully grown otters (I almost wrote 'seals' because they were so large), ducks, loons, a garter snake sunning itself. Beside two waterfalls, we ate Choke Cherries, Cracker Berries, Saskatoons, Raspberries, and some kind of black berry with hair. Not too bad for a couple of city-dwellers.

That was more wildlife than we saw during a similar time period when we were anywhere in Mexico, Central America and Panamá. We Canadians are so very lucky, even though only a few of us are fortunate enough to have good health and unlimited time to enjoy our natural resources. (If only we had a bit more money for gasoline.)

We've decided that we need to buy a used canoe. The lakes of British Columbia and the Yukon demand it.

It sure feels good to be home!

How long will these tans last?

Mexico

Ciudad Juarez
Hermosillo
Alamos
Chihuahua
Creel
Mazatlan
La Paz
San Miguel de Allende
Guadalajara
Veracruz
Mexico City
Bacalar
Acapulco
Oaxaca
Tapachula

EL BANCO DE MEXICO
5000
PAGARA CINCO MIL PESOS A LA VISTA AL PORTADOR
SERIE
GR
U 3339732

Mexico

Border Crossing: USA to Mexico

Liz and I had little trouble crossing into Mexico. El Paso-Ciudad Juaréz is a busy border crossing and it does take time to get through the paper work. Don't try to rush it, or it could take longer.

Don't take non-prescription drugs or guns into Mexico. They are illegal.

A reasonable amount of foodstuffs should pass easily. Hopefully you intend to try the local dishes or shop inexpensively at the local supermarkets (supers) and local markets (mercados).

If you have an outdated Mexican registration sticker on your window, remove and dispose of it immediately. Otherwise next time you are crossing into Mexico, you could be faced with some very, very expensive fines. You are required by law to turn in that sticker at least one day before it expires.

For those of you who wish to drive your vehicle(s) into Mexico, here is information as gleaned from personal experience and "Mexico Travelbook" by AAA, "Peoples Guide to Mexico - Winter 1994", and "Sanborns' 93/94 RV Guide to Mexico". Annually issued guidebooks will be more current.

You will need your original and two photocopies of the following.

1. Each person requires a passport, birth certificate, or naturalization papers. In addition, each child less than eighteen must have notarized permission from both parents.

2. You'll need your vehicle registration or bill of sale if you own it outright. Insurance registration might not be enough. If you don't own the vehicle, you'll need a notarized letter of permission from lienholder.

3. If you have two vehicles, you'll need a second bill of sale. If you do not own the second vehicle, then you'll need a notarized letter from its owner which states that the other person travelling with you is allowed to drive that vehicle in Mexico. One person is allowed only one vehicle, period.

4. A valid driver's licence is essential. Make sure yours doesn't expire while you are in Mexico.

5. Copy both sides of your credit card. US$ 12.00 will be charged to your credit card. Without it, you'll need a lot of cash.

6. The staff will copy your newly issued tourist card once you've got it. I suggest you take the maximum days allowed.

Double check all those registration papers! Our bill of sale listed the serial number of our RV as the chassis number, as assigned by the manufacturer. That caused problems because it should have listed the true VIN, which can be used to trace engines.

I didn't have the bill of sale for my motorcycle which I've owned for six years. I did have both an outdated and non-renewed provincial registration. After much deliberation they accepted those, and annotated Liz's papers.

Once the vehicular registrations were completed, metallic holographic stickers were affixed to the vehicles. Our paperwork disappeared. We were given back our tourist card and one set of the photocopied papers.

After the paper work was done, we waited in our motorhome for over an hour for someone to come and complete their ten-minute inspection.

It might take one or two hours to clear (1) immigration, (2) vehicle registration, and (3) customs before you cross into Mexico. We talked to one young couple who, because of faulty vehicle papers, were cleared eight days after starting the process.

All conversations were in Spanish. We found the agents and other tourists to be very pleasant and helpful. Forget the horror stories. Be prepared, be patient, relax, and expect a delay at a busy border crossing.

Insurance and Registration

We stored the original documentation, and always showed copies whenever we were asked for our papers. Sometimes we had to show originals.

Canadian insurance is of no value south of the USA-Mexican border. I understand the situation is the same for insurance that was issued in the USA.

You do not need insurance in Mexico, but is the gamble—save money and drive carefully versus have an accident and go to jail—worth it? We had insurance the first time we were in Mexico. We didn't bother the second time.

You can get Mexican insurance from Mexican agents, Sanborns, AAA and other agents. Fully comprehensive insurance can be expensive; third-person liability insurance is much cheaper. Various options exist. We tried to visit three Sanborns agents in Mexico; all addresses had expired. The cost of two months' insurance was about the same as for a full year.

One camper we met got Mexican insurance for two days' travel, hightailed it to an RV campground, then set up and didn't move for three months. When he wanted to get back to Canada, he got another two days' of highway-driving insurance. Total cost was forty dollars. Not bad for a $60,000 vehicle, not bad at all.

While in Mazatlán, the Canadian Consulate told us that the Mexicans don't care about non-Mexican vehicle registration. [Note. The same was true at all international border crossings, even the Mexican-USA border on our return trip.] We let our provincial insurance and registration expire and never had any problem with any local police. It seems as long as you have a valid vehicle permit issued at their border they could care less about the dated decal on your licence plate. But check with your insurance company to see if they care.

You might want to fix the licence plate nuts so they can't be taken off easily. This is a common practice in the case of traffic misdemeanours, real or imagined. We put our licence plate inside the back window of our vehicle.

Fuel and Propane

Diesel is considerably cheaper than gasoline. Almost every Pemex station has it.

There was no shortage of low octane, leaded gasoline (Nova) or high octane, unleaded gasoline (Magna Sin) in Mexico. New state-controlled or franchised Pemex stations were being built in large numbers. It was difficult to travel 100 km and not see at least one station.

Highway 200 from Tecomán (southeast of Manzanillo) to Playa Azul (near Cárdenas) was an exception. If you were to believe tourists and locals alike, this is an area where you do not want to run out of fuel. Carry enough fuel to travel 300 km.

Propane plants are built outside of most cities and towns for safety reasons. Usually they are readily visible from highways. Guadalajara was an exception; a plant was inside the city and well hidden.

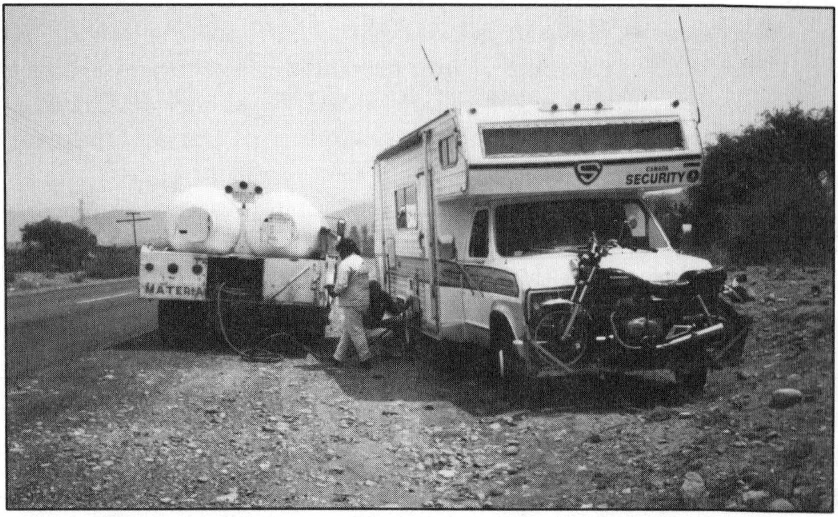

Roadside-injections saved us from searching in large cities.

Propane plants can fill permanent tanks as well as bottles. It is even possible to stop a propane truck and refill permanent tanks on the side of the road. We did that at least twice but, for some reason, we never got a receipt.

Prior to devaluation of the Peso in December 1994, gasoline prices were much lower (N$ 1.32 vs N$ 1.93) but the exchange rate was also lower. The result of the devaluation is that costs to tourists have dropped but, unfortunately, costs to Mexicans have increased.

The following numbers have been used to calculate equivalent prices in Canada. Some banks know the Can-USA exchange rate. One rate was US$ 1.00 = Can$ 1.41 = 6.32 New Pesos (N$ or NP). As of June 25, 1995, average prices are:

	Mexico	Canada
Unleaded/Magna Sin	N$ 2.00/L	Can$ 0.45/L
Leaded/Regular/Nova	N$ 1.93/L	Can$ 0.43/L
Propane	N$ 1.21/L	Can$ 0.27/L

However, this is not the true price of Mexican gasoline. Having conducted tests in more than 80 gas stations in almost every state in Mexico, the gasoline pumps were in error by an average of more than 6%, in their favour. This means you get approximately 94% of what you pay for. This value was confirmed by comparing my actual gas kilometrage (km/L) in Mexico and the USA.

First Twelve Days in Mexico

January 12, 1994 was the beginning of a memorable month-long trip from Kelowna to Mexico. We drove through wintry Washington, down the stunningly beautiful, sunny coast of Oregon, through rain and aftershocks of an earthquake in California, up and over to the cold and sometimes freezing altitudes of Arizona, Nevada and New Mexico, then finally into Texas and the border crossing at El Paso.

Liz in California Redwoods

It took us two more days of driving in Mexico to get to Creel, bypassing Chihuahua in favour of the back roads of Highway 23 through Ricardo Florés Magnon and then Buenaventura, Bachiniva, Cuauhtémoc (Coo-wow-tay-moke), La Junta, and San Juanito. We wanted to find out how those thick, thin, and thinner black lines on our AAA map related to actual roads.

They were great. All were two-lane asphalt roads without potholes. And the scenery changed form cacti-covered desert and bare sand dunes, to farmland with adobe houses and rock and barbed-wire fences, to steep, precipitous switchback canyons, to ranch land, to irrigated farmland, to evergreen forests, to huge Men-nonite farms with concrete buildings, to orchards, and to beautiful mountainous hills and valleys surrounding log cabins.

A shrine painted on a rock-face on the road to Creel.

Creel is a pioneer town, with logging and tourism being its greatest sources of income. Like the few Mexican towns we've seen, it is small, dusty, messy with litter, and full of run-down and half-down buildings, several hotels and unlimited food and pop stalls. But the obvious can be deceiving. We could make photocopies, and phone, fax, and computer-interface anywhere in North America, although not always immediately and reliably. We could also watch TV without cable, and listen to innumerable AM Mexican and US radio stations at night.

We managed to hook up to the only full-service facility in the Pensíon de Creel, for N$ 10.00/night.

Next day, Liz and I climbed up onto a rocky promontory overlooking the tiny town, and sat for an hour next to a huge but deteriorating statue of Christ. This formed a quiet backdrop while we watched a dozen turkey vultures as they climbed the thermals, made lazy circles in the sky, and swooped down within inches of the pine-covered ground looking for a meal. Laid back? Sí. So long, stress. Hello relaxation.

We saw Tarahumara Indians living in caves near Creel or selling woven belts, baskets and dolls at the train station and everywhere else. These Indians live in La Barranca Del Cobre, and have maintained much of their independence. But at a cost; they are extremely poor. The men are known as racers, and have been known to run nonstop for more than thirty-six hours. In one international race, a fifty-year-old Tarahumara ran 100 km over rough terrain, much of it with a twisted ankle, and passed the finish-line four and a half hours ahead of the next racer.

Other sights were within walking distance or accessible with a guide and van for U$ 20.00. We stopped by Arareoco Lake and its simple picnic grounds, and the Mission de San Ignacio. We also visited weathered, uniquely-shaped stones in the Valley of the Gods (or Monks), and motorcycled to the Valley of the Mushrooms where roaring waterfalls would have been if there had been any water. This was the dry season and water was scarce; in 1994-5 this area was so dry that parts of it were declared a disaster area.

In the dark of night, we heard a knock at our door which, when opened, revealed two semi-scruffy men with day-old beards. Naturally, we invited them in for coffee and conversation. As they left, they commented that the only worthwhile tour was to Batopilas. Batopilas, hey?

After much questioning we found out that we could take a van tour for US$ 85.00 (N$ 260.00) or US$ 67.00 per person return, provided there are three or four others. Alternatively, we could take a scheduled bus for N$ 60.00. The bus left every second day at 7 a.m.. Food and lodging would be extra.

Waking up to an alarm at 6:00 a.m. was no fun. Much of that night had been spent worrying about getting up in time to catch the bus, and wondering if there would be seats available for us. We got there early. There was room, directly in front of the one working speaker of a cassette player with its dentist-drill squeal. Sadistically, it played the same two or three dusty tapes at a volume that could be heard at the rear of the crowded, rattling, jostling bus.

An hour after departure, a radiator hose burst and all of us were stranded, seemingly in the middle of nowhere. Another bus wheezed by, and stopped. After a short discussion, we and several others escaped the tape recorder. Magically, we were transported twenty kilometres to a small building which served a breakfast of scrambled eggs, tortillas, beans, tortillas, instant coffee, and tortillas. We ate on wobbly, hand-hewn tables under one small light bulb in a dark and dusty room without windows. It was like being in "the bad guys' hideout" in those black and white B-westerns of my childhood.

Our original overcrowded bus arrived an hour and a half later. Shortly afterwards we were on our way, and shortly after that the blacktop disappeared. The dirt road could best be described as an occasional thin layer of dust covering rocks, with ruts where last summer's rains had washed away the smaller stones. Most of the huge boulders had been pushed onto narrow shoulders.

Then, at Quiráre, the three-quarter point of this 130-km excursion, the road got really bad. It turned into an incredibly steep, narrow, mule-train trail with uncounted switchbacks, potholes, washouts, and fallen boulders.

I have the greatest admiration for drivers of those rusted, dilapidated, scratched and bent trucks that we met on that steep path to Batopilas near the bottom of the Copper Canyon. I wouldn't park on a place where the road widens just a little, with my outside wheels within inches of a very very long drop, to let a bus go by. But they did.

And I have even greater admiration for drivers of big buses. They circumnavigate hairpin corners by rubbing the front bumper against rocks while part of the outside dual rear-wheel hangs suspended in the air. They even move closer to a crumbly roadside edge to prevent the bus from leaning into jutting rocks before inside wheels drop into washed-out ruts.

We're up there, somewhere.

Exaggeration? A little, the bumpers never actually scraped the rock walls. Do not take your rig or trailer to Batopilas.

So why did we take the bus over this road from Hell? Because we didn't know any better. But once committed to something, you may as well enjoy it, right?

To relieve overcrowding and to escape again from the cassette recorder, some of us climbed up onto the roof-rack, and sat between backpacks and boxes on hard steel-rod flooring. We were rewarded with a much better view of the canyon as we descended, bumped, climbed, turned, tipped waaay over.

We descended and descended through 1,500 m in 35 km in three and a half hours.

And what views. Especially those heart-stopping views of extremely deep canyons and far-below rivers that we saw when looking straight down over the side of a bumping, leaning bus and not seeing the road.

Nervousness of another sort surfaced when I realized that branches of an overhanging tree had huge thorns on them, and that they were going to scrape us.

But what views! Canyon walls looked like nature's own apartment buildings. Towering lava-core peaks blocked the late morning sun trying to shine on zebra-skin walls of water-stained sandstone. Slopes of chaparral and grass looked like pastel woven carpets. One promontory with several layers of different colours reminded me of a birthday cake. A half-completed dam of bright golden ochre wasn't a dam but a unique natural outcropping. Canyons turned into other canyons that turned into others. A jade-green river was fed by creeks filled with multicoloured boulders and very little water. Some trees were covered with a hundred cotton-balls of seeds which were blowing upwards, not downward. Unbelievably brilliant purple and magenta flowers mingled with at least five species or genus of cacti, some of which were bigger and taller than nearby trees. One high rockface was covered with the luminescent shimmering colours of a peacock's tail. A celestial blue canopy appeared to be resting on mountain peaks and infinity at the same time.

After eight hours, Batopilas appeared none too soon. My rump was sore, Liz's was bruised, our legs were stiff. And my hands were scraped from grasping the metal rods which, after all, weren't bent and crushed by my white-knuckled grip.

Batopilas had five hotels: Mary (N$25/person/night); Moncies (N$20//); Batopilas (N$15//); and two others we knew nothing about. You get what you pay for. Hotel Mary had two hot showers and a good a la carte restaurant. Mr. McWilliams restored Copper Canyon Lodge cost about US$ 200.00/night. Pre-registration is required. That price includes live band music, fabulous meals, outstanding rooms, and guided tours.

The Lost Cathedral is a huge mission-fortress built in the 1700's by unknown persons. They're unknown because two fires, as evidenced in the bell tower, destroyed all records. It is still being used as a church, and is slowly undergoing repairs, replastering and refurbishment. Because of missing stucco, we could see that the gigantic dome had been built by one spiral of adobe brick, in the same manner that an igloo is built.

If you walk the seven kilometres to get to the church, en route you could see dust, and the Crocodile Rock with its two black bulbous eyes just above the water surface. You should also see a twenty-foot fig tree with forty feet of intertwining yellow roots clinging onto the outside of a nearly vertical pinkish rockface. You'll definitely see goats, burros, cows, and more dust.

Across the river from Batopilas, the bottom half of a once magnificent stone wall encircles the remains of a hacienda. Near the turn of this century, these buildings were used to process more than 1,000,000,000 ounces of silver that were taken out of local mines. It reminded us of a medieval king's castle. The crumbling three-storey house must have been an outstandingly beautiful sight with its many gardens and luxurious furnishings. Unfortunately there are no pictures here, only walls and imagination.

This complex, and the waterfall-fed aqueduct that still supplies Batopilas with its water, were engineering marvels.

Because the trip back to Creel started at 4 a.m. there wasn't much to see en route except a colourful sunrise. There wasn't much conversation either, even after the Policia Nacional stopped us for a roadside check in the dark. Those who spoke Spanish were very concerned by the menacing tone and actions of the patrol but, in my ignorance, I thought it was exciting.

A day after our return from Batopilas, we boarded the Copper Canyon Railway to El Fuerte. It was a spectacular ride there, and even more so on the way back.

La Barranca Del Cobre

I suppose everyone who has driven to Mexico, or has thought of doing so, has heard of La Barranca Del Cobre, or the Copper Canyon. It is four times bigger and 400 feet deeper than the USA's Grand Canyon.

We planned to catch a train at Creel, put our rig on a flatcar, and pass through the Copper Canyon to Los Mochis. From there we'd tour the west coast beaches of Mexico. 'Twas a good plan, but impossible.

Contrary to what some articles seemed to imply, we could only ship our rig if we belonged to a caravan or a prearranged tour. [Note. In Mazatlán, I met a returning Canadian who told us that a travel agency could arrange for a one-way trip from Los Mochis to Chihuahua, possibly as part of a freight train. He hadn't done it.] The cost of tour groups we investigated started at US$ 1500-2300. All returned to their place of departure, which definitely was not for us. So it had to be from Creel to Los Mochis and return via passenger train, or ferrocarril, or FC.

At the train station in Creel, we learned a one-way fare to Los Mochis was N$ 59.00/person for punctual first class, or N$ 16.00 for the usually late second class train. One backpacker had told us it would cost nothing if we wanted to ride an unscheduled flatcar or boxcar which, hopefully, was going in the right direction.

First-class and second-class trains look the same from the outside; we couldn't see inside because of the streaky dust and dirt on the tinted and sometimes cracked windows.

We decided to travel first-class to El Divisadero, get off, walk about, peer down a sheer canyon wall, climb a nearby mesa, then board the second-class train which was scheduled to arrive two hours later. Then we'd go as far as picturesque La Fuerte, two hours short of the unexciting industrial port of Los Mochis. We'd travel part of the trip in the dark, but we didn't mind because we would see all of the canyon during our return to Creel the following day.

We boarded the Primera Classe train promptly at 12:25 and zipped along to El Divisadero. We disembarked, bought some tasty fast-food within feet of the tracks, avoided the hawkers of jewellery and carvings, and wandered over to a spectacular viewpoint overlooking one of the canyons. Then we visited a magnificent hotel; it has a public washroom. If we'd had the money, we would have stayed for supper, even though it would have meant walking and eating within inches of a vertical canyon wall.

A couple of hours later, we boarded the Segunda Classe. We sat in seats that were almost as comfortable as in first class, next to cleaner windows that we could open. This train wasn't full of tourists, just real Mexican families and hawkers of food and drinks.

As Liz and I were discussing someone somewhere who had ridden the front of a train, she looked at me, I looked at her, a spark leapt between us, and we were up and walking to the front of our train. Once at the first car, we opened the safety gate and leaped onto a diesel-stained locomotive. We worked our way up to the Engineer's cab, where we were let inside by a startled driver. In broken Spanish, we convinced him that we 'locos turistas' wanted to ride on the front of his locomotive.

Surprisingly, he agreed. Suddenly there we were, with stupid grins on our faces, hair blowing straight back, glasses tied to our shirts, and fists clamped around a single, waist-high bar. We were almost scared out of our wits as we leaned into corners at 80

All aboard!

km/hr, and crossed over trestles where we could look through the ties to water far below. Unstoppable, we sped into smoke-blackened dark tunnels with dripping water and rough blasted rock spotlighted by the trains headlamps. We laughed at the wind.

We spent four hours getting windburned, and saw some truly spectacular canyon walls, fantastic vistas, deep canyons with small but high waterfalls, railway workers fixing the same tracks we were using, and a colourful sunset that popped into full view as we left one canyon and turned into another. Darkness came quickly. With black stains on our dusty, gritty clothes, we straggled back to the same seats where we had left our knapsack. It appears as if Mexicans will not take an occupied seat, even when no one is in it and even if they have to stand.

In an overcast blackness that seems to happen only down south, we disembarked at El Fuerte. As our eyes adjusted to the darkness, we realized that there was nothing there except a train station, and one other passenger who was waving to us as he was getting into a taxi. We joined him, and 8 km and N$ 25.00 later we were in the city. With the cab driver's help, we got an inexpensive room and were asleep before thin sheets covered our shoulders.

Knock knock, at 6:00 a.m. Oscar our cabbie was ready to drive us back to the train station, in time for the Primera Classe which we didn't want.

Some animals are not stupid. During our early morning wait at the El Fuerte train station, we watched a sad, head-drooping mongrel hobble up on three legs to several people, pitifully balancing himself while holding his useless right front paw off the ground. We felt sorry for him and would gladly have fed him if we'd had something. Slowly he completed his circuit. Sadly he got nothing. So he put all four legs on the ground, raised his head until he looked like a self-assured pure bred, and proceeded to play tag-chase with two other dogs. A while later, more people arrived by taxi, and the woebegone mongrel temporarily made his appearance again. What an actor he was.

At 7:30 a.m. our Segunda Classe wheezed to a halt. Once again we boarded the Copper Canyon Railway. This time we stashed our knapsack in an overhead rack. Then we got off and climbed on at the front of the locomotive, and were allowed to stay. For six hours we stood there, and marvelled at even more of the spectacular scenery than we had the day before.

The first of many tunnels is almost a mile and a half long. We did much of it in absolute darkness, until the Engineer blinded us when he turned on the big headlight. Then I suffered endless twisting and turning vertigo as the walls raced past our peripheral vision while rough, phosphorescent and often damp rock magically appeared ahead of us. Neither of us had experienced anything like it. It was better than any roller coaster ride we'd been on.

Travelling over thirty-nine trestles, through eighty-six tunnels, and between towering canyon walls covered in dusty greens and patches of autumn colours (except where a single burst of raw rock lay sharply exposed), we laughed and smiled as two ribbons of steel stretched hypnotically into the future. All that scenery was there only for us, as we flew six feet above the ties clinging to the steel bridle of our labouring diesel Pegasus.

Reluctantly back in Creel, we knew we had to leave; there was so much more Mexico to see. Liz and I treated ourselves to a simple but delicious meal at Casa Marguerita's. During that one meal and several coffees we talked with German, Belgian, Swiss, English, and Canadian tourists. We should have gone there sooner, world travellers are so very interesting!

A day after our return, sadly, we packed up and left Creel in its dust, and headed along Highway 16 for the Pacific coast and its beaches.

We stopped at beautiful Basaseachic Falls, two hundred kilometres closer to the west coast beaches, and stayed in an extremely neat National Park. Liz had been at me about my

Relax. It's only 300m down!

protruding tummy—it's her fault, she cooks too well too often—so she decided that we needed exercise. We had to climb down to La Ventana, the Window or the View. It took nearly an hour. The view really was spectacular, even though the volume of water was minimal. The water flowed under a natural bridge and over the edge to drop 300 m (1065'). It got to the bottom as mist. The tiny pond at the foot of the falls was barely disturbed.

Slim, trim Liz was exhausted by the climb down the primitive and rocky path, so I went alone to the bottom by an even worse path. Surprisingly, the view wasn't as good as where I had left her. So back I went. I took the same time descending and climbing a distance twice greater than that which we had done together. I guess my tum-tum gave me better balance; at least she hasn't said much about it since then.

Next day, we decided that we would gamble and cut off many kilometres by not going to Hermosillo. Still, it was a full day's drive to get from Basaseachic Falls to Ciudad Obregón, over a road that drops 1,600 m in 100 km (5000' in 60 mi) and through the best highway scenery we've seen so far. It took me awhile to get used to travelling at 30 km/hr, climbing or descending, through all those switchbacks. It was nothing like the view en route to Batopilas or from the ferrocarril on the edge of the Barranca Del Cobre, but in its own way, it was just as stunningly beautiful.

A planned two-day trip had turned into eleven enjoyable days of unbelievable scenery. We saw the spectacular Barranca Del Cobre in three different ways: by bus; by train; and by motorhome. We were lucky. Time and deadlines don't exist for us. Our limited financial budget can be stretched for a long time when overnight camping is cheap.

If or when you are passing by Chihuahua, Chihuahua, Mexico plan to detour into Creel and Batopilas. You'll be glad that you did. Guaranteed!

Driving in Mexico is Easy

Don't drive at night.

Driving a recreational vehicle in Mexico is easy. Just remember that you are bigger than the cars and most trucks.

If you run out of gas or blow a tire on a main highway, one of the tourism-sponsored Angeles Verdes will be by shortly to help out. Proudly display your "I was blessed by a Green Angel" sticker. If he helped, a tip is appropriate.

Highways are well marked, with numerous directional signs at intersections. In addition, there are lots of kilometres-to-go signs, except when you are low on gas.

There are fewer accidents in Mexico than in the USA or Canada. What accidents there are, are usually fender-benders.

For more than four months, Liz and I have driven on a few toll roads (cuotas), many free highways (libres), and numerous back roads, streets and alleys of Mexico. We've seen one accident. A white truck was overturned in the middle of a highway. We guess that it left a dirt road above the highway and rolled down the steep hillside.

We were in Texas for six days and saw two accidents, a minor rear-ender and a high speed collision that destroyed two cars and an unknown number of bodies; two ambulances were in attendance. I'd rather drive in Mexico than in the United States.

Some animals are stupid. They don't realize they are at fault when they get killed crossing the road while mangling your rig's front end. It almost appears as if you are at liberty to kill any animal that is on the highway. Dusk and dark are the best times, black cows and charcoal-brown burros can't see you coming. Maybe their poor eyesight is genetic; we seldom saw light-skinned animals lying in ditches. You might want to equip your rig with one of those bull-bashing, steel-tube grills that you see on older buses and almost all trucks. Make sure that it is welded to the heavy-duty frame and not bolted to those new rubber-coated, fibreglass, dentable, flexible bumpers.

Most Mexican drivers are excellent defensive drivers. Really. They are always on the lookout for cars that unexpectedly come out of side streets and alleys, for taxis that stop on a dime to make a dollar picking up a passenger, for trucks that stop in either the left or right lane to make a delivery, for bicycles and motorcycles that slip in and out of the half-metre space between vehicles, and especially for lost and frustrated tourists. Mexicans survive by being aware of what goes on around, in front of, and behind them.

Unfortunately a few, particularly taxi drivers, also believe in the military dictum that a good defence is a good offence.

Mexican drivers seem to do what they want to do. Oh sure, there are laws – I understand Mexico uses the Napoleonic Code – but they are used only in law courts. Since you are automatically assumed to be guilty, it seems laws are made to be broken, to be used only as guidelines.

On highways, when a truck in front of you turns on his left signal light it means it is safe to pass, if you are not being passed and if you are quick. In the cities, when the same truck driver signals left, it means he is going to turn left. Sometimes drivers forget where they are or they forget to turn off the signal, so use common sense.

The continuous line in the middle of a highway does not mean you can't pass. It's a reminder to speed up when passing uphill on a blind curve.

Newer buses often have a 95 km/hr speed displayed on their vehicles. Any bus driver worth his salt knows that is the minimum speed expected.

No one stops at railway crossings. They merely reduce speed, look, and keep on going. Some crossings are topes in disguise. It's always wise to slow down.

Every village has at least one pair of the dreaded topes (pronounced 'tow pez'). Expect them, be alert, and you won't have to replace springs and muffler.

Driving in Mexico is easy, and so is parking. Just park wherever you want, even if it slows traffic in crowded, narrow downtown streets. Just don't block traffic completely. The worst that will happen is that you'll hear a few horns honking, at first. But your vehicle quickly becomes just another of many objects to drive around. If you feel conspicuous, open the hood and look like any other broken down vehicle owner.

Getting lost in a city is even easier. Just follow your map or rusted detour signs. Mexicans don't take down detour signs, maybe they'll be needed again.

If you do get a map, get a good one that shows all of the streets. Don't worry about being able to read the street names. You won't find the faded street signs anyway because they've been painted over, they fell off, or they're hidden behind trees and vines. Use your map to count the number of intersections you pass, then turn when you get to the right number.

If you have to turn around, do so immediately, even if you are in the middle of the street. Mexicans understand.

Any wheeled vehicle on the street is allowed to be there, licensed or not. Horses and burros are permitted too. But pedestrians have no rights whatsoever. It is their responsibility to avoid damaging your vehicle.

Most drivers play Chicken poorly. Let me give you an example. After fifteen long minutes behind three overloaded trucks slowly and noisily climbing up the side of a canyon, I had to pass when I saw a quarter kilometre of straight highway. So what if there were five cars coming toward us? I selected second gear, put the pedal to the metal, checked the mirrors, changed lanes, and turned on the signal lights, in that order. I got past the first two trucks easily enough—I was up to 55 km/hr—but then it started to look a bit dicey.

The first oncoming car flashed his lights. I returned the signal indicating that I wanted the right of way. I kept accelerating until I was just past the third truck then immediately swung back into the right lane. By then, the first car had pulled so far to the right it was almost in the ditch. But what the heck, it was at least two seconds before we were side by side. Close, but safe.

Liz doesn't play Chicken very well either. All she said for the next couple of minutes was "Oh . . . oh . . . Ohoh . . . uh . . . oh" as she sucked in great gulps of air.

I got my comeuppance in Manzanillo.

As usual, I had taken the wrong turn and ended up in the old part of town. "Old part of town" means very narrow, one-way, rough and broken streets with no street signs; lots of traffic, parked cars and trucks; telephone poles jutting out from the edge of sidewalks; buildings with balconies or low overhanging roofs; and innumerable people with innumerable bags walking everywhere.

I was trying to make my escape when I came face to face with a legless man in a wheel chair. I slowed down, he speeded up. I stopped, he passed. I started to move, Liz yelled. I stopped, he didn't. He kept trying to squeeze by, even though his left wheel was rubbing against the foot-high sidewalk and his right wheel was jammed between the side of our motorhome and the leg of the awning.

He kept trying to revolve those wheels, but neither of us was going anywhere. I had to get out and, with the help of another driver, we picked up the wheelchair, carried it and the man over the sidewalk, and put them back into the street behind the motorhome. He was neither scratched nor hurt, but he was not pleased. I guess he wins at Chicken so often that it has become a bother playing the game.

When you are driving in the mountains, the chances are your motorhome will be in second gear as you climb. A good policy is to keep it in second gear when going downhill. Use your transmission to provide braking, and use your brakes as little as practical. If you don't, they will heat up and you won't have them if and when you really need them. Remember your brakes are hotter than usual already, certainly hotter than they would be in Churchill, Manitoba in February.

Which reminds me, one Canadian told me he was used to driving with below-recommended air pressure in his tires so that he could get a better grip in snow and on ice. When he was in southern Mexico, his tires overheated and two of them blew apart. I think it's better to have slightly higher-than-recommended pressure when driving where it is hot.

If you drive down a one way street the wrong way, which is easy to do because of the lack of legible signs, you are liable to get a ticket. Mexicans know this. When they want to go the wrong way, they do so in reverse. I never saw anyone get a ticket for performing this bit of optical illusion.

Driving in Mexico is easy. Know the rules but use them sparingly. Being bigger gives you an advantage. Drive alertly, defensively, and keep your eyes on the road. Use common sense in doing what you want to do, when you want to. Pass quickly but cautiously on hills if the truck in front of you signals left. In cities and towns pedestrians will avoid you. Park anywhere. Forget about maps.

And take your time. Mexico is a wonderful country.

Pemex, State Controlled Gasoline . . . Oh Yeah?

In theory, the government determines what the price of gasoline will be anywhere in Mexico. At this time of writing, the price of unleaded, 92-octane Magna Sin was N$1.32 per litre.

Being state controlled, all the pumps show these figures. Therefore, that is what you pay for gas, right? Oh yeah. Sure.

Mexicans are noted for their resourcefulness and ingenuity. I became aware of that ingenuityvery quickly while in Cuauhtémoc. The second time I filled up in Mexico, I put more gas into my two tanks than I had ever managed to do elsewhere, and one tank had been a quarter full. "Shuckens Darn," I thought, "I've been suckered. I guess I really do have to watch those gas jockeys carefully, just as I'd been warned."

And so for the next few days, I unlocked my gas caps then stayed to watch and make sure that the meter was reset to zero, and that the price charged agreed with what the meter displayed. And I enjoyed practising Spanish with the attendants and trying to explain that we had come from Canada and were going to spend several months in Mexico before going on to Central America.

I stopped enjoying that when I realized that while I was distracted by chatting, the attendant could tamper with the meters. Usually they would stop pumping and reset the meters to zero, giving some excuse I couldn't understand. Eventually, I cottoned onto the fact that when the pumps are reset they do not have to go all the way to zero before gas can flow. Naturally, the attendants would start pumping gas as fast as they could. I learn slowly.

Weeks later, one attendant got me good. I had carefully watched him wait until the meters were set to zero before he was allowed to start pumping, and I wouldn't allow him to reset. When he was done, I crosschecked the final price and paid him one hundred pesos. We chatted for a few seconds then, as he showed me the several bills I had given him, he said "These don't add up to N$100.00." And he was right, they didn't. So I gave him an additional N$10. Shortly after I drove away, I became suspicious and checked the money in my pocket. It is never very much, and I realized that I was ten pesos short. He had exchanged a twenty for a ten and made it look as though I had not paid enough. He did not say I owed him more money, I voluntarily gave him some. Slick.

But even with all my precautions—locked gas caps, watching the meters carefully, not talking while filling—my gas mileage still seemed to be less than I used to get north of the Mexican border. Why?

So I got myself an American gallon jug, which is equal to 3.766 litres, or 3.8L. I marked a line on the neck, and began to fill up the jug with gasoline before I unlocked any gas cap. The first five jugsful, all from different stations, gave the following results: 3.85, 4.18, 4.35, 4.2 and 3.9. I took the lowest to be the most accurate, after all, why would the gas station give gas away? It wasn't exactly 3.8L, but I'd probably drawn the line too high up the neck, so I assumed it to be 3.9L. Close enough.

After I started filling the jug before filling my tanks, if a meter showed more than 4.1L, I bought only enough gas to get me to another Pemex.

When you drive up to a Pemex and you notice that there's an empty lane, even though several vehicles are lined up at other lanes, ignore the arm waving and get in line behind the other vehicles. I'd wager those drivers know where the best 'bang for your buck' is.

By the way, if you drive up to a gasoline station and it is not very busy, then there is probably another Pemex in town that is. And it will be busy because it gives the most gas for money received. Consider driving about until you find it, then fill up at one of the more honest Pemex stations.

Unexpectedly, we had to return to Texas. I filled my little jug to the line a couple of times and, wattaya know, the pump's meter registered exactly one US gallon. Now I fill up my tanks only when pumps indicate less than or equal to 4.0L.

By June 1994, I had recorded 22 jugsful. The minimum amount displayed on the meters was 3.81 litres, the maximum amount was 4.35 litres, and the average was 4.03 litres. That average means that in Mexico, even if you are scrupulously careful, you will be getting 6.7% less than you pay for. A price of N$1.32 is really N$1.40 (C$0.64/L). Our calculated consumption of 2.82 Km/L is really 3.0 Km/L, and those 13,625 Km we've travelled have cost us Can$ 163.50 more than it should.

A couple of months previously I read the premier edition of the "Travel Mexico" newsletter. It also discussed this problem of litre-fixing. Based on seven readings using a calibrated 19L container, they found the average price to be about 8% high. At the end of our return trip, I had recorded 92 jugsful in every part of Mexico. The average error was 6.8%.

If you are doing a lot of driving with a vehicle that gets poor gas mileage, as Liz and I did, you might want to start using the jug-test method. It will save you money while improving your gas mileage. And it'll make for some interesting conversations in español; the buck-passing comments are quite ingenious.

Like me, you might also send off a letter to the Department of Tourism and to Pemex head office, specifying what each station's meter read after filling up your jug. I don't know what good I did, but it made me feel better.

The Dreaded Topes

"Topes" is the plural of "tope" (pronounced tow-pay).

"Tope" is defined in the Larousse's Diccionario Básico de la Lengua Española as "Tope (m): Pieza que impede la accion o movimiento de un mecanissmo; freno, obstáculo, límite". My translation is "a piece that impedes the action or movement of a mechanism; a brake, an obstacle, a limit". But the real meaning is "Slow Down. Now."

Topes are speed bumps between 10-15 cm high, about a metre wide, and usually extend completely across a road. They can be made of bricks, concrete, blacktop or a row or two of shiny steel hemispheres. To quote Sanborns' Mexico Mike "Think of them as speed bumps with a desire for revenge. They are a gregarious bunch and come in 2's, 3's or even 6's. When you see one, keep your eyes open for three or four others. If you don't slow to a crawl, they will TEAR YOUR SUSPENSION APART!"

A not-so-dangerous variety, called vibradores, are only 5-10 cm high and about two metres wide. They consist of several grooves cut into a concrete pad and can give your rig quite a noisy shaking.

Although not a tope per se, when you see a sign indicating "vado" where a dry river crosses a highway, slow down. These miniature concrete valleys are designed to handle the runoff during the rainy season. Some of them are remarkably deep and steep. It is easy to scrape the rear of your rig as you begin to climb out the other side.

I drove over a topes—most everyone uses the plural as the singular—at high speed only once, and that was once too many. It is much wiser to creep over them at 15 km/hr or less.

The unmarked tope was hidden in the shadow of an overhanging branch of a leafy tree. I was too late in applying the brakes. The front of our rig reared up like a bucking bronco on its hind legs. The seatbelt yanked me back into the driver's seat after my thighs crashed into the steering wheel. When the rear wheels struck the tope, the back of our motorhome became airborne then crash-landed on the highway, flattening the springs and squishing the shocks. My exclamation was cut short because I bit my tongue as I rocked forward. Another more descriptive comment followed.

The rear bathroom cupboard opened its door to let most of its contents spill on the floor, which was now wet because the toilet vomited up its few ounces of clear water when the seat and cover flew open. One Venetian blind clattered to the floor, as did pieces of our aluminum coffee pot and tea kettle. Fortunately my computer was fastened down by a seat belt and stayed on its place. Dust escaped from everywhere, and joined the cassettes and oranges as they were ejected from open boxes.

Eventually we stopped bouncing about, and stopped. But then we had to drive a short distance before we could pull off the-two-lane highway and check for damage. Amazingly nothing was broken. A few minutes later, cupboards were repacked and order was restored. Thank heavens for a one ton frame with heavy duty springs above oversized tires.

So . . . How can you tell when topes lurk ahead?

In cities, you can guess that a tope is near when you hear trucks accelerating. That noise is the only good thing that comes from those innumerable vehicles without decent mufflers.

Outside of cities and towns, watch for signs. Some hand-painted boards—probably put there by local victims—will say Topes. Believe them, and immediately begin to slow down. Official highway signs will show two bumps, sometimes three, together.

Of a different nature but just as important are the following highway signs. 40 Km/Hr Maximo signifies a 99.9% chance of a tope very soon. 60 Km/Hr Maximo means a 95% chance of a tope within a minute. Signs with names of villages or towns are usually near a tope. Pay particular attention when you see signs such as "Cruz Escolar" or "Cruces del Escolares" (School Crossing), or a black on ochre drawing of a child walking.

Also, look for people selling drinks or hawking goods on the side of a highway; they stand where you have to slow down. Because of construction techniques watch out for bridges and, sometimes, bridges under repair.

Other unofficial things to look for are: long skid marks (on either or both sides of the road); rocks piled up on the shoulders (to prevent cars from going around the topes); white or gold zebra stripes painted across the highway (only in some considerate states); cars, trucks, and especially buses, that suddenly brake and slow down; and any vehicle in front of you whose front or rear end bounces up and down. Sometimes you'll even see scrape marks where newer cars test the durability of their mufflers or oil pans.

When driving in Mexico, let your navigator enjoy the scenery; you keep your eye on the road. Often you'll be able to detect that slightly darker line, or sometimes that lighter line, that is a tope in disguise.

And, of course, there are invisible topes. Really. I hit one that was placed in between the tracks of a railway crossing; luckily I had slowed considerably. Another time, I braked for one tope, rode over it, and fell into a deep groove that was dug out of the blacktop; obviously somebody was PO'd about something. Yet another time, I hit a tope that wasn't even there; someone had dug it down to a depth of several inches. Occasionally I've slowed for a tope, only to pass right through it because somebody dug trenches for wheels to pass through. Because of our large diameter tires, our rig doesn't have a problem with that, but many low-slung cars had scraped their undersides.

Topes are very effective in controlling vehicular speed. Considering how some Mexicans drive, this is a good thing. But they certainly affect how far one can travel in a day. Be aware of, and beware of, the dreaded Mexican topes.

Aahhh. Now this is the lazy life, a dream come true.

Besides, what's the hurry. You can always get there mañana while enjoying the scenery today.

Playa Amor

I've died and gone to heaven. Well, no. Actually, I'm alive and well, so is Liz.

We have a full hookup in the extremely clean "Playa Amor" RV park, 18 km south of San Blas, Nayarit, Mexico. We're resting on real grass between ripe coconut palms, with the sun setting in a lazy, hazy pacific-blue sky while waves are lapping on the grey sand and rocks. To seaward, pelicans, frigate birds and cormorants are feeding on the many fish rippling the ocean's surface just beyond the small breakers.

Pinch me.

On second thought, don't you dare.

I'd never realized how graceful a pelican can be. Those aeronautical engineers who developed the F-111 must have used a gliding pelican's silhouette in their initial designs. Those flesh and metal birds were meant to be in the air. With their wings outstretched and noses and beaks straining for new adventure, they slide effortlessly through the unimpeding air.

The F-111 is expert at skimming over mountains and valleys just a few metres above the tree tops. But the pelican does it better. Huge wings fully extended, with the tips curving downward, they'll skim over the ocean surface within centimetres of the water, flapping their wings only after covering many tens of metres. Though the birds were less than ten metres away, I had to use binoculars to prove to myself that their wing tips did not touch the water. Pelicans use the ground effect so efficiently that they can glide and glide and glide on the updraft just ahead of and parallel to a wave as it builds into a breaker. They climb only when the crest of the wave roils over into white water.

An F-111 can rotate its wings backward and tuck them in to form a high speed delta wing. A pelican circling five to ten metres above sea level, having spotted a fish near the surface, turns, dives, and tucks its wings in so tightly that when it cleaves the water to catch a fish, there's no splash until it bobs up on the surface. They spend only a few moments to tuck away their catch, then back into the air they go, taking a mere one or two flaps before their dripping feet clear the water.

They are spell-binding, especially at sunset when their black bodies are silhouetted against an orange sky splashed with purple clouds outlined in flame red.

On the other hand, the frigate birds with their long split tail and double dihedral wing, like WWII Stukka dive bombers, search from on high then plummet down and swoop with only their beaks slicing water to ensnare their unsuspecting victim. Most times. Occasionally they splash crash to an undignified halt, but even then usually end up with a small, wiggling thing in their beaks.

About the only time they flap their wings is to climb back to altitude. They work thermals so well that much of the climb and all of the soaring are done with wings held stationary. Effortless, efficient, they're exciting to watch.

I'd like to know the name of those small white fishing birds that "shimmie-shake" their body and tail feathers after they splash in and fly out of the water.

Somewhat less spectacular but just as efficient, cormorants, or diving ducks, paddle about near a school of fish then suddenly disappear below the surface and bob up 15-20 seconds later somewhere else. I watched one resurface and struggle with a silvery fish for several minutes. It just couldn't seem to get the fingerling in the right position. The bird even dropped it a couple of times. Then, in the blink of an eye, the fish disappeared at the same time as the bird's throat momentarily doubled in size. The cormorant shook its head, droplets sparkling in the sun, looked around, and disappeared.

I never did see it again because I was surprised by a Vee of Canada Geese, not Pelicans, flying directly overhead. Unbelievably, every bird was flapping its wings in synchronization with each other, almost as if one bird were seen many times through a kaleidoscope or in a house of mirrors.

It amazes me how one's perspective improves when there is time to smell the mango flowers. I thought a pelican was a stupid looking bird, a frigate was a boat, and cormorants lived in New Brunswick. I'm learning otherwise in nature's immense schoolyard.

Who pinched me? The sun has set. Jejenes, those noseeums, those flies with a jaw, those piranhas of the air, are successfully attacking my ankles. It's time to go inside.

Will I be able to live my dream again? Sí. Tomorrow.

The Green Flash

From the Pacific beaches of Mexico, almost every clear night Liz and I watch the sun sink into the ocean, and we see the green flash. It occurs only in the last second, or part of a second, as the sun disappears completely. The sun turns green. Really. It does.

We've seen it several times, and so can you.

Although you can occasionally observe this astronomical phenomenon with only your eyes, it is better to use binoculars. Of course, you must always be extremely careful when looking at the sun, and especially when using binoculars which increase the chance for eye damage. It is also very important that you do not stare directly at the sun for more than a few seconds, because your eyes will register reverse colour—a greenish image which moves with eye movement—and this could mask the green flash.

Watch the sun out of the corner of your eye until the last few seconds.

After the sun is at least three-quarters hidden, when you can focus on it, you should see the edges start to turn to lime green, and then the remaining gold quickly changes into a flash of green. Often the colour is a very pale jade, reminiscent of unripe lemons, but once in a while the last visage of the sun will shine like a fluorescent emerald. Once there was an inversion layer, and it caused the setting sun to split in two during its last two or three seconds. There were two green flashes, the top being the brighter.

An 80-year old vendedor of small bananas & warm eggs.

Much more rarely, the green will spontaneously transform into amethyst-blue. The only time we have seen that, the brilliant blue collapsed in on itself and disappeared into a pinprick of light which was two to three degrees above the horizon. It was how I imagine a star collapsing upon itself to form a stellar black hole; astronomically beautiful.

The green flash is real. Look for it.

Ciudad Guzmán, Modern Mexico

Ciudad Guzmán is at the junction of Highway 80 (libre, free, rough) and Highway 54D (cuota, toll, four-lane luxury). Each highway is a link between Guadalajara and Colima. Take either, but do stop for a day or so and explore this pleasant, clean, friendly, modern and prosperous Mexican city. We came for a half day's rest, stayed for the long Easter weekend, and regretted having to move on.

It being very warm, Liz and I drove Highway 80 from Guadalajara to Colima, because the AAA map showed it to pass by the south end of a large lake. We wanted to have a swim. The lake does exist, but it is dry sand many months of the year. It is so dry and shallow that it has a blacktopped highway passing through its middle. I've heard a story about one traveller who was on that highway. He couldn't believe it when the bus driver wouldn't slow down when the wind was so high that the entire 5 Km of blacktop disappeared in a sand storm that would have done the Sahara Desert proud. It seems that he was afraid of somebody driving into the back of his bus.

Our secondary highway transformed into a narrow street enclosed by clean, well cared for buildings. Several were under restoration. One of the first things we noticed in Guzmán was that the paved streets were free of litter, dust and obnoxious odours. Our street led to a large, grass-and-trees zócalo (sew-ka-low), or central plaza. Four churches, the tourist information office, and many stores, shops and markets were within easy waking distance from there. As tourists, we were allowed, nay encouraged by the local policemen, to park next to the plaza all day and overnight. Some local vehicles were ticketed for expired parking meters.

If you want to avoid Americanized cities, visit Ciudad Guzmán. It is not a tourist town—Liz and I were the only visitors—but a town by Mexicans for Mexicans.

It took us two days to find the "Balneario de Katrina", a commercial swimming complex ten kilometres north of the city. It boasts three pools, shaded eating areas, food stalls, lots of grass, and hundreds of happy Mexican families. We had our swim.

But the best part was the city itself.

The four large churches of Guzmán are worth visiting because of the diversity of architectural designs. Each is different. The cathedral with its domes and buttresses is magnificent, albeit on a smaller scale than the one in Guadalajara. One church has beautiful stained glass windows depicting the story of Our Lady of Guadeloupe; all of its high ceiling frescoes and intricate designs are painted on plaster. See this one on a sunny morning. Another is very abstract-modern, plainly painted, but with Grecian-style concrete pillars. Yet another is old and garish, with huge rafters of logs, reminiscent of the ancient missions.

Behind the cathedral the enclosed mercado, or local market, had an exceptional variety of vegetables, fruit, fish and other seafood, pork and beef. And it was clean. For the first time in Mexico, I truly enjoyed walking down the aisles. And it seemed to me that I was charged the same as everyone else in the city. Of course, prices are determined by what the vendor figures he or she can charge, so it always pays to haggle a little.

Surrounding the mercado, like the layers of onions, are shops selling clothing, pharmaceuticals, hardware items, shoes, electrical and electronic items, and furniture. And surrounding these, many booths were selling candy (including a fabulous confection of sugar and nuts), watches, cassettes (many pirated and with photocopied labels), helium balloons, beach wear, belts, pancakes, fried bananas with exquisite sauces, hot dogs, hamburgers, succulent cactus, fruit cups soaked in lime juice, and so many other things I can't remember. But, saving the best for last, the Churros — a sweet dough formed into a long spiral, fried in boiling oil, then coated with cinnamon sugar — were absolutely scrumptious.

We found the Bull Ring, and the Cock Fight Pit, and we stumbled across the weekend flea market. We even joined a couple of parades, one with fireworks.

Mexican women and children will look long and hard, and stare unabashedly at whatever has their attention; the men are not quite so bold.

Mexicans will go anywhere that they can. We've had several people walk under our awning because it was the quickest way to get somewhere.

We discovered that unkempt exteriors can mask lovely interiors, especially if a satellite dish is on the roof. The rich live next door to the poor and refuse-filled empty lots. Almost all buildings have ornamental ironwork on the windows and doorways. Many buildings are falling apart or never finished; we were told no taxes are paid on untenanted property. There were areas of the city that were better than others, but we didn't see a Snob Hill area.

A block of houses is just that, a wall of houses. If there are any grassy areas, flowers or shrubs, they're inside private courtyards.

By the way, many of the shopkeepers speak much better English than Liz and I speak español. Although they seem pleased with our attempting fractured Spanish (I dasn't yet call it español) I get the impression that they would prefer to practise their English. Their pronunciation is almost always perfect but, of course, they do stumble over unknown words.

During our third day there, two young gentlemen came by and asked us to speak to them in English. The end result was that they got a tape and photocopied pages of expressions in English, and we got a tape in español, including the alphabet.

Mexico is more than sun and tropical beaches and quaint, dusty villages and tourist traps designed for Canadians and Americans. There are also fabulous colonial and heritage towns; there are prosperous business cities.

Ciudad Guzmán is one of the latter, and we enjoyed seeing yet another aspect of Mexico. If you're travelling in the area, drop in and drycamp for a day or two. It's not exciting, but it is modern Mexico, and worth a visit.

The Making of a Tortilla

Tortillas are to Mexico as Maple Syrup is to Canada and Coke is to the United States.

Have you ever wondered how tortillas are made?

They can be made by hand, as described by Steve Rogers of Deadwood, Oregon, USA, in the Winter 92/93 issue of "The People's Guide Travel Letter". The following was excerpted from that magazine.

"Combine two cups of [unrefined] tortilla flour with lukewarm [purified] water until it becomes a stiff dough in your hands, then let it rest for about 20 minutes. It should then break cleanly but still be damp enough to hold together. Experiment to get it right.

"You need a metal or wooden circular press (available in Mexico, of course) and a clear plastic bag with the edges cut off. Pinch off a chunk of the masa dough, roll it into a ping pong ball, place it between the plastic sheets in the press, and slowly flatten with firm steady pressure. Experiment to get the right thickness.

"To remove the tortilla from the plastic, hold it in one hand, slowly remove the upper plastic sheet, invert the tortilla into the other hand, and peel off that side. If it cracks, roll it into a ping-pong ball, etc. Now the trick is to get the limp tortilla onto a hot griddle without folding or wrinkling it. Experiment until you get it right.

"The griddle or cast-iron pan should be dry—no oil—and hot enough that water droplets dance on top. At the perfect temperature, the tortillas won't stick, and if they do smoke it shouldn't be very much. Experiment until you get it right.

"Flop the tortilla onto the griddle and when you see that it has begun to cook through, flip it with a spatula or with bare fingers like the Mexican women do. Some scorching and smoke are okay. Cook the other side for the same amount of time, then flip it back to side one and cook it until the tortilla begins to inflate.

"This is what separates authentic tortillas from the chewy fakes; if everything is right, moisture in the dough will turn to steam and magically inflate the tortilla like a balloon, cooking it on the inside.

"Making real tortillas isn't all that difficult, especially if you already know how to cook. Merely repeat the above instructions several thousands of times, or until you consistently get it perfect!"

Bah humbug. "... a tortilla is a melancholy form of nourishment." Viva Mexico by Charles Flandrau (1908).

What really happens? How are tortillas really made? Liz and I spent five days in Ciudad Guzmán, and we think we learned the truth.

A beat up, rusty excuse for a truck with four bald tires and no lights smokes into town, and a bewhiskered old man drives up to the grist mill. He's paid a couple of pesos for a tattered bag full of overly ripe, hard as a nut, kernels of corn, which he drops on a dirt floor.

As he leaves, a woman picks up the bag and starts to add his corn to a wide, flat hopper, spreading it with a stick while looking for what shouldn't be there. Slowly the corn vibrates down to a narrow opening, where clear but unpurified water—from a rusty tap at the end of a lead pipe—is slowly dripping and wetting the corn. Both corn and water disappear into a grinder—driven by twin belts and an extremely large electric motor—from which emerges a doughy, sticky paste called masa. Every part of the corn is used, but it's ground so finely that there is nothing to get stuck between your teeth.

The masa is scooped by hand into a large reusable plastic bucket and tamped down until it's full. Then the bucket is weighed and covered with a damp cloth to keep the moisture in and the bugs out. Eventually a bucket or two are transferred to a three-wheeled, motorized, open cart and delivered to restaurants, tortillerias, and who knows where else.

A tortilleria makes and sells tortillas, early in the morning and often in the middle of the afternoon. If you walk through any Mexican town and see a long queue of women and children with buckets and towels in their hands, you have probably found a tortilleria.

Tortillas are mass-produced in a simple and ingenious machine. At the beginning of the day, some damp paste is placed into a hopper, the propane gas flames are ignited, and the machine squeaks and squeals after it is turned on. Slowly some of the paste is squeezed out onto a steel mesh conveyor as thin disks of uncooked corn meal. The operator rolls up the first few into a big ball and puts that back into the hopper.

At some magically determined moment when the disks look right and the oven and plates are hot enough, the thin disks of masa are allowed to fall onto another conveyor of linked ceramic plates which pass over two metres of gas flames. Side one is lightly cooked. Just before they disappear, the plates come together with a second set of linked plates, trapping the disks between them. The disks are turned upside down, and both conveyors pass through the flames again to finish cooking and scorching. They emerge as hot, lightly browned, soft and flexible cooked pie crusts and fall onto a third conveyor which delivers them to a woman who puts them on a scale for weighing.

Total time for one tortilla was about 50 seconds. For 20, about two and half minutes. I guess it takes about sixty tortillas to make up a kilo, and almost everyone I saw bought at least half a kilo, and more often than not, a kilo or more. Which explains why the queue of women and children is so long.

Twice Liz and I gave up waiting to buy our daily order of seven or eight tortillas, but when we did make it to the scales, they gave them to us. Oh, I forget to mention that tortillas cost two or three pesos per kilo, the best buy in all of Mexico.

So . . . If you want a tortilla in Canada, don't buy bags of crispy chips, use Steve's recipe and experiment until you get it right, or you run out of money. Or spend that money to drive to Mexico and when in Mexico do as the Mexicans do. Line up and buy inexpensive, warm and nourishing tortillas fresh from a tortilleria. They really are quite tasty, if you use them to wrap up refried beans, flavourful rice, spiced meat, or cheese and green peppers.

Playa Azul

Just like hot pigs in cool mud, Liz and I are wallowing in Mexican luxury at the Hotel Playa Azul, in a Pacific beach resort village of the same name. Our ever-faithful gasoline-guzzling Class C is fully hooked up between two clean and well maintained swimming pool complexes. One has a poolside restaurant, a bar, real grass, and shade; the other shows off a waterslide, a poolside snackery, an in-pool bar, and shade.

The ocean beach with its young surfers and a rusting, grounded freighter is only fifteen metres (yards) away. It is accessible through a gauntlet of palapas, ramadas and tiendas full of exotic foods, cervezas, tropical shell-figures, and colourful clothing.

We drycamped for 19 out of the last 21 days. Until you've done that in semitropical heat, you have no idea how luxurious it is to be on level ground that is raked each day, to be able to hose down the dust, to be surrounded by numerous shady shrubs and palms, to have showers each day without worrying about precious water, to be able to wash and rinse the dishes properly, to be able to launder more than the unmentionables, to be able to flush the john (that's okay, that's my name) long enough to get rid of all the stains, and to be able to turn on every amazingly-bright light while the radio is playing. That's luxury.

And for me, the 'coup de gras' means I can compute while the air conditioner is blowing on my sun-browned back and pool-damp forelocks.

After heading south from Tecomán to Playa Azul, we had to drive nonstop through 330 km (200 mi) of up-and-down, isolated, winding, twisting blacktop. If I were to believe only half of the three warnings I was given, the road is full of poverty-stricken, rifle-carrying bandidos who put logs across the road to stop rich gringos. I was so nervous that I wouldn't stop at any of the three beautiful, uninhabited, and fantasy-fulfilling south-sea beaches that magically appeared from behind hills or plantations of coconuts. When our short-range CB occasionally sputtered with Spanish, I had nightmare visions of modern-day Robin Hoods organizing an ambush.

Imagination can be an awful thing, and that day it was. Intellectually I knew better, Mexicans have proven to be a very warm, pleasant, friendly and helpful people. But both Liz and I heaved deep sighs of relief when we finally found the beautiful Hotel Playa Azul.

We did have one problem. New found friends from Cuyutlan told us it was a three-hour drive. The North American AAA map indicated the distance was 200, which we assumed was 200 kilometres. After a leisurely, late-morning start and a partial fill-up, we were on our way. Six hours later we were forced to stop at Caleta de Campo and buy exorbitantly-priced gasoline from battered 45 gallon barrels.

Even though we had an hour left before sunset in which to travel the remaining 50 km to Playa Azul, we stayed overnight. We do not drive at night because of slow-moving cars, overloaded trucks and ATC's, many without headlights and taillights. There's been many a morning when we've seen freshly killed animals—cows, horses, mules and dogs—on both sides of the roads. Cows and horses don't have tail lights.

Looking back in safety, it was a fun drive. We saw a lemur, two snakes, five iguanas (one in a tree, two captured and offered for sale by children, and two scurrying across the road), and several different birds. We also heard a monkey or a parrot screeching in a jungle that was encroaching on the narrow highway. There was enough tension to ease the monotony of driving on an uninhabited two-lane highway, and enough variety of green tropical plants to make us really aware that we were below the Tropic of Cancer.

Neither I nor Liz would change a thing because we are fulfilling an eight-year dream. This journey is the destination, and right now we are truly spoiled! We're loving every luxurious moment in Playa Azul.

Ixtapa: A Cotton Candy City

As a child, do you remember going to a fair and buying Cotton Candy. Remember how big it looked, and how great those first bites tasted. But then remember how disappointed you were when you realized all that fluff was gone, and you couldn't remember eating it? Ixtapa is like that.

Once it was a real city, but that was destroyed by the forces of nature and its oceans. Then it was redesigned and rebuilt by architects, computers, and marketeers.

It is an extremely beautiful city, but without soul. Like the photography in the underrated movie "Edward Scissorhands", it is clean and sharp and empty. It reminds me of the newest gambling houses in Las Vegas, all paint and glitter with no substance. It's like a three-dimensional, computer-generated virtual reality; it exists, but it's not solid.

Tourists live there. Mexicans do not. There are fantastic hotels and excellent restaurants and air-conditioned malls selling overpriced trinkets. There are no mercados or tiendas or wagons selling tostadas and tacos on the square corners. There are no children hawking belts, hats and serapes on immaculate streets. The buildings are painted in matching and complementary colours, and the streets and sidewalks are continuously level and clean. There is no litter. There are no bare brick walls with splotches of mortar filling the cracks. There are no dirt soccer fields or plain concrete basketball courts. There are immaculate golf courses, fenced-in tennis courts, and a neat marina with white boats contrasting against walled-in blue-green water.

It is a great location for an escape from winter snows. It is a place to sleep, to have a martini (shaken, not stirred), to go deaf in a disco, to stroll in air conditioned malls, and to eat a hamburger with Pepsi and fries. Ixtapa is for Americans, Canadians, and Europeans; it is not for Mexicans.

But an 11 km trip to Zihuatanejo will bring you back into real Mexico. Rent a car or ride one of the many buses or taxis to get there. That's where the casual beachfront restaurants have menus in español, although English is understood very well. That's where you can dicker in the vendor stalls for a great variety of souvenirs. That's where you can look through an open door or window and see the magnificent furniture that stands on the other side of a stained and dilapidated wall. That is where people are vibrantly and busily alive. Zihuatanejo is Mexican.

One of our nearby neighbours at Playa Linda.

We drycamped on a long ocean beach at Playa Linda, only a few kilometres outside of Ixtapa. It is not a trailer park, but a picnic area with coconut trees providing shade for the likes of Twiggy, and three restaurant-bars providing drinks and snacks under thatched ramadas for the likes of us. Nevertheless, motorhomes are welcome to park and stay overnight. Police do patrol the area twenty-four hours a day, when they're there.

At night, twinkling stars and bright planets dazzle and dance in the black sky, unhindered by lights. There is no electricity even though a transformer is only metres away. During hot, sunny days several crocodiles float almost submerged in a nearby river or hide on shaded banks. Colourful birds fly and squawk overhead. All are protected from over zealous tourists by a chain-link fence.

Ixtapa is a luxurious cotton candy city that should be admired and tasted at least once. But for a more fulfilling and satisfying adventure, drive to and explore Zihuatanejo.

Hasta Luego.

Acapulco: Why?

To my way of RV thinking, the only good thing about Acapulco is the Acapulco Trailer park which isn't even in the city. It is 10 km to the north, in Pie de la Cuesta.

This is a nicely maintained, secure park with full hookups (but low water pressure) and access to a fresh water lagoon and a Pacific beach . Be careful. Sometimes it is dangerous to swim in the ocean near Acapulco because of undertows.

In addition to having owners who speak reasonable English, this park has a store with all of the necessities at reasonable prices. There are also clean bathrooms and showers, local and long distance telephone services, boat launching into a lagoon and bird sanctuary, and nighttime breezes. There are also some really spectacular sunsets, many which rival those in Arizona and New Mexico because of their brilliant oranges and purples.

Quinta Dora is another reasonable, slightly cheaper nearby RV Park, also with access to both bodies of water. There are also two grassy RV parks on the south side of Acapulco. But they do not have beach access, and are even less accessible to the centre of Acapulco. A fifth RV park is situated downtown but we weren't able to find it during three days of motorcycle driving; because of other concerns, we didn't look too hard.

There are so much smoke and grime in the city that when we wiped perspiration from our faces the cloth turned black.

Acapulco is an overgrown city that believes its own public relations advertisements. There are several expensive places to go, to see, and to be see in. And it does have several lovely, sandy beaches, two of which advertise that riptides are usually not dangerous in the afternoon and swimming might be okay. Amid heavy traffic, pushy drivers put those in Montréal and Québec to shame.

Acapulco would probably be enjoyed most by those who own condominiums or who rent hotels with all of the facilities of expensive North American hotel resorts. Following is a quote from the booklet 'Acapulco Inside 1993' ". . . All this is aimed to keep Acapulco with its everlasting versatility, to offer service not only

Beautiful to look at, dangerous to swim in.

to the most demanding tourists – the rich ones – but also to those ones with a limited economy . . . ". This city is not for Liz and me.

Granted, we are biased. We left Kelowna because it was getting too big when the population started to exceed 90,000. I've read that Acapulco residents number two million. I've also read that they number only a half million. I wonder how many tourists are rushing around during a busy winter season?

Although you might like Acapulco, we'll not be going back. Several Mexican acquaintances are of the same opinion.

The Caves of Juxtlahuaca

If you were to drive approximately 65 km north of Acapulco on Highway 95, then travel another 35 km eastward on a winding, paved but potholed road which includes three long and narrow cobblestone village streets with overhanging roofs, you would arrive at the village of Colotlipa. Seven km further and you could be parked at the entrance of a large and exciting cave complex.

The cave is locked to ensure that vandals can't get in and destroy or steal some of the natural wonders. It also ensures your safety because to get in, you must be accompanied by a qualified and properly equipped guide.

As you enter Colotlipa, you will see a hand-lettered sign "Información de Grutas" that points to a gate in a wall on the right of a two-burro-wide street. Drive about thirty metres more, while avoiding gutters down the middle of all streets, then park beside the central plaza across from the church. Lock your vehicle, walk back, bang on the gate until someone arrives, then ask about going to the caves, or grutas.

Waiting in the shadows, a national pastime.

What you hear will be something like this, loosely translated. It will cost a group of one to twenty people eighty New Pesos. A guide will accompany you. He will carry at least two Coleman lamps, extra mantles and matches, and a waterproof flashlight. The group must provide their own vehicle to get from Colotlipa to the Grutas de Juxtlahuaca. (Because we had a motorhome, Liz and I drove with three charming senoritas in their VW Bug.)

Chartered groups and Mexican tourists arrive almost every weekend, so you can save money by being there at that time. Not knowing any better, we arrived Thursday afternoon. We spent Friday wandering around the village and being taught Spanish by a group of kids who just wouldn't go away. Early Saturday morning we browsed in a market which wasn't there on Friday, then joined up with a group of explorers about 10 a.m. We left at 11:30 because three federal bureaucrats were late.

We were lucky that we wore shorts and running shoes, and that we took along drinking water and a snack. Unlike the caves near Nakusp, B.C., where ice forms on the cavern walls, the humidity and temperature in this cave increased as we descended. The floor was slippery and damp in several places. Our spelunking adventure took more than five hours, and the snack was greatly appreciated by all when we sat down for a rest.

We also brought along our flashlight, which proved very useful whenever both Coleman lamps were hidden around corners or behind columns of calcite. Although some steps and levelled walkways have been created, walking in the dark or shadows can result in banged shins, a minor stumble, or a bruised cranium.

We didn't bring our Spanish-English dictionary—remember it is dark in those caves—and we missed most of the comments, discussions and jokes by our affable Mexican guide.

The cave complex is at least two kilometres long. The series of interconnected caves and passageways vary from a mere metre and a half high to 75 m high, from less than a metre wide to 125 m wide. The floor changes from smooth, sandy soil to smooth, slippery rock to rough, jagged stones; and from flat to manmade steps. There is one spot where you have to slide or crawl down a couple of metres of [seemingly] treacherous calcite.

What lurks in the darkness?

At the end of all this are two clear-water lagoons, one of which you will walk through and get your knees wet. You can go for a swim in the shallow water, but watch out for submerged stalagmites.

As I walked along in the middle of our group, with gas lamps hissing at each end of the procession, I was reminded of the scene in Snow White where the seven dwarfs cast grotesquely twisted shadows on the walls of their mine. So did our group, and sometimes those shadows would disappear into a cavern or tunnel, sometimes they would tower over us, and other times they would slink around a silvery or rose column of calcite like living Spandex. Or there would be no shadows at all, just black shapes silhouetted by a ghostly white light flickering between the stalagmites and stalactites. (When you're not sure which is which, think of ants in your pants; when the mites go up, the tights go down.)

The variety of shapes was surprising. Of course, there were many of the standard, cone-shaped stalactites and stalagmites. Some were joined and looked like the parts of a gigantic pipe organ, or a waterfall of frozen ice. One group resembled brain coral, supposedly transplantable to anyone who wanted to stay in the caves for a week. Other areas were formed of wavy, kelp-like fronds of calcite. Some of these were hollow and when rubbed or slapped in certain places, would produce musical notes that sounded as if they were made on calypso drums. Another area, high overhead, had produced stunning translucent rose-and-pink opal; think of it, we were walking inside an immense geode.

In addition to all of these natural beauties, and more, there are several paintings that date back to the 1000 BC era of the Olmecs. And there are even two skeleton remains which have turned into stone.

We enjoyed Las Grutas. The off-the-beaten-track trip there and back was challenging, but worth it. Happy spelunking.

Ghost Town or Town Alive?

Real de Catorce and Taxco are two Mexican towns which exist because of silver. One is dead and the other is lively. Which should you see? Both. Spend four hours in one, four days in the other.

To get to Catorce—so named because of 14 bandidos that plagued the area—entails driving on 20 Km of new, bumpy and winding cobblestone highway. Once there you must park your RV at the entrance of a narrow 2 km tunnel which passes through a mountain and takes you to the town on the other side. A low

Class B might be able to drive through, cars and trucks can. (If you do, remember to use the intercom to ensure that no one is coming toward you.) We recommend you take a bus from nearby towns, such as Cedral on Highway 57.

Real de Catorce is a ghost town with two churches, a thousand inhabitants without a noticeable source of income, and innumerable broken and crumbling walls that define where homes, businesses, two mints, and an opera house used to be on steep hillsides and river frontage.

This cemetery is so crowded the graves abut the stone steps.

There are two or three hotels but only one seemed worthy of the name. It was on the far side of the almost empty village, and across from a tiny church whose wooden floor is made up from the tops of interred coffins. Liz and I couldn't get into the others. They might be lovely on the inside.

The town is quiet. It's so quiet that while Liz and I were wandering about, we thought we could hear horses walking on gravel but couldn't see any. Then a whistle made us look up to a ridge one or two kilometres distant, and we saw four burros working their way down a rocky path. Eventually the quiet got to us. After an hour, we were talking in whispers so as not to disturb the silence. It was marvellously and unexpectedly relaxing.

We stared over partial walls with cacti and trees growing out of them. We looked over crooked streets, cul de sacs, and footpaths where winter rains have washed away many cobblestones. We wandered inside rooms partially filled by collapsed roofs and second-storey floors. Looking at miniature ruins on the sides of nearby valleys and gorges, it was impossible not to try to visualize what this once thriving town of 70,000 people had been like in the early 1900's.

It must have been a beautiful city, with its walled haciendas and grand homes of the mining aristocracy, waterworks, electric lights, an opera house where Caruso sang, and when thousands of people lived in active, crowded, organized confusion that seems to personify the Mexican style of living.

Real de Catorce is a town in which your imagination can and should run freely in the ghostly silence hovering over a maze of rock, adobe walls, and unnamed streets.

On the other hand, faraway Taxco doesn't need your imagination, just your appreciation. It is full of lively artisans and silversmiths with their own artistic imaginations converted to touchable and valuable silver 'objets de art'.

The most amazing piece of sculpture I've ever seen is polished silver inlaid with turquoise and jade, artistically formed to create an illusion of the Madonna by letting one see what is not there. Absolutely astounding!

Do visit the store-factory "Los Castillos" and marvel at some of their other art, too. When in the back rooms, talk with the artists, especially the older ones who can tell some very intriguing stories as they transform metal to magic.

It takes a couple of hours of winding, climbing, twisting driving on a narrow, smooth, two-lane, blacktopped highway to get to Taxco, which is held onto rugged hillsides by silver mines which cling like the roots of a fig tree. But it is worth the trip. If you can't drive there, take a first-class bus.

Once in the city, there are very few level places, very few. In this city we've seen VW Bugs which couldn't make it around steep uphill curves, a motorcyclist who had to leave a passenger behind while he struggled to the top of a hill, and a 1972 Ford that had to back up twice to squeeze around a corner. This is not an RV paradise. But it is a visual one.

There are literally hundreds of shops making or selling silver. (If you want to import and sell some in Canada, telephone or write to El Presidente, or the Mayor. He will definitely respond.) Many of the pieces are stamped out by the thousands, then hand-polished. However, there are also several almost-one-of-a-kind pieces, too. Prices are negotiable, of course. It's best to visit several shops before buying anything, provided you can remember what you saw where.

Enjoying a snack in Irene's rooftop restaurant.

Artists in silver begat artists in wood, paint, bronze, gold, and literature. This is a town for those who appreciate created beauty, or even a discussion about the merits of this piece, or that picture, or this or that. And what better locale for a chat than on a wrought-iron balcony overlooking the main square, or in Irene's restaurant hidden in a rooftop courtyard, facing a wall covered in a tiled, Mayan frieze.

The second night there, Liz and I walked to a spot that overlooked a myriad of hazy city and house lights below us while hiding the pinprick of lights and stars above. It was a marvellous sight, and a magical minute. Next day as we were wandering through a gallery, dejá vu almost struck me down. The same scene, painted on burlap and hanging on a wall, complete with all my emotions, was there. "Every picture or object contains meaning; however, like a dream, it does not explain itself. Author unknown" It didn't have to. And it was for sale.

The museum displaying the winners of the annual international silversmith competition is a must-see. Bring along a magnifying glass so you can study the detail on some of the smaller pieces.

The baroque Church of Santa Prisca on the plaza is another must-see, even if you are an agnostic or fear pipes will freeze in July if you dare to venture inside. Beautiful, bizarre, obscene, miraculous, overwhelming, fantastic, amazing . . . these and many more adjectives are used to describe the visual onslaught that awaits you.

The restored buildings and grounds of Hacienda del Chorrillo are now the Governor's summer guest house. It is open to visitors. If you can find the kitchen, you might even get a cool drink to enjoy next to a fountain.

Casa Humboldt or Museo de Arte Virreinal, Convent of San Bernardino, Museo de Plateria, Museo William Spratling, tour guides, native markets and other sights and delights await you in Taxco.

Real de Catorce and Taxco are two towns separated by time, the vagaries of politics, and several hundred kilometres. Each owes their existence to silver, and you owe it to yourself to spend a little silver to see them both.

The Jewel of Cuernavaca

The Diamante Trailer Park & Club is just as its name implies, a diamond, a real jewel.

Each campsite has electricity, water and sewer, and a concrete pad beside a gravel parking area. Paved streets run between real grass, flowers and shade trees. All of this is kept watered and trimmed by four grounds keepers.

What a pleasure it is to wake up to the musical chirps of birds or the muffled thonk thounk of someone playing tennis instead of the raucous crowing of a rooster.

In addition to the night-lighted tennis courts there are handball courts, a gymnasium, and three chlorinated swimming pools.

Both rectangular pools are quite small, although the bigger one does have submerged stools next to a bar. The third is a 25 m kidney-shaped pool which is unique. In the middle there's a barely submerged island surrounded by deep water. The outside quarter of the pool is only inches deep, except for an imbedded Jacuzzi. I enjoyed swimming in the deep part, then being able to lie down in the shallow water to keep cool while the tropical sun warmed and tanned my relaxed body. Unfortunately, to tan my back without drowning, I had to get out and lay out my towel on the nearby grass within arms-reach of a cerveza fria (cold beer).

But no place is perfect. Because this campsite is only 100 km from Mexico City, there is no ocean beach within walking distance.

In compensation, only minutes away there is a truly huge K-mart department-pharmacy-grocery store. A little further to the south, off the first exit on the highway, there's a Commercial Mexicana complex with a well-stocked supermarket and several other stores. If you were to travel south along Avenida Diana for a short distance, there is a very large, very modern shopping mall with hundreds of shops and sun-blocking underground parking. Centro, or the old town, is slightly farther away.

Once the smoke and blue haze from all the burning was washed away in a couple of good thunderstorms, we were surprised to see two snowcapped mountains. Like seeing several types of cactus growing among leafy trees, it just doesn't seem appropriate to see snow in the tropics.

If the Diamante RV park sounds like just the place for you, stay on the autopista coming from Acapulco or the airport, then take the K-mart turnoff and put the store behind you. Drive along Calle Diana for approximately a kilometre, then turn left again at the Diamante sign. We stayed there three times.

Most of the 150 sites are permanently occupied, but we always managed to get in. There is also a parking space for a caravan, but it doesn't have the ambience of the rest of the park. In the middle of a week there may be only four or five families there, but during the weekend many people drive down from Mexico City to relax in this quiet oasis.

This is one place to which Liz and I will return again, even if we have to fly down and rent a trailer. Perhaps we'll meet you in this jewel of Cuernavaca.

Recreational Vehicles are Convenient

Full time RVing is an amazing lifestyle. Until Liz and I had this opportunity to travel for as long as we want, we never realized just how invigorating and relaxing a stress-free vacation can be. We have no concern about deadlines nor do we need to cover a certain number of miles per day. Sure there are frustrations. Where can we get propane? Why did we park on top of an ant hill? Do we have enough gasoline? Do we have enough extra money this month to go there or do that? But there's no rush. We're travelling like turtles, slowly and inside our own home. We have RV Convenience.

We met a young college man carrying only a back pack. His summer job was to determine that lodging, restaurants and other facilities were as advertised in a popular "travel-cheaply" guidebook. His monthly expense account was the same as ours; he was surprised to realize how inexpensive RVing could be. But we wouldn't change places with him, even if we were paid to do so, because someone would be telling us where to go.

A young couple travelling by bicycle averaged 60 km/day, while carrying their tent, stove, utensils and clothes in two saddlebags. On their best day they managed 100 km. We met a man travelling by motorcycle who had to average 325 km/day for two weeks. He carried one small bag lashed to the passenger seat. But we wouldn't change places with them, this was the rainy season. Besides, we like to set our own pace.

A retired Spanish-speaking couple from California were travelling in a compact station-wagon all the way to Tierra del Fuego, which is at the extreme southern tip of South America. Like us they have unlimited time, but twice the monthly budget that we do. Nevertheless, we wouldn't change our roomy motorhome for their overcrowded car. We never did find out exactly what they spent on gas, lodgings and meals, but we're certain it was considerably more than we spent. They'll keep hotels and restaurants happy, we'll bring smiles to owners of Pemex franchises and vendors in mercados.

Often we have to save money to keep within our budget. Sometimes we want to spend it on something extra special that would blow our budget. So we drycamp wherever we fancy, at little or no cost.

At night we sleep together in our familiar double-bed, on our own puffy pillows, and between sheets that we washed.

We get up when we want to, not when some tour guide says we must, or when a hotel maid mistakenly opens our door.

When nature calls, we know the bathroom is clean. A night-time call can be answered without having to get dressed to go into a public hallway or to the building next door.

Our showers are warm, not cold.

Breakfast in our pyjamas can be coffee, bacon and eggs, toast and jam; or cereal and milk; or a dish of sliced mangos, papaya, plums, apples, bananas, oranges and yoghurt. Or we can get dressed, go for a wake-up walk, and enjoy a morning special at a restaurant or cantina of our choosing.

We buy fruit and vegetables and put them in the fridge until we want them again. We don't have to eat them all in one day before they spoil.

While driving, if we see an interesting sideroad or a road-side market we can explore it rather than wistfully passing by in a bus. If we want to stop for a hot coffee, breakfast or lunch, we do. All we need is a reasonably flat pullout, preferably a mirador, with a view of a green jungle valley or a roaring river gorge.

Anytime we want some grapes, cookies, chocolate bars, a cold beer or a pinch of ocean-salt and water, we can get it immediately. We don't have to risk driving into a city to find a store that might have what we want, and then haggle over the price. Most times we don't have to stop at all.

We can brush our teeth after each and every meal and snack, if we want to.

When it rains, we can sit under our awning or go inside to read or play games. We don't have to head for a restaurant and buy something we don't really want, just to keep dry.

Our dresses and pants are hung up, not packed away in a too small suitcase or a stuffy duffel bag. When electricity is available, we can iron our clothes.

To us, convenience is freedom to do what we want, when we want. We have the freedom to choose a destination, and arrival time. And, if we think we might see something special en route, we can stop and enjoy an unexpected diversion. We never have to worry about where we'll sleep.

Fulltime RVing has given us this convenience and freedom. We wouldn't exchange it for anything.

Addictive San Miguel

San Miguel de Allende (Ah-yen-day) is addictive. Liz and I came for two or three days, stayed ten, and will return.

I can resist almost anything. But a dynamic and growing city that has been declared a national historical monument, a charming city with old world elegance, a city with a local newspaper in English, a city with hotels and restaurants and vendors that span entire financial and taste-bud spectra, a city which is one of the internationally recognized centres of art, a city with potable water and two RV parks and, believe it or not, a city with an active computer club, was almost too much to resist. Nevertheless we did manage to get away, eventually.

La Siesta is an RV park on the edge of town. It offers full hookups, a swimming pool, and accessibility to the services of a hotel of the same name. Lago Dorado is a quiet RV park about 4 km outside of the city. It offers full hookups, a laundry area, shady trees, green grassy sites, and a small pool. The price for either was N$ 30.00 per night for two, with reduced weekly and monthly rates. Whichever you choose you will need transportation to the city centre. Your vehicle could be a taxi, a bus, a passing truck from Lago Dorado, or your own bicycle or small car.

We were disappointed in both when we visited them at the end of May, which was well past the winter tourist season. Full services were not available but their rates didn't change. The electrical system of La Siesta looked terribly unsafe (as do most in Mexico, but they do work) and the deep pool was empty. At Lago Dorado, the laundromat was inaccessible and the filled pool was too murky for us to want to swim in it.

Although the road to it is rough cobblestone, we stayed at the Lago Dorado on two different nights to empty our tanks, top up our water supply, and recharge our batteries. We also recharged ourselves with really deep sleeps. At night we extinguished the campground lights and luxuriated in darkness. During early morning hours, only a few bird chirps mingled with the distant bray of a lonely burro. We were too far away to hear claps of thunder generated by continuous fireworks; San Miguel seems to have at least one or two festivals a week.

Are you asking "But if you spent ten days in fabulous San Miguel, and only two nights in an RV park, where did you stay?" Good question. We drycamped on a street that encircles Parque Juarez, beside the wall of a hotel that charges about N$400 per night, in the shade of several large trees, and within walking distance of the centre of the city.

We didn't plan to. Liz thinks I'm foolhardy, stubborn as a burro, etc., etc. But, being the competent, adventurous driver that I am, I thought that we should drive to the central plaza and park there while we had a quick look around. Within a minute of being in the southern edge of the city, we had to detour off the main street which was under construction. Within two minutes even I knew that I had made a mistake. The sideroad changed from flat rock to uneven cobblestone, and the pink walls closed in at an alarming rate. We stopped in the first wider-than-usual spot we found, pulled our 7.5 m (23') rig far over to the right, and hid behind a telephone post. Cars, taxis, vans, large trucks and buses squeezed by, often waiting patiently as approaching vehicles passed first. Nobody honked nor asked us to move, so we didn't. After the second hourly police patrol went by without stopping, we knew we were safely ensconced.

Such might not be the case during a busy tourist season.

Liz and I spent several days and evenings in our adopted front yard. Our "yard" was a large park with several footpaths bridging a small stream which meandered between ferns, flowers, basketball courts, and fountains. Overhead, leafy trees were full of colourful and happily noisy birds.

Thanks to schedules and articles in the English newspaper Atención, we ate in quality restaurants such as La Princesa, attended concerts in Bella Artes, and visited art openings, art shows and galleries throughout the city. I recommend you buy a painting by Lubben before its price becomes astronomical. Portraits and sketches by El Syd soothe the eyes.

As always, we toured cathedrals, churches and chapels. We thoroughly enjoyed the truly unusual murals in an ancient church in Atotonilco, 18 km outside of San Miguel. We also visited museums, open mercados, enclosed mercados, two simultaneous rival political rallies (briefly), and three tiny street festivals. And our taste buds kept demanding more of the delicious offerings of sidewalk foodstalls and mobile street vendors.

In fact we were so busy we started to make plans on a calendar. That's when I knew we had to get away.

Frustratingly, we tried to use many public telephones, but they took our money and gave nothing in return. The telephone system was being updated to fibre optic technology; Latadel and its direct-access-card capability were not there yet. Eventually, thanks to the ex-Canadian owner of the Santa Clara ice cream store, we were successful in our monthly attempt to communicate with our children, by fax.

Even using a calendar we couldn't see everything we wanted to. We'll have to go back to modern 19th century colonial San Miguel de Allende and its many treasures and pleasures. We escaped this time, but will we want to after our next visit?

Some Days are Better than Others

Yesterday was the pits.

Liz and I got off to a late start. We couldn't fill up with water. On a whim we changed destinations, then suffered through several hours in above-average midday heat looking for a winery that 'makes the best wine in Mexico'. None of the locals knew of it. We got lost. I got mad, barked at my tired wife, and had to apologize. Liz calculated that we had covered 196 km to travel 63. And after all that, we were forced to park in a Commercial Mexicana parking lot where the lights were on all night.

Today was better, much better.

But it got off to a lousy start. We hadn't slept well, and woke up to the noise of parking cars and slamming doors. We couldn't shower because the remaining water was needed to do the dishes. I dislike sponge baths. Liz had decided it was time for cereal and tea and, no, she was not going to cook bacon, eggs, hash-browns and coffee. I dragged out my computer, opened our expense spreadsheet, and confirmed that once again we were going to be over our monthly budget. It was time for a walk.

Silence. Two people walking side-by-side, glad to be outside together but saying little in an effort to avoid an argument.

Hey, an open door. Maybe it leads to a fancy courtyard. Let's explore . . . Too bad, this building is some kind of school, and its grubby courtyard isn't worth the effort. Look, a bulletin board. What's on it? Looks like a newspaper page advertising several activities. Darn, in español. Wait. I think the last one concerns a performance by the Ballet Folklórico, sponsored by La Universidad Autónoma Querétaro, on the 4th. Remember the video that Marvin showed us of the Ballet and the majestic Degollado Theatre in Guadalajara? Their performance was superb. Tonight's the fourth. Let's stay for it.

We have to move our rig anyway, so let's drive to the address and park there. Oh yeah, we don't have a map, do we. "Señor, por favor. ¿Donde está el Central Unión? .... Muchas gracias. Adiós". Liz, can it really be that simple? Ready? Right, we're on our way. Drat. This road deadends in another block, now what? "Señor . . . Adíos".

Well, we finally made it. Hey, guess what? We're in the deadend I avoided before.

But this is an elementary school, what gives? Quick, ask him. He just came out of the building. "Señor . . . ".

Mexicans are certainly helpful. Imagine a principal taking time out of his busy schedule to drive about and bring someone who can speak English.

"Buenos Días, senorita." ... "Thank you, we're pleased to meet you too." You say the principal is a priest who speaks Italian. And there are two activities with almost the same name on the same day. It's no wonder our conversation was so confusing. Tickets? For us? Free? "Muchas gracias, padre." You mean you want us to park in the fenced-in school yard for the night. And we can fill up our water tank? "Sí. !Muchas gracias!"

You know Liz, it's hard to believe people in this upper class neighbourhood are so concerned about our safety. Considering some of the places we've parked our rig, this should be like parking in the bonded lot of the Policia. Maybe those walls, gates, and ornate ironworks aren't just for looks after all.

Liz, while I move our motorhome, why don't you go with Margarita? Don't give me that look, she really seems to mean her invitation to come to her house. I'll be along shortly.

Ah, parked and filled. Now, where's the address? Shoot, Liz kept the card. Darn.

Hi. Glad you're back. I was getting worried, and hungry.

A birthday party? We're invited to a birthday party for a four year old grandson!? But won't we be in the way? You're sure? Well, we've always said it would be interesting to see the inside of some Mexican homes. Okay. . . .

You know, I really enjoyed that couple of hours. They're marvellous people and the food was delicious. Just think. Her father is a wine salesman for a company in Ezequel Montes; we missed the winery by 7 km. That bottle of Cava Antonelli Burgundy was surprisingly good. So was the Hidalgo Blanco. Oh, that's right, that one's made here in San Juan del Rio.

Now we get a chance to return the favour. They did agree to come by about 9:30, after the Ballet, didn't they. I know, I know, it's time to tidy up.

That didn't take too long. Let's go. . . . You know, this private school just doesn't seem to be the place to hold a performance of the professional Ballet Folklórico. I thought we would end up in a concert hall, or at least a theatre. You don't suppose this is a school play of some kind?

Here we are standing in the schoolyard, and all we can see are parents and families. Do you think they are staring at us because we're tourists, or have I torn the seat out of my pants again? Is this going to be a "pig-in-the-poke"? Oh migod. That kindergarten kid is dressed up with vest and sombrero. And that one, she can't be much more than ten years old! I think we goofed. I didn't even like going to school concerts for our own kids.

It's nice to get out of the wind that came up from nowhere. These seats are a bit hard and slippery, and that sure looks like a small stage. Ouch. For people who speak so softly, they do like their music loud. Maybe we should leave. Never mind. I think they're about to start.

Hey, they are all grownups. ... You're right, those costumes really are fantastic. They're so colourful. The dresses must be made out of silk because they flow so beautifully. They remind me of Chinese banner dancing.

Look at their footwork! And listen. Eight couples and it sounds like only one or two people. Superb timing. Sixteen dancers, and they all stopped at the same time. Amazing. This is no school play! These guys are good. Yes, the women are good too.

Oh oh, he lost his sombrero. I hope they can continue to dance around it. Astounding how they just leave it there.

Listen, a Mariachi band. Three guitars, three violins, and two trumpets. Crikie. Look at the size of that bass guitar. The trumpets are a bit loud, but by putting my hand to my ear I can hear the violins. Is that ever lively music. I'm glad we came. Applause.

Look at those two love-birds dance. Is he ever snotty. Talk about macho. Their feet are a blur. How can they keep it up for so long?

Look at those dresses! They're even fancier than the last ones. Who has time to do all that sewing and embroidery and quilting?

Notice how they've changed costume from the upper class to a lower peasant class? This dance reminds me of the plaza where the men walk around in one direction and the women in the other. Ah ah, he lost another sombrero, now he won't be able to kiss his partner in feigned secrecy.

That is one sweet Indian maid, pretty and so timid. I hope he gets to kiss her. Reminds me of when we were courting. You sure did have me wrapped around your little finger. We're lucky nothing has changed, I still love you.

Applause, and curtain. Now they can get rid of those dumb hats. Hey, somebody is handing out confetti. Of course I'm going to get some. What'll I do with it? I don't know. Curtain and applause.

A wedding feast! Look. Behind us. Here, throw some on them as they come down the aisle. That's one crowded stage for-twenty-six people. Look at them move. How can they keep avoiding each other without missing a step or a beat? Those two kids sure look cute. Why are they coming down between the seats. "Lo siento, no hablo español." Me, you want to dance with me? Sure, why not? . . . This is fabulous. Oops, sorry. I don't know this dance. Its like a polka but different. Thanks, that was a lot of fun.

Applause, applause, whistle, applause. Curtain call. More applause. That must be the director. Hmm, they could use a bit more practice learning how to leave a stage. Applause.

Liz, I'm going back there and let them know we thought they were great. Come on.

"Anyone speak English? Thank Heavens. Oh, it was your daughter who danced with me; she was good. I hope her foot isn't too sore. We just wanted to say that, even though we're

Canadienses who don't understand the intricacies of the various dances, we thoroughly enjoyed the evening. All of you were great. Really professional. Thanks. Adiós."

Too bad we have to walk back in the rain, Liz. Wait, someone is calling us. It's the woman I talked to backstage. "The dance troupe wants us to join them for supper, for real Mexican food!? We'd love too, that's very kind. Lo siento, we're sorry. We can't. We might have guests coming over. Adiós."

I hear Margarita's Volkswagen. I'll unlock the gate. "Come in, pase, entre. Thank you, we like it. It has everything we need. Intimate? Yes, I guess it is. Coffee or tea? . . . Buenas Noches."

Sharing RV-hospitality with new friends.

You know, Liz, even with their daughter and son translating much of the conversation, I'm tired. If we feel like this after an hour, what is it going to be like taking Spanish lessons for four hours a day in Guatemala?

There, the dishes are done. What a fabulous day! We just don't know what's going to happen, do we?

Good night, my Love, I'm exhausted.

Hmm, that's my favourite perfume you're wearing.

Massive statues in Tula, near San Juan del Rio.

About to be Discovered Puerto Escondido

Puerto Escondido, Oaxaca is 410 km south of Acapulco and worth the trip over bumpy Highway 200.

It is even worth an eight-hour trip on Highway 131 from Ciudad Oaxaca. But unless you like travelling over 106 km of twisting, bumpy, washed-out, under-construction, often-one-lane, dirt and rock road, I suggest you take another road to picturesque Puerto Escondido. We took 131 because of a misunderstanding in español.

Liz and I think this tiny fishing and tourist town, with several beaches and 8,200 inhabitants, must be like Acapulco was before "the movie". And before international money turned Acapulco into a beach fortified against attack with walls of concrete called hotels and with defensive mobile machinery spewing forth noxious gases and black soot.

Puerto Escondido's tarnished-silver and bronzed-gold beaches and multi-hued aquamarine bays are accessible to all visitors. Although parts of some beaches are dangerous because of white waves crashing against huge black rocks, they are still beautiful. Between the several swimming areas and the rocks, ah, that's where the young muscular surfers dare to ride the silvery manes of Neptune's breaking waves.

Between 8 and 10 a.m. watch out for fish-laden vessels that literally fly over the breakers and skid to a halt halfway up Puerto's main beach. But don't worry about that stampede of women with empty buckets and baskets heading toward the boats. Somehow they'll get around you and get there before you do, without appearing to rush.

To visit the more distant beaches, you might have to hire a taxi. But you can walk to the local beaches.

Wander down streets and past three-wheeled wagons selling delicious tortas, tacos and tamales. Skirt by beach-side stalls selling inexpensive T-shirts, swimming gear, and souvenirs. Stroll through a small disco or cosy bar or hotel lobby or aromatically-tempting restaurant. The managers will be glad to see you. They know you might stop to sample their hospitality.

Once on your chosen beach, you'll have to decide whether or not to bypass vendors trying to rent you a shady umbrella for N$ 10.00/day. You can ignore children and adults hawking handmade jewellery, more cotton beach wear, tasty ices, and cool drinks, or you can buy a memory. You can lie on the beach and soak up the sun's rays, or you can plunge into the salty water. Or you can do both. Decisions, decisions. Life can be so demanding.

In mid-June in early afternoon in the swimming areas, waves reached a towering one metre. That was just the right height for a prairie-born landlubber like myself. Even so, one of several successful attempts at body surfing resulted in a topsy-turvy ride and eventually a scraped hip and a jostled shoulder.

How do Sneaker Waves — those occasional, extra large waves that soak your running shoes as you scrunch along the beach — always seem to know when you have your back turned toward the ocean?

Whenever rivulets of sweat began to pour down my back, I got up and dove into the ocean. I didn't have to stop to splash frigid water on my wrists and the back of my neck to avoid thermal shock. Water temperature in the mid-seventies is a perfect complement to a golden orb blazing from a cloudless sky.

During one of my aquatic excursions, I surfaced beside a school of small fish and was astounded to see them seemingly trying to breathe air through their gasping mouths. Another time I had to borrow a bucket to capture a dead Puffer fish — an amber and brown balloon with stinging spikes — then deposit it on the beach. It quickly disappeared, probably to reappear on a display counter somewhere. But most of the time, swimming meant floating in undulating waves beyond where they begin to break upon the shore. Occasionally I got a chance to admire Pelicans two arm-lengths away or a Kite bird majestically gliding through the air above.

In addition to clean beaches and clear green-blue water, Puerto Escondido has a long concrete path below its lighthouse and along the edge of its rocky cliffs.

During our first stroll, Liz and I hadn't realized how long a walk it was. We spent twenty minutes blindly retracing our way back in the sudden pitch-black darkness of early evening. We had stopped too often to admire the sunset, and to watch black crabs clinging to wave-washed boulders, and to wait until a fisherman caught a fish using only a minnow and monofilament line wrapped around a block of wood.

During our second walk, we stopped near the mouth of the bay. Initially we thought we were seeing an oil spill, but eventually we realized that the dark spot was fish moving against the wind. Hundreds? Maybe even thousands. There were so many fingerlings that the water changed from turquoise to tire-wall black.

Every so often, like a randomly spouting geyser, fish would explode out of the water, silver shards contrasting against dark shadows. Why? Because big fish knew where the little fish were, and came to feed. We could trace the submerged paths of those hungry hunters because the line of explosions resembled those made by skipping stones on the water's surface.

But all is not perfect in this paradise. Good RV camping facilities are sparse.

Many advertised trailer parks exist in name only. The Neptuno and Palmas de Cortez trailer parks are situated downtown, abutting the principal beach, but their trees were too low and too close together for our Class C. Smaller Class B's and vans would have no problems weaving between the palms. Electricity or water might be available in a few spaces, but not sewer. Comments and facial grimaces from people who stayed in those campgrounds indicated that the bathrooms were filthy.

On the western outskirts of town, the Escondido-Carrizalillo Trailer Park provides 150 level lots, a third of which have full hookups. There's always plenty of grassy spaces available.

Unfortunately, when we arrived in the off-season, we had to drive through five metres of broken glass in burnt garbage. Then we talked to the owner, the only rude person we met in Mexico. Even though the pool was empty and the sites had no water and little shade, we would have been charged N$ 40.00 for the night. It wasn't worth it. We've heard that the price for a lot can be as high as N$ 75.00 during busy times such as Semana Santa. (Many months later we talked to a German couple who thoroughly enjoyed this park. Maybe the owner had a bad day when we were there.)

This campground is situated on a bluff overlooking one of the better, if not the best, golden sand-and-shell beaches. The steep path down to the beach makes for a long walk under a tropical sun, but who's in a hurry? After you arrive, you might be lucky enough to relax in the shade of one of three public palapas.

All Mexican beaches are federal public land, and tourists and locals have the right to use them freely until 7 p.m. Because of the owner's attitude, we drycamped for several days, without cost, on the wide paved road immediately next to his RV park. When we wanted to, we made up a light snack, took along a few pesos to buy coconuts or refrescos, and locked our motorhome. Then we walked through his campground, down the bluff, and spent a lot of time on the warm beach and in the clear waters of the bay.

Puerto Escondido will, undoubtedly, become another major tourist area. It is going to be developed by the Mexican government. Rather than RVing, you might consider buying or building a house and spending several months every year in this idyllic location. Be extremely careful when buying land in any foreign country. Nevertheless, if you want to explore this possibility, you can contact Robert Dezbeck, an ex-BCer who recently and successfully built there.

If you don't want to camp, you might consider staying at the five-star Aldea del Bazar hotel. Hotelling is not our thing, but we were so impressed by its immaculate grounds and Arabic appearance that we gave it a good look-over, both inside and out. If we were to spend N$ 250.00 per night, we would do it there. Second choice would be the downtown Hotel Barlovento with its large rooms, and small book exchange library. Its owner and manager, Helen, spent twelve years in Toronto and is always happy to see a Canadian.

In June '94, Puerto Escondido was a quiet, sleepy Mexican fishing village with its many facilities used by only a few visitors and tourists. Its gorgeous beaches were almost deserted; the swimming was fabulous. So too were the fresh fish, shrimp and pulpo (octopus). The prices of food, drink and trinkets were reasonable.

Visit Puerto before it is converted into another Ixtapa or Huatulco or, heaven forbid, another Acapulco. It's a town movies should be made in, with you seen tanning underneath a coconut tree.

The "O" Town

If you can pronounce Ocozocoautla properly, then you won't have to call it the O-town. To me it will always be the latter. No matter how often I've tried to say O-co-so-co-owt-la, my tongue continues to trip over my right eye tooth, and gibberish and tiny water drops fly from my mouth.

For me, the only reason to visit O-town is to stay at Hogar Infantil on its outskirts. There was no charge, but they did accept donations. This orphanage is a project subsidized by some generous people in Texas. Carmen, the manager, spoke some English.

If coming from the west, turn left at the O-town junction. Do not concern yourself unduly with the hundreds of yellow hemispheres imbedded in the highway. If you were flying by at an altitude of 150 m you might be able to discern a pattern. Just drive over them, travel about 200 m, then take the first left turn onto a narrow blacktopped highway. Drive another kilometre or so, and turn right at the Hogar Infantil sign. Hogar Infantil translates as Infantile Home, or Orphanage.

We slowly topped up our tank with low pressure water. (Almost all water in Mexico is non-potable, although a capful of Chlorine bleach will make it safe to use.) We were allowed to plug into an electrical outlet in one of the rooms. Before we left we tried to use their septic system, but we were unable to get close enough.

A small group of interesting and interested children.

The kids were great. Our first visit stretched to four days. Part of that time I taught them a few computer and word processing techniques. We also visited their farm animals, walked through cultivated gardens and fields, watched their games, and sang songs with them at night. The second time we were limited to a single night of renewing acquaintances. The percentage of these young people who go on to university is way above the state average. If you have any English story or text books that you'd like to donate, they could use them. Also, if you have computer equipment or disks that you no longer use, they could use them too. The first time we visited, they were expecting to upgrade from a single XT to a couple of 386's. These hadn't arrived when we returned six months later, but they'll get some eventually.

Liz and I enjoyed our visits there. I don't usually endorse organizations, but . . . If you are planning on driving by or dropping in, before you leave the USA you might want to contact Hogar Infantil @ 3500 NW 1st Avenue, Mineral Wells, TX, USA 76067 or try calling (817) 325-3641.

We enjoyed our time near Ocoz... Ocozoco ... Ocozocoautla. Oh you know, the O-town. You might, too.

Tuxtla Gutiérrez

Tuxtla has at least two great places to visit.

It also has several shopping malls and large grocery stores. After eight months without any, I found dry roasted peanuts. So I bought four kilos (10 lb) of them.

First, visit the tourist office, on the right of Highway 190 just as one enters the city from Ocozocoautla. We got excellent maps and information, much of it in our native tongue. The agents we met during two visits spoke good English. Both Liz and I think it was the best staffed, best equipped tourist information centre in Chiapas, maybe even Mexico.

Second, visit the zoo located in the south east corner of the city. Admission is free. This zoo was what every zoo should be: shady; well maintained; and natural. The fenced areas were large enough for the animals but small enough that we found them. Some animals and birds were free to roam about. There were concrete walkways, snack shops, and an abundantly-stocked souvenir store. Although wheelchair-accessible, some paths were steep and might be difficult to navigate in a wheelchair.

While in the zoo, do try 'Cerveza de Raíz' and a tostada or two. Plan on spending a minimum of two hours enjoying exotic animals and birds in quiet tranquillity. Four hours or more could slip by unnoticed. We stayed a full day.

We parked overnight near the zoo entrance, under a street light in a gravel parking lot. Police patrolled the area. Next morning we planned to go back in, but the zoo wasn't open. We knew we'd be back.

During our return trip, we revisited the zoo, which is called Zoologico Miguel Alvarez del Toro. We saw a colourful, long-tailed Quetzal, which is the national bird of Guatemala. When we got to the pond where a slow-moving Cayman had been covered in mud and live plants, we were disappointed to discover that he had cleaned up his act.

While touring the park, we met a couple with their son. They asked how to get to el Cañon del Sumidero. Because we were going part of the way and because we had a map, we led them across the city. When I drove down a rough dirt road through an empty field, then travelled a couple of hundred metres along the side of a highway against the traffic flow, they thought we were lost. We weren't. I had been, but when I could see where I wanted to go, I went there. I told them I had learned how to drive properly when we were in Central America.

The family carried on. Liz and I camped at the entrance to Parque Nacional Cañon del Sumidero, which is on the north side of Tuxtla. If we hadn't needed gasoline, we would've driven the 22 km and stayed at the canyon lookout, which is reported to be excellent.

During our first visit, several of us had rented a boat in nearby Chiapa de Corzo, and enjoyed four hours of travel up and down the awe-inspiring canyon river.

San Cristóbal

The following paragraphs were copied verbatim from a brochure that had been translated from español into English. The English could use improvement, but the idea was correct. I've included them as an example of the dichotomy that exits in that country. Many Mexicans speak good English, yet a glossy tourist brochure didn't. No doubt about it. Mexico is interesting as well as frustrating.

"San Cristóbal de Las Casas, is it a colonial city and a excellency place, a place of privileige of haigh lands of Chiapas with a variety of turistic atractions.

"This city was founded in the 1528 year for the spanardian Captain Diego Gaspar de Marzariegos and since conserve the colonial architecture divide in 'barrios' (neighborhords).

"It is the most important city in the Haigh Lands of Chiapas. The city with spanish desig, with its stone-paved roads, with roofs of terracotta tiles, houses with patios and fronts with many architectonical influences is a place of peace and tranquillity. The surrounding woods are mostly pine and its climat is pleasant the whole year trough. San Cristóbal can be the center of tourisic activity for tourist who are searching a different adventure."

San Cristóbal is a pleasant, modern and altogether cool city to visit. Every year, thousands of Europeans do. We're glad we followed in their footprints.

I gave the following description to a downtown tourist office.

"San Cristóbal de Las Casas is the most important city in the High Lands of Chiapas, and yet a place of peace and tranquillity. It is an excellent colonial city, a privileged place in those high lands of Chiapas, with a variety of tourist attractions. The surrounding woods are mostly pine and its climate is pleasant throughout the whole year.

"This city was founded in the year 1528 by the Spaniard Captain Diego Gaspar de Marzariegos, and since then has conserved its colonial architecture, including the division of this city into 'barrios' (neighbourhoods). It is a city of Spanish design. Its roads are stone-paved; houses have patios, courtyards and roofs of terracotta tiles; and building facades show several architectural influences.

"San Cristóbal can be the centre of tourist activity for those travellers who are searching for a different adventure."

Liz and I agree. We toured 28 of 32 states of Mexico; we liked Chiapas the best. We'll be back someday. We'd be there right now if we could snap our fingers, or wiggle our noses, or command "Beam us there, Scotty." And again we'd stay in the full service RV campground within the walls of the Best Western Hotel.

A Potpourri of Ideas about Mexico

Following is a collection of random thoughts, comments and incidents. They came to us during the more than five months we spent in marvellous Mexico.

Canada, Cañada, Canadá. Canada is the name of a Mexican chain of shoe stores. Cañada is one word of several in español that means canyon. Canadá is the land of ice and snow north of Estados Unidos.

What a contrast. On one side of the road is a John Deere tractor pulling a five-bladed plough. On the other side is a pair of oxen lugging a single-bladed, wooden plough.

Another contrast. Looking down this street we see a centuries-old church steeple dwarfed by a modern, multi-antenna microwave tower.

In many churches, it is common to see birds flying around rafters or resting on high ledges. All those we saw were toilet-trained.

I've been told that a Mexican male can be very chauvinistic, and it might or might not be true. However, whenever a caballero spoke to us, he always said "Buenos días" twice, once to me and once to my beloved.

Perhaps you are familiar with the "Mexican Miracle". No? It's a common occurrence during weekends. A Volkswagen Bug or other similar small vehicle pulls up at a beach or picnic site, and eight to ten people get out. Then these two or three families proceed to unload a cooler, a bag of groceries, a baby chair, a canopy with four poles, and numerous assorted odds and ends. I truly believe that many Mexicans would not understand the joke 'How do you get seven elephants into a Volkswagen? ... Two in the front, two in the back and three in the glove compartment.'

Writing this makes me realize why Mexican parks and hotels charge by the person. If they didn't, it's conceivable that one space or one room could be home to a dozen or more persons. Unlike in Canada, one vacationing Mexican family often includes parents, children, grandparents, uncles and aunts and nieces and nephews.

Although Mexican highways are mostly blacktop, and a large percentage are without potholes, they are anorexic. Two lanes means just that. There are no shoulders nor safety lanes.

If you have the money and time is critical, use the new four lane toll roads. They are in excellent condition, and you can really speed along safely. However, they're not as much fun as the free roads.

Driving down Mexico's spine, in one of its northern desert areas, we noticed a sign saying "Don't buy wild birds and animals. Protect our wildlife." That's a nice sentiment. But within five minutes both sides of the road were filled with natives selling live birds, iguanas and many, many snake skins.

After ten minutes of chugging and twisting our way up a mountainside, we came across our first 'dangerous curve' sign. Even though it was a switchback, the curve was only marginally worse than many we had already encountered. Another time we were on a four-lane divided highway and came across a similar sign, but we had to move the wheel a mere eighth of a turn. Danger, like bravery, is always relative.

During April and May, we observed hundreds of fires, some large, some small. Garbage was constantly being burned to reduce the possibility of disease. There were so many fires that the horizon disappeared into a murky blue at 5-8 km. We began to think all Mexican hills were grey-blue. Then came the rains, and suddenly the hills were green, brown and a profusion of other striking colours.

When driving through mountains, you are usually at or near the top of a hill when you can see a microwave tower nearby.

In the mountains of Mexico, if you see spruce, pine or cedar trees along the road side, you're probably at 2,000 m or more above sea level. You might continue to see cacti there as well.

If you used second gear to climb a hill, you will probably have to use second gear to go down the other side. Using your motor for braking saves those warm brakes for when you really need them. Pull-offs are not common; runaway lanes don't exist.

Our misconception that cacti grew only in dry desert lands has been replaced with the knowledge that cacti, evergreens and deciduous trees can coexist in the same patch of land, at sea level or above 2,500 m. We've even seen cacti growing in riverbanks.

Once Liz and I drycamped next to a manmade lake. During late afternoon, we saw a black zigzag move slowly across grey gravel. The entire snake was black as pitch, and almost as shiny as solidified tar that's broken by a hammer. It was one beautiful reptile. I think the last few centimetres were corrugated; if so, then it was extremely poisonous. But it didn't bother us and we didn't bother it, so we'll never know.

I hope we can get used to adults staring at us with the intensity of young children.

Mexicans seem to be able to adapt anything to their use. During siesta one fellow was comfortably resting in a wheelbarrow, which has the same shape as a Papasan chair.

We have seen horses and burros in the centre of cities of one or two hundred thousand people. How do they get there, and where are they kept?

When asking my beloved navigator if I should turn left or right at an intersection, I'm no longer surprised to hear "I don't know, I haven't been here before! .. Go right. No, no. The other right." Fortunately for both of us, we've adopted Carl Franz's motto "Wherever you go .. there you are." We've certainly seen some unexpected vistas.

A muddy detour around a washed-out bridge.

Regardless of the colour of its coconuts, do not park directly beneath a coconut tree. Even green ones can fall and dent an aluminum roof.

Plan ahead. Get yourself some calling cards, with names and a mailing (not house) address. It saves time when you want someone to write to you when you get back home. But of greater importance, presenting your calling card puts you a step above regular tourists.

Our first cards were simple black on plain white, but they saved me at least one fine from a motorcycle policeman. He stopped me because my motorcycle went into one of its really bad smoking fits; it probably killed every mosquito in Cuernavaca. He was happy to put my card with the many others he had. Then, instead of giving me a ticket, he returned my driver's licence.

After that lesson, whenever we were stopped by people in uniform, I smiled, asked "How are you?", and gave them a calling card before they could say a word. Yes sir, the best defence was a good offence.

If you are going to be in Mexico for a couple of months, buy a big 25 Kg bag of oranges and a juicer. Then you can have fresh orange juice every morning, cheaply. Citrus fruit such as oranges, limes and lemons might get hard but they don't spoil, unless they get wet. Which is why limes were used on British sailing ships to combat scurvy, and which is why the British sailors were called 'Limies'. Only once were we able to find lemons in Mexico.

Having been in twenty states, we think Chiapas is the prettiest state in Mexico. Tourists from Canada and the United States are vastly outnumbered by Europeans, who come by plane and travel by bus and van. Older folks are usually part of a tour package. Younger folks get about using backpacks and the excellent and inexpensive bus system.

Poor Mexicans think nothing of coming up to you and begging a few pesos. Children as young as four will ask for moe-nay and look angry if they don't get any. Sometimes they can be annoyingly persistent. Mexicans seldom give to beggars. Our official tour guide in Taxco was angry at a beggar lady because she has a husband and well-to-do family to look after her.

In city intersections, boys and men wait with soap, water and a squeegie. As soon as a car stops for a red light, they are up on the car hood and soaping the windshield. Because of the dust, grime and black smoke, they really are doing a service. They charge only a peso for a good job. However, no windshield needs to be cleaned four or five times a day.

In San Cristóbal we had to sort through our seldom-used attic, which is underneath the trailer floor above the holding tanks, and get out our heavy sweaters and windbreakers.

We toured Chiapas during a time of political unrest. We saw many armed men in khaki and helmets. But the only problem we had was the time spent at road blocks. These courteous soldiers inspected us to make sure we weren't carrying anything illegal. We think most of them wanted to see inside our motorhome, because they seldom opened a cupboard or a door. A couple of officers did take our name and address, which could have been comforting in the unlikely event that anything happened to us.

After the last major earthquake in Mexico City and the havoc caused by exploding liquid petroleum (LP), many of the propane distributors have been moved to somewhere outside of city limits. In San Cristóbal we drove 18 km toward Palenque to a propane plant, only to be told to return to the downtown office, pay for propane, then come back to get it. Sheesh.

The cave near San Cristóbal provides an interesting optical illusion. We found "mirrors" in strange places.

Most Mexican drivers are excellent drivers. On highways they have to avoid potholes, small chunks of rock and huge boulders in the middle of the road, and washouts and missing roadsides. Sometimes they have to swing around a landslide that has covered half of a highway for weeks. They have to miss tourists who don't know where they're going, to pass overloaded trucks crawling up steep hills, and to bypass trucks or cars broken-down in the middle of a road. They also have to miss horses, cows, burros, and goats who frequent the roadsides and frequently panic. On city streets they need to be good drivers too. They have to avoid men pushing ice cream carts in the fast lane because it is smoother, trucks stopped to unload cargo, motorcycles that zip in and out, women carrying monstrous baskets on their heads and babies on their hips, drunks weaving their way to oblivion, and more lost tourists.

Mexican drivers are good drivers because they have to be. They would probably die of boredom driving the highways in the rest of North America.

In Chiapas, beware of unusual highway traffic. We've seen men and young boys coasting down hills while sitting on top of firewood in a go-cart swaying above tiny, wobbly metal wheels. They slow down by yanking on a stick scraping underneath a square wooden axle. Now I know what causes those strange wavy lines in the blacktop.

Many of the free highways have lots of curves and dips and bends. Liz and I learned to coordinate her going back into the kitchen to get something from the fridge. When I'd ask for something, she'd make a smart-aleck comment such as "Why didn't you think of that when we were stopped five minutes ago?". Then she'd sigh loudly, watch for a straightaway, bound out of her seat, duck below the crashbar, and race to the back of our Class C. As she rummaged about, my responsibility was to let her know whenever a curve was imminent. Occasionally I'd be too busy trying to stay on the highway and I'd forget. Shortly thereafter, I'd hear a thump or a thud, quickly followed by vocal explosions of exasperation. After such occasions, I've learned that it pays to be extra nice to one's navigator, at least for a couple of hours.

In Chiapas, we were surprised to see that many of the gutters on the sides of the country highways were blocked by small dams. The reason became obvious when we saw poor native women using the dammed-up water to wash their clothes.

We discovered a new type of "tope". It's made out of dirt or, occasionally, tree branches. It warns there's construction ahead and you had better slow down quickly. By the way, construction often means that several men are working on one side of the highway but rocks, sand, cement and barrels of water are stored in the middle for easy access. Often these men were building retaining walls to prevent more washouts and disappearing lanes of blacktop.

Leaving Mexico, the First Time

Our tourist cards were running out, and we had to leave Mexico. It had been five and a half months of frustration, fun, frolic and new friends. It was even relaxing once I learned to think like Mexican drivers. A north-south zigzag course through Mexico, while crossing mountain ranges at least seven times, had advanced the odometer almost ten thousand kilometres.

This trip has meant hooking up in some great, many good, and an occasionally "should we stay here?" trailer parks. When nothing was suitable or available, we would drycamp on beaches, next to town plazas, in front of churches, or beside a new acquaintance's house.

It has meant sunning and swimming on gold, silver and volcanic-black beaches; sipping cocktails while floating in hotel pools; and enjoying the sights and social activities of historic colonial towns. It has also meant bartering in big and small markets, and eating delicious local foods from dusty street-vendors and street-corner kiosks which couldn't pass health inspections anywhere in Canada. We feasted on tortillas, tacos, tostadas, tamales and sweet churros. We picked mangoes from trees. We enjoyed an unlimited supply of fresh papaya, pineapple, oranges, melons, apples, peaches, plums, guavas, and other fruit we never could name.

When we felt like Canadian food, we visited giant supermarkets.

Every day another page of Liz's diary got filled with memories and, once in a while, an article or description would be stored in my computer.

As we looked over a verdant valley or at craggy rock walls above a rushing river, as we lay on warm grass or sandy beaches, as we floated in clear blue-green ocean water, or as we held hands walking in a park full of colourful flowers and grey-topped statues, we pondered our limited financial situation and wondered "What are the rich folks doing?". Inevitably our answer was "Probably working in an office trying to save money for a two-week vacation."

Of course, not everyone could, would or should do what we are doing. (There should be more.) Thank heavens not everyone is as crazy as we are; the roads and highways would be so very crowded.

Enough reminiscing! Mexico will soon be behind us, and another new adventure awaits us in Guatemala.

More Random Thoughts in Mexico

After nine months in Central America, we have returned to Mexico! We feel like we're home. It's as if we'd escaped from a psychological pressure cooker. Unless it was because of the constant warnings about thieves, I don't know why we feel this way. Except for border crossings, we enjoyed Central America.

You will need some United States of America currency at each and every border crossing. Bring enough or, better yet, buy some at city banks or use the money changers at the borders. Offer ones and fives rather than tens or twenties.

Mexico should not be known for its Tequila. It should be remembered for its topes, vados and vibradores. My Gosh, they're everywhere. A lot of money was spent on building these damnable nuisances, and rebuilding the ones that the locals have levelled. If that money were available to the federal government, the crushing national debt would be reduced. And cars and RVs wouldn't suffer squashed springs and squished shock absorbers.

The coastal highway from Rincon de Guayabitos past Los Mochis and up to Navojoa is not the Mexico Liz and I like to remember. That area is expensive, and almost all prices are quoted in American dollars regardless of the exchange rate. I feel sorry for those persons who do not see other parts of Mexico.

Travelling westward from Veracruz through Mexico City to Tepic, we suddenly became aware that we were once again in road-kill territory. The number of dead dogs and horses on the sides of Highway 15 is unbelievable. We had forgotten that trucks sported huge animal-bashing grills made from thick steel pipes. Seeing them again was like seeing excerpts from the movie "Mad Max".

In June, Highway 15 is a multi-sensory experience. Dusty green trees leap out from a background of hot and tired yellows, ochres, greys and pale browns that disappear into a blue haze of smoke which hides distant hills. Jake brakes disturb the whisper silence of new cars whizzing by us and overpower the rattle of rusty trucks we pass. Our olfactory nerves were subjected to the most unusual odours in most unexpected places. Factories, pig farms, chicken farms, dead animals, and undetected sources contributed to an unpleasant tapestry of aromas. Chiapas — with your thought-provoking tranquillity, your winding and curvaceous black roads, your verdant mountains, and your crisp blue skies — we miss you.

Tapachula

After months in Central America, Tapachula impressed us as a clean, bustling, modern city of a quarter million people. Because of its many wide one-way streets and avenues, its visible street signs, its functioning street lights, and its considerate drivers, we had no problems driving in this city.

But first a short story, with a moral.

As we were leaving Guatemala, we heard some weird sounds. Our brakes became semi-effective and a brilliant red warning light stayed on. After five repair stops in Central America I was fed up with the quality of their work. The CA-2 highway from Esquintla to the Mexican frontier was filled with potholes. We couldn't go very fast so we gambled on safely making it to

Tapachula, Mexico. About 50 km from the border, our brakes went back to normal. I guess all those bumps shook something back in place.

We crossed the border into Mexico—quickly, easily and inexpensively—and drove on a good highway to Tapachula. For 90+ km the brakes worked perfectly. Anxious to get to Yucatan, we were debating about driving on. Suddenly, instantaneously, our brakes failed completely as we were coasting to a stop at a red light. I wheeled into an empty dirt lot and scrunched to a halt. I barely missed the stopped car in front of us. I avoided falling into a deep, unseen ditch. My dear wife exclaimed, "Thank you, Lord!". For once I agreed with her wholeheartedly and unconditionally.

We decided to get our brakes fixed.

A local business man suggested MANZUR on 8th and 8th, so I drove there in a taxi. Yes they had parts for a 1979 Ford F350 and yes they could work on it right now. Their parts department was so big I think they could have fixed anything but airplane brakes, and maybe even those. They called a tow truck and the Transit Police. I returned to my stranded motorhome as a passenger on a police motorcycle.

It cost us N$ 150.00 to have our five-ton casa rodante hauled inside a huge building with a clean concrete floor without blowing dust. Parts and labour cost another N$ 431.33. Three hours later Liz and I drove out with a new set of front disk brake pads and a completely rebuilt left rear drum brake. We left behind several interestingly shaped chunks of worn down metal, torn rubber seals, one badly gouged brake pad and about 15 cc of old brake fluid.

On 20-20 hindsight, I am amazed at my stupidity and how easily I was blinded by goal fixation. Every other time, brake or tire problems were fixed immediately. But our travelling time had been shortened by three months because of our son's recently announced wedding, and there was still so much to see and enjoy in Mexico. That decision to delay repairs almost cost us a lot of money, time, and possibly time in jail. On a highway it could have cost us lives, ours and others. Idiotic.

Happily, this story had a fairytale ending.

If you are passing through Tapachula and you are concerned about your brakes or your clutch, drop by MANZUR and have them checked out. I think you'll be pleased with the result. We were.

When passing through Tapachula, drive up to the Hotel Loma Real. It is located just a few metres off and above the northern part of the Periferico, or Calle 17A Norte.

Hotel Loma Real is a five star hotel with a guarded and level parqueo that has five RV sites with electricity and water. You'll need a long electrical cord and a long hose to use them. There are eight more sites with water only, and space for a couple more dry campers. Hurray, there is also a blackwater dump station.

For N$ 50.00 per night you get to camp in an area that overlooks the city. The view was especially lovely one evening during a thunderstorm, even though one palm tree partially blocked the view. You can use the hotel's tennis courts, weight room, small Jacuzzi and swimming pool. And, of course, the restaurant and bar are also at your disposal. You can even fill up a 19-litre container with purified drinking water and ice from the bar.

We were told that there is a propane plant nearby that can fill both bottles and fixed tanks, but we didn't check it out. The information came from a friendly Mexican couple living and travelling in an older Class C; I expect this information is accurate.

Pailfer, at 2nd Avenue and the northern Periferico and a block from Banamex, is a well-stocked supermarket. Actually, like Gigante, Ley and Commercial Mexicana in northern Mexico, it is a grocery store, a clothing store, and a department store all rolled into one air-conditioned building. Pailfer accepts international Master Card and Visa credit cards, even on weekends when all the banks are closed.

Tapachula would be a pleasant place to stop and rest before going into, or after leaving, Guatemala via CA-2. It has most amenities that any RV traveller would want, except a white-sand Pacific beach.

Tuxtla to Villahermosa

Highway 195 east of Tuxtla to Villahermosa was quite a trip. The blacktop was in excellent condition and there were no potholes. But it took us six hours to travel 293 km, the last flat 85 km took an hour.

It reminded me of Highway 131 and the eight hours it took us to go directly from Oaxaca (spectacular churches) to Puerto Escondido (fabulous beach), except that 131 was under construction and not yet paved.

An open-to-the-public monastery near Oaxaca.

With sufficient engine power and travel time, this winding, twisting road was a pleasure to drive. There were some beautiful valleys and vistas. But several times I wondered "How would a driver born and raised in southern Saskatchewan, suddenly transported to Hwy 195, survive? Or "How fast would a Saskatchewanite drive: 25 km/hr, 15 km/hr?". Thank heavens I had practised in those towering mountains of Beautiful British Columbia. At one spot we had to wait for a half hour while two tow-trucks worked on a tractor-trailer that had rolled a hundred metres down the side of an embankment.

Every kilometre a distance-to-go number was painted on the road surface. Liz thinks that was because there is almost no room for signs in the nonexistent shoulders on the sides of this narrow road. A couple of the signs that were there had been hit, bent and twisted.

At Kilometre 140, there was a most amazing sight. Right in the middle of the road was 140 m of short white lines. It was legal to pass!

At Kilometre 65, or thereabouts, there's a pleasant and clean looking hotel-balneario called El Azufre. On our return from the Yucatan peninsula and its archaeological pleasures, we diverted there and regretted the decision. The balneario was filled with murky, dirty lukewarm water.

Close by are the spectacular caves, Las Grutas de Coconá. . We carried on to the caves and were glad we did.

One of many stone carvings in "La Venta" in Villahermosa.

Ciudad del Carmen

Driving from Villahermosa to and along the Gulf of Mexico coast road was a pleasure. The road was narrow but good, except for those dreaded Mexican topes. Sadly, there wasn't a lot of picturesque scenery to see.

Seen at dusk, Ciudad del Carmen appeared to be clean, with a large, pleasant central park. We didn't take time to check out the city because of our time-limited return journey and the great number of kilometres we had yet to travel in Mexico.

Playa Norte (North Beach) was a great place to park and dry camp when it was hot and humid because of its sea-to-land and land-to-sea breezes. By parking parallel to this almost white beach, refreshing mini-hurricanes blew through every window.

As in other coastal cities, tasty fish or shrimp dinners were available in many restaurants. Eating out sure beats sweating and slaving in a kitchen with four propane burners heating air that could be bottled and sold as portable saunas.

On the down side, the different costs of two toll bridges were vexing. At the south bridge we were charged as if our rig had four axles. In other parts of Mexico we'd been charged for three axles (tandem and dual wheels are considered the same) which is all right because the motorhome certainly weighs more than a car or small truck. But four is excessive, and at N$ 40.00, expensive. At the north bridge, however, friendly folks there charged us only N$ 15.00 because we had a tourist vehicle. On average, the toll charges were reasonable but I wished they were more consistent.

There were no Pemex stations in the 90 km between Frontera and Ciudad del Carmen. One in-city Pemex station had configured its pumps to read 4.25L for one US gallon. Another in-city Pemex—SG Badillo Literas, # 0370—had set its Magna Sin pump to 3.88L, so we filled up. Besides giving value for dollar, people in this station went out of their way to be friendly and helpful. It is no surprise why this gas station (or gasolinera, pronounced ga-so-lee-nay-ra) is so busy, and expanding. There's also a Pemex on the highway, immediately past Ciudad del Carmen, but we didn't turn in.

Bahamita Trailer Park, 16 km northeast of Carmen, has room for about twelve RVs. It provides 110V electricity, potable water hookups, and a blackwater dumping site. Access to an unshaded, sandy parking area is a bit tricky. Across the highway is a lovely white beach, palm-thatched palapas, and the cool inviting Gulf of Mexico. El Sr Longinos Acosta speaks understandable English, certainly a lot better than mi pobre español.

The coast highway really is a coast highway. Several times we were tempted to stop, walk over white seashell sand, and go for a swim in the isolated blue-green waters. We didn't, and I'm sorry we didn't. There was a clean palm-roofed restaurant at the junction of highways 180 and 186, near Sabancuy, which provided a pleasant break from driving, cool beer, and a beach for swimming.

In Champoton, La Palapa restaurant (second one on the left when driving into town) served delicious sea food cocktails. But beware. The entrance stairs are smooth and slippery, and the doorway onto the balcony is only 1.7 m (5'6") low. Look for a cranium-shaped dent in the concrete beam, at eye level if you are two metres tall.

One of the 1000-year-old intricately carved walls in Uxmal.

Liz and I turned off the coast highway onto Mexico 188, just before the toll road into Campeche. This time we weren't trying to save money. We were heading off to see Ruinas Edzna, en route to Kabáh, and Uxmal and other archaeological sites.

Edzna is a large complex of semi-restored buildings and temples, reminiscent of Palenque but not quite as large. Some temples are honeycombed with sealed passages; the buildings are not always solid rock. I wanted to break into some of them to see what was inside. There were one stelae and some small carvings in the rocks. Two faces or masks show men with an extreme overbite; one of them is cross-eyed. This site is worth seeing, if for no other reason than to climb to the top of the 30 m high astronomical temple and view the surrounding lands.

We joined up with Mexico 261 after Edzna and drove through Hopelchén. It was a pleasant town with a lovely central plaza, and it has a Pemex. But Liz and I drove on and stopped at Sacbe Trailer Park just before Santa Helena a few minutes before day switched to night. And after our eyes adjusted, night turned to day under a full moon.

This is in Ruinas Chicanna

There is only one sign, immediately adjacent the gated entrance, advertising Sacbe Trailer Park. This cared-for park has spaces for several RVs, with three-prong electrical hookups. No air conditioners please. There were laundry facilities, water taps, clean showers and bathrooms, some tenting spaces, and a small information centre. (On Sunday, entrance fees are reduced. Do you want to know about a short cut to Chichen Itzá? It does save kilometres.) All in all, this was a pleasant place to have to ourselves or to share with others.

After two days and hundreds of kilometres, we were looking forward to a couple of days of short-distance visits to several nearby archaeological sites.

Ticul

Ticul, first town in the short cut from Santa Helena to Chichen Itzá, has a Pemex station. That and my motorcycle caused the accident.

As always, the first thing a Mexican gas attendant must do is fill up my plastic jug, which holds 3.8L. With a rip-off pump reading of 4.15L, I told him that I'd get only N$ 50.00 worth of

Magna Sin. That was enough gasoline to let me drive to the next town without undue fear of emptying both tanks.

The gas attendant put the pump on automatic slow and let gasoline pour into the front tank. While I was unlocking the rear cap and pouring in gasoline from my test container, he left.

Later I found out he had gone around to the front of our motorhome to look at my motorcycle. All I knew was that he had disappeared from my view. As I emptied the jug, I looked uneasily at the pump, and realized that the meter was going to pass N$ 50 very soon. No way was he going to get more than N$ 50.00.

I moved over, pressed the handle to stop the gas flow but, because there was no spring, it immediately went to and locked at maximum flow. Without thinking—easy after months of vacation—I pulled out the nozzle and turned it over to see what was the problem.

My chest, face and eyes were immediately doused in gasoline splashing off the side of our trailer, and I went blind. It was an instinctive reaction to close my eyes, and to keep them closed. They stung.

From somewhere the attendant appeared, flipped a switch, and gasoline stopped pumping. But I couldn't see. All I could do was taste and smell gasoline.

Water. I needed water. He grabbed me and led me, unseeing and stumbling, across level ground, pulled my hands out until they cupped water from a tap, and let me slosh handfuls of water on my burning face and squeezed-shut eyes.

I thought it would feel better, but it didn't. The more water I threw on my face, the more it seemed to sting. Nevertheless, I knew I had to keep doing it.

I moved closer. He said something sharply in español. The ground disappeared. I fell. Miraculously, I kept my eyes closed. After he grabbed my shoulders and pulled me up and after I finished splashing water on my face, only then did I dare open my bloodshot eyes.

I had fallen into an eight-foot deep hole, an excavation in preparation for another gas tank. I would've fallen to the bottom except somehow I became entangled in some water pipes and dropped only four feet.

Nevertheless, I scraped my right leg on some concrete and ripped off about an inch of epidermis, dermis and flesh from my big toe. Why did it have to be the same leg I had injured previously? I was tired of limping.

But my face was still stinging badly. We walked back to the trailer. Liz got some Vitamin E cream and covered my face with it. I don't know if any other cream would've worked, but that stuff did. Within seconds, the stinging ceased. Completely. My eyes still hurt and my sinuses demanded to be blown clear, but the pain was gone.

Then I realized that my waist and male parts were on fire. I quickly divested myself of my colourful Guatemalan shorts, washed myself down with soap and water, used more vitamin E cream, and slipped into a dry pair of shorts. Things were getting back to normal.

When I heard the attendant laughingly tell another customer about my accident, my only comment was "Ho, Ho, Flipping Ho!"

Later, when I went to get my gasoline-impregnated shorts which were stinking up our rig, I realized I'd thrown them on top of a Styrofoam cooler and that they had melted into the plastic. I yanked them free, taking a little of that white stuff with them. It took two days to get rid of the smell, a week to get rid of the Styrofoam.

After almost all was said and done Liz, who was now driving, spoke the final words. "John, I guess you have to have an accident at least once a month just so I can continue to practise my nursing profession. Thanks a lot."

What's next? When?

Ruta Maya (in part)

We avoided Americanized Cancun and Cozumel, choosing instead those vivid blue, bright turquoise, pastel green and milky beige waters of Bacalar. After almost two weeks visiting various archaeological sites in the Yucatan Peninsula, we were amazed at the variety of different carvings and designs.

We were also surprised at the great distances we had to drive to get from site to site. After being in those small countries of Central America, we had forgotten how big Mexico is. Fortunately, the roads were excellent and free of potholes. Although they were narrow in places, I could set cruise control at 80 and relax.

Relax that is, until an occasional village or town was announced by signs warning of topes. Only one was unmarked except for black lines of rubber on asphalt, to which I added two more. We bumped over it and crash-landed without spilling or breaking anything.

Sacbe RV Parking, on the western outskirts of Santa Helena, is centrally located for Uxmal and four other Puc sites: Kabáh, Labná, Sayil, and Xlapak. Sacbe means 'a white road'. The ancients had several straight roads of limestone between their many cities. We saw the arched beginning (or end) of one after we walked a couple hundred metres across and past the highway at Kabáh. We spent a day at Uxmal and another at the other four sites. Each was similar, yet different. Uxmal was the biggest and best, but we enjoyed them all.

When exploring these sites, bring along a small flashlight for dark rooms and narrow tunnels, a sombrero or parasol for a blazing sun, and sun glasses to darken brilliant white limestone.

The nighttime light and sound show at Uxmal is supposed to be excellent, even better than at Chichen Itzá. We didn't go because we discovered our motorcycle light was erratic; I soldered a loose wire next morning. If you can, go early for the español version, walk around under a full moon, then watch it again, in English.

Piramide Inn Resort in Pisté is a mere one kilometre from the entrance to Chichen Itzá. There was space for our RV in its parking lot, close to electricity and one water tap. Temperatures were blast-furnace high. When we walked that short distance, we were reminded of a desert scene from "Lawrence of Arabia".

This clean and charming hotel offers guests a glimpse of the service of friendly people and well-maintained beauty of the mid fifties and sixties. It has a gallery of old archaeological photographs, and a lovely backyard with its own unrestored Mayan building and cemetery. Most important, at least when the temperature hovers around 40-42^{0}C, or 103-108^{0}F, it has a huge swimming pool with one end being ten feet deep. (I know, I know. I should write three metres. But that pool was built when I was much younger and grams, centimetres, kilograms and kilometres were something only Europeans used.)

Chichen Itzá is truly amazing. It is also a very large site. Actually it is two sites (each of which could easily occupy a full day of exploration) plus some more distant buildings. Remember to bring a flashlight and parasol. If you can, hide a collapsible ladder among your camera equipment. Then you might be able to sneak up into El Caracol, the circular observatory with an internal spiral staircase that starts two metres above ground.

After climbing that monster pyramid in Uxmal, Liz and I were disappointed in the height of the main temple in Chichen Itzá. But we were grateful it wasn't nearly as steep as the one in Uxmal. That temple, El Castillo, was built over another temple. Near midday, custodians unlock a door to allow tourists inside. Two marvellous carvings can be viewed at the top of the pyramid inside a pyramid.

Not wishing to retrace our coastal route back to Villahermosa, we chose to head to the Caribbean coast. We drove a few kilometres to Grutas Balankanche, which I enjoyed but Liz didn't. Then we drove a few more kilometres to Cenote X-Keken, or Dzitnup, where we enjoyed swimming in its refreshingly cool, subterranean waters. We almost made it to Bacalar, but darkness caught us at Señor. We parked in front of a general store, talked with locals, learned some Mayan words while laughing a lot, and finally went to sleep.

Cenote Azul

Cenotes are sink holes, usually caused by an underground river dissolving limestone rock close to the surface. The Yucatan Peninsula does not have rivers. Most rainwater disappears into the ground and into massive underground rivers. Cenote Azul accesses an underground river that is more than 90 m deep. I wished I had a miniature submarine to explore this aquatic tunnel.

Cenote Azul, a few kilometres south of Bacalar, was a great place for a swim, fresh seafood and inexpensive beer. Being a Mexican restaurant that advertises breakfast, lunch and dinner, it seems strange that it opens at 9:30 a.m. and closes at 6:30 p.m. Tired of swimming, diving and snorkelling among tiny fish, we paddled our way across to the other side on two inner tubes, then let the gentle breeze blow us back to the restaurant while we tanned under a tropical sun. We stayed for two tranquil days and nights.

Cenote Azul Campground is only a few metres away. It has clean spaces for several RVs, well water for topping up tanks, and electricity (small air conditioners only) for most afternoons and evenings. There is also a dump station. Cost was very reasonable: N$ 15.00 without electricity and N$ 26.00 with electricity. Antonio was very friendly but spoke no English.

We visited nearby Hotel Laguna, where we had stayed three years before. Once again we swam in the lagoon's clear blue water, ate lunch in the hotel's restaurant, and reread humorous sayings imbedded in glassy tiles.

Hotel Laguna near Cenote Azul and Bacalar.

Chetumal

Chetumal is a large, free-zone city south of Bacalar, Cenote Azul and the romantic Hotel Laguna. Chetumal is very close to Belize. Except for Pemex gasoline, we didn't find prices that much cheaper than elsewhere in Mexico. Mind you, we didn't shop around that much because of our annoying time constraint.

If you can get downtown to the modern mercado—as distinct from the huge, dirty old mercado, which is worth a short visit anyway—you might find a nearby tourist information centre where you can get a city map. Why can't those kiosks be on the sides of highways on the outskirts of cities?!

Propane can be purchased across from the airport, which you can't see. As you drive toward Chetumal, bypass the first turn off with its divided boulevard and stay on the highway. Within a couple of kilometres, on the right, across from a hedge of trees which hides the airport, you will see a wall advertising a propane company.

Turn in here if you have a fixed tank that must be filled by hose. You might have to argue with a guard who will peer over a solid metal blue gate from up high, who thinks you should go elsewhere, who can't hear you because of traffic noises, and who doesn't speak English anyway.

If your RV has removable bottles, proceed two blocks further, turn right onto a residential street and keep on going even though it quickly turns into a narrow, potholed road seemingly going nowhere. Eventually, probably after you decide that you are lost, you should see another and much grubbier fence to your left. Behind that fence you can get your fill of propane, if your bottles have the correct fittings.

Having relaxed for two days at Cenote Azul, having filled all tanks in Chetumal, Liz and I headed for Belize.

Highway 180

Just after passing from Tabasco into the state of Veracruz, on the right at kilometre 38.5 on highway 180, There is an excellent trailer and RV park called Rancho Hermanos Graham.

The owners were very friendly and, I think, they speak some English. I say "I think" because now Liz and I are understanding sufficient basic español that we're not always aware which language is being spoken. However, when I speak and stammer, I know.

This park has been built to provide space for more than 150 RVs and to provide several ancillary services. Each spacious lot has its own electricity and water, which is not always the case when a campground advertises them. More than half also have sewer. The cost was N$40.00 per night.

The pool, with a deep end, showers and bathrooms, would be crowded if all camping spaces were filled. When we were there in mid-May, which is long after the usual tourist season, the pool had not been maintained. The bottom was visible through green water.

In addition to the pool, there were a few palapas providing shade for tables and chairs, at least one bar and food stall, and ample grassy areas for games.

During the tourist season I would expect Rancho Hermanos Graham to be an RV park well worth visiting.

Catemaco

Catemaco is about midway between Villahermosa and Veracruz, on the edge of Lago (Lake) Catemaco, near the Gulf of Mexico. It is definitely a tourist town. But on May 22, 1995 it was a tourist town without tourists.

As Liz and I walked along the street that borders the dark grey beach, we saw many restaurants with empty tables and chairs. Next to them were kiosks with only their salespersons looking at the trinkets for sale. On the beach, dozens of passenger boats were tied up while special sights, monkeys and mud baths on some of the islands were unvisited. Catemaco was a ghost town.

But it does have two places for recreational vehicles, a campground and a hotel. Solotepec Campground no longer exists.

The first, driving in from Villahermosa, is La Ceiba Restaurant and Camp Ground. It is only a block or so down the first street to the right. If you can't find it, a licensed guide (often a teenager on a bicycle) will spot you driving around; he'll offer his services, and take you to where you want to go. Dorio and Rafaela, the friendly owners, speak a little English.

For N$30.00 a night, La Ceiba has a dump station, space for 18 rigs, electricity for all sites, and drinkable well water for topping up tanks. Although reasonably level, most sites require some use of levelling blocks or jacks.

I doubt that 18 crowded RVs could use electricity simultaneously. We were the only off-season guests. We tried using our small air conditioner but quickly switched to fan-only when we heard the labourious chunking of its compressor.

La Ceiba is on the beach street, which can be hazardous to your dignity. This wide paved street is lined with tall overhanging trees which are home to hundreds of birds. Many of the branches are white on the top, just as much of the surface of the blacktop street below is chalk white. From first head experience, guano rains from above in copious quantities. It is thin enough to flow from a widow's peak, across a cheek, down a neck and into and onto an open shirt collar.

As an alternative to La Ceiba, the Gran Hotel (also called Casa Hotel) on Playa Azul might be worth a 2-km exploratory trip. If coming from Villahermosa, stay on the highway and drive past the first Pemex until a sign indicates Catemaco to your right. Turn right. Follow the green and white directional signs until you leave the city and come to the hotel entrance. Turn in, being careful of the centre post and its chains. If they are accepting RVs and temperatures are high, the cool clear chlorinated waters of their swimming pool should make this an excellent choice.

Reception charged us N$50 a night, assigned room 54, and allowed us to park on a well-shaded street in front of a complex of rooms. Electricity was provided by our passing a 15 m (50') extension cord through a special hole in a screen and into an outlet in our assigned room. In addition to 120-130V electricity which easily powered our air conditioner, a shower, a bathroom and colour TV were available. Potable water was available from a distant but easily accessible tap.

We were told that the hotel would accept up to four rigs that used electricity, and more without. From their familiarity with RV requirements, I'd guess that several caravans have been welcomed there.

Camping in Catemaco at La Ceiba, or near this tourist town at El Gran Hotel, is not for those expecting first class accommodations. But both provided clean and quiet spaces at reasonable prices. After our time in Central America, where we found or heard about fewer RV parks than there are countries, these accommodations were greatly appreciated.

Veracruz

Driving from the tourist town of Catemaco toward Veracruz was very slow going for the first 100 km or so. We drove along a busy and narrow highway, and through many small towns with their inevitable topes and vibradores.

Veracruz is a large modern and commercial city, of 1,000,000 or more residents. It's a great place to get a replacement hydraulic hose. A Ford dealer is located at 2100 La Fragua, just south of Avenida Colon.

Mocambo Balneario and RV Park is a campground on the south side of the city. Actually, it's in Boca del Rio. It is hidden directly behind the Mocambo Hotel and next to a beach on the Gulf of Mexico. Cost was N$30 per night with water hookup and little shade. An extra N$ 12.00 per person gave access to one or more nearby swimming pools.

These clean pools are open to the public. If you want only to swim and camp elsewhere, public parking costs N$ 4.00.

We didn't use the campground because, when we found a Ford dealer, my power steering pump was making so much noise that I parked in front of their building and immediately turned off the engine. We were parked beside a divided boulevard where noisy ambulances, roaring trucks and whispering cars raced past, and horses and buggies slowly clippity-clopped by.

For supper, Liz and I had the honour of being the first guests during the grand inauguration and opening night of Tacos Arabes El Oriente. It was only a block away from where we were stranded. The flavour of roasted spiced meat wrapped in corn or flour tortillas with side dishes of fried onions, thick cream and piquante salsa certainly bested that of greasy hamburgers and fries. But we never did figure out why there was a tope behind the ninth table. This clean and whitewashed nook didn't appear to have been converted from an alleyway.

Liz and I dislike large cities. We seldom know where we are, which is another way of saying that we get flipping lost and easily frustrated. We left as soon as the leaking hydraulic hose was replaced (the dealer had a new one made) and the bill was paid.

Tlaxcala

Tlaxcala is a clean, quiet city worth a visit when travelling east of Mexico City. A stroll along the landscaped river and past a small zoo, or a snack in a sidewalk café surrounding the zócalo, can be very relaxing.

Tourists can park next to a small park close to the zócalo, or central square. We were directed there by a transit policeman. Parked directly below a 'No Parking' sign, it took a few minutes for my Central America-induced paranoia to subside. Eventually I realized that I wasn't going to get a ticket or be asked for a refresco (mordida). I guess the sign was meant only for locals.

Several downtown streets were one-way. There were no signs indicating which way to go, but there are several arrows painted in the streets. All of them were pointing in the direction opposite to the flow of traffic. Confusing.

This is not a big city, we could walk to everything we wanted to see, and did. The hills reminded us of our time in fabulous Taxco.

A should-see is the Basilica Y Santuario de la Virgen de Ocotlan. We think it is best approached by foot via the Capilla del Pocito de Agua Santa (its paintings were being beautifully restored) and a long uphill path between tiled walls. The ornate outside of this basilica is covered with red-orange tiles and a white sculptured facade. The inside is gorgeously baroque with lots of gold leaf. The altar is remarkable as well, especially if you can get to walk around it. But the best part is behind the altar, inside a small room used for christenings and other more private functions. This is one ornate room! Liz, who has visited the Vatican, said she had seen nothing like it.

But do not visit this backroom immediately before mass starts. We did. The only way out was through a sacristy, past some dusty old paintings, and into a courtyard of an attached convent. With the assistance of a nun, we finally escaped through a locked gate leading into a busy marketplace.

The post office is near the zócalo. It opened at 9:00 a.m., precisely! And it had stamps of sufficiently high value that only one was needed for each envelope. The tourist bureau, only two blocks from the post office, gave us a city map and complimentary tickets to a piano concert that same night.

There was some confusion about a Plaza de las Artesenias (which doesn't exist even though advertised in a brochure), Casa de las Artesenias (which does exist and is filled with very good handicrafts), and Centro de Artesenias (which is a fair ground and open stage on the other side of the river). We walked for a long time, got conflicting directions from policemen, taxi drivers and people in the street, but we never did find the Plaza. Tired and frustrated, we finally paid to climb aboard a public taxi, or combi. We travelled three blocks to the Casa, which was a mere two blocks from where we started.

Upon our return to the tourist office, we got a much better city map, and much needed clarification about Plaza, Casa and Centro de las Artesenias.

The city's shop owners, government workers and policemen were extremely friendly and helpful. Liz and I felt welcome in this city. We would have liked to stay longer.

Teotihuacán

Teotihuacán is a very famous tourist attraction about two hours north east of Mexico City, and only a minute from San Martín del las Pirámides. I think it is overrated. Liz thinks it was impressive. However, there is no doubt it was and is a very important archaeological site.

This site is open every day, and free on Sundays as are most Mexican attractions. Teotihuacán covers a lot of ground and gives a good indication of what that ancient centre might have been like. I would expect city planners would really enjoy this place. Except for a single facade on the Templo de Quetzalcóatl, one small area with carved pillars and a couple of partial murals, and two underground excavated sites, there is little to do except walk, climb the two pyramids, and walk some more.

Fortunately, this area has other sites and sights to offer.

There are five entrances from the circumferential road around the main site. Between entrances One and Two but closer to One, Restaurant International y La Casa de Cabrito (goat is their speciality) might let an RV or two park overnight. They let us do so, and also provided some very useful information.

In the same building as the restaurant, an unnamed store offers a large selection of souvenirs and trinkets, some of which are made on-site. There are several other restaurants along the external road offering similar food and souvenirs.

There were many kiosk-restaurants near entrance Five that offered typical Mexican food. We arrived during the off-season and had to drive carefully to avoid hitting men and women who rushed into the road to wave us into their kiosk. Some handed out menus displaying maps of the main site.

On a dirt sideroad immediately adjacent to Restaurant International, about 50 m in and to the left, is a swimming pool complex. It looked clean and inviting, but it was a frosty 23^{0}C when we were there. Coming from the Yucatan Peninsula and two weeks of 40-43^{0}C temperatures, we had to wear sweaters and sleep under a quilt to keep warm.

Slightly farther along this dirt road are two small archaeological sites well worth seeing, Tetitla and Atetelco. Take the very first turn on your right; by the time you read this the sign might be put back up. It is only a short distance to both sites, easily walked or driven. In each site there are some excellent murals. Liz and I enjoyed these more than those at the main site.

In Atetelco there were two buildings being fully restored, with original pieces of murals being included in those amazing restorations. What a pleasure it was to see homes with more than just plain stone walls. Oh, by the way, ask el Sr Hermanez Fortina where four skeletons were buried, or where a thigh bone was discovered in May '95.

In the mornings at entrance One of the main site, men in local costume risk life and limb as they swing around and down from a 25m pole. While four swing, the other dances and plays a flute on a tiny platform way up there. These men are the celebrated Valadores de Papantla from Veracruz State.

Near entrance Four, Tepantitla is another site with murals that might be worth a visit. Heavy rains precluded our going there.

Entrance Four is a stopover station for a tractor-driven train that drives around and between the pyramids and museum. This ride offers a welcome break from walking and climbing. There are other on-site locations where one can catch a train.

Also near entrance Four is a museum, on the lower floor of a building built in the early 1900's. It is closed on Sundays.

These brave men were resting between their bi-hourly show.

Liz was more enthusiastic about Teotihuacán than I was. However, we did enjoy our time in that area because we visited more than the main site. Tourists who don't visit the other sites will miss some unique discoveries.

As an aside, when you leave Teotihuacán and head for Mexico City, take the cuota. The cost of the toll is a small price to pay to avoid getting lost – once, twice or three times – on the back roads.

Mexico City

Mexico City was a pleasant surprise, not at all what we expected. We will be back. Of course, Liz and I used the Metro rather than drive our motorhome or motorcycle in heavy traffic and that might have contributed to our positive attitude.

We had driven through Mexico City three times – South to North via Avenida Insurgentes – with no problems but one. There is one glorieta, a roundabout, with six exits and once we took the wrong one. We quickly realized our mistake, stopped, and then were led back to Insurgentes by a taxi driver who would take no money.

Most major tourist attractions can be reached by inexpensive Metro. We think the best is Museo Nacional de Antropologia.

If in Mexico City, plan to take at least one full day walking through all its exhibits. Two would be better and less memory-overpowering and mind-numbing. Reasonable food and drink were available at the cafeteria.

Nearby Bosque de Chapultepec is a bustling, pleasant park, filled with families, young lovers, bewildered tourists, boat rides, ducks, swans and hawkers of food, drinks, mass-produced plastic toys, handmade (formed in moulds and hand-painted) souvenirs, and magical dreams. This is the way big city parks of old might have been before disinterest, vandalism and drugs took it all away. Liz and I felt perfectly safe strolling hand-in-hand in the cool darkness of a starry evening

Mexico City by Metro

Mexico City is big and bustling and easy to drive in after practising in Guatemala City. But why drive in a large city you don't know? Why risk getting lost or getting a ticket? Why experience the frustration of seeing that special place you hope to visit go whizzing by on the other side of a divided highway?

Drive past or stop before getting to Mexico City then set up your RV in the Diamante Trailer Park in Cuernavaca. After an early morning game of tennis or a swim, take a taxi to the nearest Pullman bus station and buy a bus ticket to Mexico City. Once aboard, spend an hour relaxing in first class, air-conditioned comfort while being driven to Tesqueñas, the southmost Autobus and Metro station. Study your tourist guide book with its cramped miniature printing or your glossy pamphlets with their too bright photographs. Walk past the kiosks and up the steps to the overpass, study the Metro layout, pay 40 centavos (10 cents) and ride to within a couple of blocks of your destination.

Master the Metro and enjoy Mexico City. Mexico City is modern and ancient and beautiful and lively and clean and filled with great eating places and sights and sites to see. It was also almost smog free when we were there.

Get back on Metro before 11:00 p.m. and take Line 2 back to Tesqueñas, walk 100 m to the bus station, and get a Pullman bus to Selva, Cuernavaca. They leave every 15 minutes. Rest your weary legs while someone else does the driving. As long as buses are scheduled to arrive, taxis will be waiting to whisk you home. Each cabbie has his own route; they are all different.

Total cost for two people to use taxis, buses and Metro should be less than 100 pesos each day. That is probably less than it will cost to drive your motorhome to Mexico City. And you won't have to worry about curvy, mountainous roads, accidents, vehicle safety, parking fees, topes, overheated brakes or transmission, missing a red light hidden behind a traffic sign, and overzealous policemen.

Visit Mexico City by Metro, not motorhome. It's fun.

Guanajuato

If you miss Guanajuato, you miss one of Mexico's treasures.

In the lobby of Hotel Santa Fe adjoining Parque Central.

If you've visited Taxco, then you might have some small idea of the richness and verticality of Guanajuato. If you visited San Miguel de Allende, then you might have a small idea of Guanajuato's colonialism and architectural wonders. If you have travelled the subways of Mexico City or the tunnel into Real de Catorce, then you might have some idea of what it's like to drive through the labyrinth of tunnels of Guanajuato. If you've watched the valadores of Veracruz, then perhaps you can imagine looking down from the Pipila of Guanajuato. If you've ever dreamed of being a wandering minstrel or a pied piper, join the weekend crowd following the medieval estudiantinas. If you've never seen and heard a Mariachi band, you can in Guanajuato.

Even after spending months in Mexico and Central America and becoming used to, jaded by, and bored with mostly-good-some-bad aspects that make Latin America what it is, Guanajuato was an unexpectedly pleasant surprise. Guanajuato is a colourful rabbit warren, a three-dimensional ant farm with five and six storey houses, a mad scientist's maze of streets that become sidewalks where lovers kiss. Guanajuato is Guanajuato.

Guanajuato must be experienced, not read about. Go there.

There are two places I will never return to because I don't want my first impressions destroyed by a second look: Tikal and Guanajuato. Disfrutelos . . . enjoy them.

Highway 15

Highway Mexico 15 from Puerto Vallarta to Nogales on the Mexico-USA border is 1656+ kilometres of boring driving. I wrote "+" because if one takes the free roads instead of toll roads the distance is a little greater. But the cost is considerably less and one often drives on the same stretches of highway. Why pay more than necessary to drive unending stretches of blacktop that, in June, are reminiscent of driving in southwestern Alberta in parched mid-August?

For many first-time travellers escaping from cold Canadian winters, it looks like paradise. When Liz and I travelled overland from Creel and joined Highway 15 at Ciudad Obregón and travelled south from there, we thought it was great.

But no more. It's good but it's not great. Having travelled through southern Mexico and the much smaller Central American countries, the beauty of this strip of land is exaggerated and prices are exorbitant.

To begin with, the beach at Rincon de Guayabitos was okay, although public beach access was limited. But we were upset at being asked US$ 20.00 for 15 Amp hookups in a tiny dust-and-concrete location with no shade and no swimming pool. But of course we were next to a beach on the Pacific Ocean. The US$ 20.00 rate was the same in the off-season as it was in the tourist season, and the same before and after devaluation. We preferred Cuernavaca with its large shaded lots, full 30 Amp hookups, grass, tennis courts, and three swimming pools in lieu of salt water. In a city with lots of shopping, it cost only US$ 5.00 per day.

Ten kilometres south of San Blas, Playa Amor was a basic and inexpensive campground on the Pacific Ocean. It was a great place to relax, to do nothing.

Mazatlán, and Playa Los Cerritos where the campgrounds are, has a clean, kilometres-long, beautiful white beach. Tourists can enjoy the sights, a mercado, and souvenir sellers. One campground charges about US$ 10.00, which is the same price that it was before devaluation. We didn't check out the others on our return trip but they likely will cost the same or more.

If you use Mexico 15 to return to the USA or Canada, drive on. If you use highway Mexico 15 to head south to warmer weather, enjoy the beaches en route, but keep on going to Puerto Vallarta and beyond.

Alamos

Many people told us that we had to see Alamos, a beautiful colonial town only 50 km from Navojoa. So we did. Why did we bother?

Of course, our initial impression was tempered by an all-day outside temperature near 38°C. There was no green on dull brown and ochre hillsides. Our rig's temperature gauge was hovering at the very high end of normality for the first time since we left Canadá. Without air conditioning the temperature in our truck cab was stifling. We were disgusted with the high cost of everything along the Tourist Strip called Highway 15. And there were no more signs after the one which said "follow the arrows". It led us to an empty, dusty, dry, dusty, bumpy, dusty river bed in the middle of Alamos.

In June, this town was empty. There were no tourists rushing around ooo'ing and aaa'ing and self-consciously spending money. There were no street-side hawkers bursting forth in an almost unintelligible singsong that so easily assists the exchange of cheap goods for expensive dollars. There were no Mexicans anywhere, except a few old men in the small park sitting beneath trees hiding from a white hot orb blazing in a cloudless, washed-out-blue sky. There was no dark cantina with an interior hidden behind a temporary wall of posters. There was no music, no sound. There was nothing, no hay nada. There was only the silence of a hot, exhausted ghost town.

Fortunately, Liz and I did manage to find the Acosta Trailer Rancho hidden behind a cemetery. We ignored the instructions in our guide book as well as the advice of two policemen in a white truck who treated us as newborn, wet-behind-the-ear tourists. We also ignored the advice of a local man who told us the streets were very narrow; hah, he should drive in the cities and towns of El Salvador. We drove into Centro, around the plaza, and discovered a black-on-yellow sign that displayed 'follow the arrows' instructions.

After a few blocks of stone and cobblestone streets then two more blocks of winding sand and rock road, we arrived just as a dust devil swirled by and around us and blew fine pulverized dust into our overheated cab and stinging eyes. We didn't care. We had seen a pool filled with water!

Ten scorching minutes later we found Maria in a private house behind a wall of stuccoed stone. She quoted a rarely offered seasonally-adjusted rate, we agreed, and she gave us permission to set up and use The Pool.

Once our bodies cooled down to a comfortable fifty degrees Celsius, and the water stopped sizzling whenever we dived in, we wandered back to our home-on-wheels and plugged in to — yes it's true—30 Amps. We turned on the air conditioner immediately. It still worked.

I think Heaven must have air conditioning.

Next day we returned to the village of Alamos and replenished our supply of liquids: 19 litres of agua purificado; bottled orange, apple, pineapple, mango, and tomato juices; Coke, Pepsi, Fanta, Squirt and 7-Up; Tecate and Corona; and something a little stronger. It is truly amazing where one can find an oasis in a parched desert.

The village had been transformed. The hot dusty streets became clean cobblestones. The concrete plaza was sparsely shaded by tall trees. Colonial buildings had Spanish arches, red tiles, multi-hued walls, and huge colourful pots with green plants. People were standing in the shade of open doorways. Entrepreneurs were selling drinks, hot dogs (hot dogs!?), hat bands, jewellery and whatever one could want.

The ghost town of Alamos was alive, barely. But it would survive until the next tourist season, a few months from now.

Notice the picnic table and Bar-B-Q pit. This is not Mexico!

Guatemala

Tikal
Coban
Puerto Barrios
Quezaltenango
Antigua
Panajachel
Guatemala City

BANCO DE GUATEMALA
GUATEMALA CENTRO AMERICA
A5031800B
CINCUENTA
CENTAVOS DE QUETZAL
Q0.50
A5031800B

Guatemala

Mexico to Guatemala, and Return

There are two major highways joining Guatemala and Mexico: the PanAmerican Highway (CA-1, also known as Mexico 190) and the Pacific Coast Highway (CA-2, aka Mexico 200).

Heading for Panamá, we travelled east on Mexico 190 in Chiapas state, passing through Tuxtla Gutiérrez to Chiapa de Corzo to San Cristóbal de Las Casas to Comitán and then to the border cities of Ciudad Cuauhtémoc and La Mesilla. Although a trip from Tuxtla to La Mesilla can be done in one day, Liz and I needed almost ten.

In Comitán, the last important Mexican city on our PanAmerican (also called TransAmerican) route, we chatted with a friendly, informed ex-Vancouverite who was working in the tourism office. Because she told us that we couldn't get vehicle importation papers at the border, we visited the Guatemalan Consulate. In 20 minutes, and upon receipt of US$ 10.00 (or NP 35.00) for each passport, we were given visas to enter Guatemala for up to 90 days, but our vehicles were permitted a maximum of only 30 days, period. To get a vehicular extension we had to go to Guatemala City. Darned nuisance!

Later we stocked up with enough gasoline to travel 400 km, then drove onto the highway for a nonstop drive to the border. We sidetracked 80 km to the Lakes of Montebello but were disappointed, we've seen more and bigger lakes in southern Saskatchewan.

The highway from Comitán to Guatemala was straight and level, but not smooth. I think the Mexican government is trying to discourage travel between the two countries. But, finally, we were at the border!

On our return trip from Panamá to Canada, we travelled west on CA-2 in Guatemala then on Mexico 200. CA-2 was not the best of roads but, being south of CA-1 and closer to the Pacific, it led to some interesting places.

Mexico 200 was excellent because we got to travel a modern, four-lane Cuota (toll road) for nothing. Because there were no libres (free roads) the government was forced to open up the Cuota to everyone. We thoroughly enjoyed the city of Tapachula and the full service campground at Hotel Loma Real.

When we return to Guatemala, we will use both roads again, but spend much more time exploring the Pacific coast. Our hoped-for Pacific adventures were somewhat curtailed because of dangers posed by more brake problems.

Fuel and Propane

In Fall '94 there was a price change at the pumps, slightly downwards surprisingly. Unlike in Mexico, there are lots of pumps everywhere with all fuels available. Competition is alive and well, with several companies offering various prices in the marketplace. A United States gallon measures as a United States gallon.

The following values have been used to calculate equivalent prices in Canadian dollars. In October 1994, the exchange rate was U$ 1.00 = Can $1.38 = Quetzales (Q) 5.65, and 1 US gallon = 3.76 Litres.

	Guatemala	Canada
Unleaded/Premium	Q 8.05/USgal	Can$ 0.52/L
Leaded/Regular	Q 8.55/USgal	Can$ 0.56/L
Diesel	Q 6.25/USgal	Can$ 0.41/L
Propane	Q 4.60/USgal	Can$ 0.30/L

Propane bottles could be filled almost anywhere, but some of the bottles had a different connector than the ones we are accustomed to: P.O.L. or the more recent Q.C.C.1. A little looking around might be necessary. If essential, an adaptor can be made; Central Americans can make anything. Although safe, it might be wise not to use a jury-rigged adapter in the presence of North American inspectors.

The only propane plant facility that we found was in Guatemala City, or Guate. We were told that there was another midway between Guatemala City and Antigua Guatemala, or simply Antigua, but we drove by three times without seeing it.

In the capital, Tropigas is located near Calle 21 and on Avenida Petapa in Zone 13, in the southwest of Guate. Watch for a small sign, a narrow entrance and a long driveway. If driving into the city from the south on CA-9, I suggest you turn right on 31st street (also the Periferico), turning left when it ends, then carry on to the plant.

Border Crossing: Mexico to Guatemala

Our first impression of our second country came an hour before crossing the Mexico-Guatemala border on the PanAmerican highway. Liz and I had seen mountains in Mexico, but the wall of vegetation and rock towering behind the Mexican plain was intimidating. It wasn't so much that they peaked at 3,600 m as it was that they were so steep and so close together. This time, our 7.5L engine was really going to get a workout!

Leaving Mexico was easy. We merely removed the window sticker and handed it and the vehicle papers to the waiting personnel on the Mexican border. Within 10 minutes we got half of the paper back and had travelled 15 metres into Guatemala.

Once there, it took 15 minutes for defumigation of both motorhome and motorcycle, plus 30 Quetzales (Q 30.00) or, at an approximate ratio of 4:1, about Can$ 7.50. We could probably have avoided the odourless interior fumigation by claiming an allergy, but we wanted it because somewhere we had picked up a zillion black ants. However, they and one housefly weren't bothered in the least by the fumes.

We had been warned to make sure that we left nothing out that might tempt the fumigator; for your safety, he'll insist on being alone inside your rig.

Another 15 m drive and we were at customs, for over an hour. They type very slowly. Because each vehicle must be assigned to only one person, Liz, who cannot drive our motorcycle, had to accept responsibility for it. I don't know what they or we would have done if we were also hauling a boat or another "moto". The customs/aduana personnel tried to charge us Q 175.00 for both vehicles, but since the Guatemalan Consulate had told us it would be only Q 125.00, that is what we paid. When we finally got our papers, they included receipts of Q 30.00 *exactly* for each vehicle, or less than half of what we paid.

Yep, you got it. It seems the consulate was helping his countrymen make a living. Later we found out that the cost of a visa was only US$ 5.00, so he might have been pulling a scam too. Although a government tourist guide book in the tourism office in Guatemala City showed a fee of US$ 5.00, the sign in the consulate looked very authentic. Maybe the tourism book was out of date.

Oh well, when we went into Central America we expected to pay more than we should, for everything. We minimized the overpayment by haggling, which they accepted, but always we let them have something extra. If we hadn't, or if we had got angry, we could've been stalled for several hours at border crossings.

After passing through customs and federal police offices, we moved to a third shack to have our papers completed. I don't know if anything was done or not, but that took another ten minutes and cost an unreceipted Q 16.00.

Make sure you carefully check all documentation before you leave! Liz discovered that our vehicle permits had already expired, even though they were just issued.

When . . . I could have written 'If' but I truly hope you will visit some of the countries south of Mexico.

When you travel to Guatemala it will be difficult to get Quetzales in Mexico, so make sure you know current rates for Quetzales in exchange for United States dollars and Mexican New Pesos. Tourism offices or banks should be able to tell you. American cash will be all right, but probably you'll lose on the exchange rate or on an inflated price when you use it in stores. Being guests in their country, Liz and I preferred to use local currency.

You *will* have to deal with moneychangers at the border in order to get some Guatemalan cash. These border moneychangers are fairly honest businessmen, unlike some we heard about in city centres but, nevertheless, buyer beware. Get many small bills, not large ones which could be counterfeit and which also are hard to use. Count them carefully, one at a time; a folded bill can look like two. A New Peso (NP or N$) is worth 1,000 Old Pesos (P); both are legitimate currency so examine all bills carefully.

Bartering is a must. We and some European backpackers started out at NP 1.00 to Q 1.20. They finally got a rate of Q 1.50. We, who were there longer and didn't care when we left, got

Q1.60. If you exchange a lot of money, you should get an even better deal.

I wonder if all border towns are dirty? Fortunately, La Mesilla is a small village and we could pass through it quickly. The good news is that this portion of the mountainous Guatemalan highway CA-1 is much cleaner than some in Mexico.

Unfortunately, the blacktop is narrower and rougher, with huge potholes deep enough to swallow a complete tire, or at the very least to inflict the need for a front end realignment. Also, an occasional sharp edged rock or boulder will show up, usually on a corner. Guatemaltecos drive faster than Mexicans, and are much more apt to cut corners and cross the white lines. Thank heavens I've learned to study the road ahead, far and near, constantly.

Because we got off to yet another late-morning start, by the time we finished at the border dusk was just a shadow away. We pulled off at an ESSO station—competition is alive and well in Guatemala—about 10 km (6 mi) from the border and spent a quiet night there.

The attendants enjoyed helping us learn a few words of español. We bought something we didn't need at a little tienda, or shop, across the road and satisfied their curiosity as to who we were. Our hand painted Mexico-Central America map sure helped.

These people are poor. A cleanly dressed young man offered to take our garbage to a nearby can, then we saw him going through it. He seemed happy to find a beer bottle and a large coffee tin with an airtight cover.

Next day, we drove up through a spectacular canyon, so spectacular that we congratulated ourselves for choosing not to use the coastal road. Of course we had to drive slowly, with no problems except near the top. At 8,000 feet above sea level and a 17% grade (!?), even our gas-guzzling engine missed the occasional beat. Nevertheless, we seldom drove slower than 35 km/hr unless we were temporarily behind someone.

Three times we were stopped by highway patrolmen who wanted to check our papers. Although they never asked for anything, I suspect that these delays would have been much shorter if we had offered them a gift, una mordida. Being friendly Canadians, having accurate paperwork, not being in a hurry, and being barely able to understand any Spanish, seemed to frustrate them and eventually we were sent on our way.

Away we went to high Huehuetenango to get some much needed money from a bank or bank machine, unsuccessfully, and then onto chilly Quezaltenango where finally we could use our credit card.

There is a feeling in Guatemala that is pleasantly different than in Mexico. Actually, it started in Chiapas. It seems we have left behind medieval Spanish attitudes about race and workplace and we've been welcomed back into the 20th century.

It felt good to be in Guatemala.

On the other hand, when we returned to Mexico after several months in Central America, Liz and I were extremely happy to be "coming home". Attitudes can certainly vary.

Random Thoughts While in Guatemala

In Mexico, most of the buildings and walls had signs painted on them, some were professionally done, most were done with whatever colours and materials were handy. There were few billboards. That changes immediately once in Guatemala. Of course, some walls are still painted with advertisements, but highway, city, and village billboards are everywhere, advertising almost anything.

How surprising it was to see "Foremost" products in stores in Guatemala. Foremost has a plant in Esquintla, on CA-9 South.

Visa and Pepsi seem to have the majority of this marketplace. Kellogg's cereals – mostly of the kiddie's flavoured-sugar kind – are here also. Gasoline is sold in US gallons, meats and vegetables are sold by the pound. Refreshingly, there aren't hordes of insistent vendors of food or trinkets clamouring around us as we walk through the streets and markets.

Oh how easy it is to misunderstand a second language. We were camping in front of our Spanish instructor's home. It was in a new subdivision consisting of three houses and several empty lots. Construction had stopped a year ago because of a change in zoning laws. Liz and I were studying our español lessons when a well-dressed woman knocked on our motorhome door, and asked us the price of corn. Oh oh, we thought, somebody is up to something. We got a package of corn on the cob we had just bought at a super market, and showed her the price. Once again she asked how much does corn cost. Ah, come on, lady! A few frustrating minutes later she left the subdivision.

Next day we saw a new sign advertising building lots for sale in our subdivision, and realized that the woman was asking the price of "el lote" (the lot) and not "elote" (corn). She must have thought we were crazy, quoting five quetzales each for what was advertised as Q 40,000 and up.

Chicken meat is not as yellow as in Mexico. Maybe these people don't put up with 'fattening' chemicals being included in chickens' feed.

Topes no longer exist. They've been replaced with tumulos and potholes. I thought topes in Mexico were bad, but compared to the monsters in Guatemala they were nothing but elongated ant-hills.

A visit to a cemetery in Central America - while you are still alive, of course - can provide unexpected beauty.

There are so many potholes—huge tunnels halfway to China—that there is almost no need for tumulos. Cars and trucks exceed 50 km/hr at their own risk. And tailgating is crazy.

We were caught in a heavy rainfall while riding our motorcycle and didn't see a pothole until too late. Both front and back rims, which are made of a very hard alloy, now sport large dents. Thank heavens I had put inner tubes inside those tubeless tires.

City streets and two or four lane highways seldom have white lines indicating lanes. Why waste money painting the blacktop when nobody pays attention anyway? Potholes don't respect those white lines. So why should drivers, when they can jump lanes and avoid paying for another wheel alignment?

On our return trip the roads didn't seem nearly as bad, especially CA-9 south of Guatemala City which had been repaired.

Almost all city streets are one-way. That way, two cars can simultaneously slip by a parked or dead-in-the-road vehicle, with a motorcycle or scooter weaving in between them. A highway designed for two lanes of traffic will often see three and sometimes four vehicles side-by-side, with a motorcycle slipping in between them. It is impossible to count the number of adjacent vehicles on a nominal four-lane highway.

It seems Guatemalan truck drivers have yet to learn that regular maintenance is cheaper than fixing stalled or broken vehicles. Of course, if everybody looked after their trucks, then there would be nobody left to stop in either or both lanes, put blocks behind wheels, then proceed to try to change a tire, to fix a broken driveshaft, to adjust transmission linkage, to wait for his engine to cool down enough to go another few kilometres, or to get a ride to and back from the nearest gas station. (When thinking of CA-9 south of Guatemala City, try to imagine a roofless repair shop that is ten kilometres of blacktop.)

It appears that drivers have yet to learn that overloaded trucks slowly creeping uphill are more expensive to run than a truck with half a load going much faster. Of course, if there were no overloaded trucks, then there would be no buses doing 7 km/hr passing trucks doing 5 km/hr in either lane, or more often than not, in both lanes. Poor motorcyclists, they'd have nobody to pass but themselves.

In Guatemala City Trebol means cloverleaf, as at the junction of CA-9 to Esquintla (and Turicentro Auto Mariscos) and Boulevard Roosevelt (and Antigua Guatemala). It is not a district, subdivision or colonia. We learned this on our second last time in Guate. Sometimes we were not too bright.

Wherever you find two or more buses together, you will hear incessant name calling. The names will be of cities and towns.

Each bus driver's assistant will be yelling at the top of his voice, trying to get people on his bus.

Diesel in Guatemala is of a special variety. In trucks, and especially in buses, it does not burn. It produces energy and motive power by evaporating inside engines and turning into a cloud, a plume, a jet of coal black dust which is expelled from an exhaust pipe in copious quantities. Not having the proper scientific measuring equipment with me, I can only estimate that each gallon (un galón) of diesel fuel produces 300 m^3 of sticky black soot. This estimate is based upon the fact that after only one hour of city driving on our motorcycle, every stitch of clothing and every square millimetre of our exposed flesh needed to be washed twice.

Liz and I wear glasses. Using motorcycle helmets without visors has resulted in our calling ourselves Mr. & Mrs. Raccoon.

Bus drivers hate motorcyclists. At least, I don't think they are picking on us alone. Buses use manual transmissions, so when they change to higher gears they have to push the accelerator to get more power. Guatemalan bus drivers have gear changing down to a science, and beyond into an art. They can gauge within millimetres when a motorcyclist is beside their exhaust pipe, and pick that exact moment to change gears and feed more diesel to their engines. A perfectly timed gear change will result in any passing motorcyclist being enveloped in a cloud of black soot, and then kept there while the bus lurches forward, matching velocities with the cyclist for a few seconds more.

Guatemala City is dirty! Not messy, but dirty from all that black soot. Most Guatemaltecos probably suffer some lung diseases. In general, Guatemala has less litter than Mexico. And there are relatively few buildings in disrepair that take two, three or four years to build or fall down.

Population estimates of cities seem to include those people who actually live in cities plus those who live in the surrounding areas. Why else would people say 5,000, 12,000, 6-7000 when asked?

Sidewalks are not level. Tree roots lift up great slabs of concrete, rain drains are missing, access to entrance ways are ramps cut into the foot high sidewalks, and piles of sand can completely cover a sidewalk. And yet Liz and I adapted quickly. We no longer have to look down but know instinctively when to take an extra high or extra long step.

People of all sizes ride bicycles. Adult men will ride BMX bikes with 15" wheels and a two-foot seat extension. Six or seven-year-old boys will ride ten speeds with 26" wheels, constantly endangering their future manhood. Just as often as not, there is a passenger on a crossbar or standing on axles extending from the rear hub. A seated male passenger usually steers while the other person pedals.

Woman passengers on bicycles or motorcycles, or more often scooters, almost always seem to look very dignified as they sit side-saddle on a crossbar or rear seat. How they maintain their balance and composure is something I doubt I'll ever understand.

In their colourful traditional dress, the native women are colourful walking rainbows.

Guatemala in 1994 was more pleasant, more laid back, and considerably cheaper than Mexico. The people seemed friendlier and were certainly less aggressive in stores and mercados.

Quezaltenango

Quezaltenango is cold, colder than that notorious arctic oasis within the tropics: San Cristóbal, Chiapas, Mexico. Quezaltenango is also called Xela (Schay-law), which is a lot easier to say through blue and trembling lips. Make sure you bring sweaters, a winter jacket, gloves and a toque when you pop down (actually up, at 3,000 m or so) to this quiet city of language schools. In winter, bring even more clothing.

We wasted our money and a week with INEPAS. They presented too many lessons much too rapidly, using photocopies of lessons overwritten with handwriting, some of which was illegible. We told them so. I believe we would have been much better to have gone to ICA for lessons in español (Spanish) but we choose to go to Antigua where it was warmer.

Hotel Modelo was a great place for our anniversary supper. Liz looked lovely in the shawl she bought in the native Indian village of San Juan Chamula in Mexico.

Neighbouring Salcajá has a friendly and well-stocked market, or mercado. I was told by other tourists it is the only source of an original and unique drink called Rompopo. Mass-produced imitations exist, so make sure you get yours in a recycled ketchup bottle because it is more likely to be authentic.

San Francisco el Alto is noted for its huge, busy market. It is also well known for its pickpockets. Keep your cash, credit cards and valuables securely hidden in a money belt inside your clothes, or inside tight pockets in skintight jeans, or leave them at home. A team of three pickpockets (los ra-tone-ays) were persistent; it took them three tries before they got my wallet. Fortunately, I was able to report the loss within two hours, and nothing was charged to my account.

The beautifully restored courtyard of the Palacio Municipal.

Totonicapán

Totonicapán was both interesting and boring during its "Festival of the Dances", a one day event. For us, that was July 31, 1994.

In the main plaza several groups of dancers and acrobats performed their specialized acts several times during the day. Each dance represented some historical event, religious activity, or hunt. Originally, many dances and costumes made fun of those conquering Spaniards of long ago; other dances were traditional ways of Indian expression and education. I wish we knew more of their traditions. We should have read more about that country before going there.

Their native, Spanish, animal costumes were made with brilliant colours augmented by sequins and pieces of mirror in strategic places. All those in costumes wore face masks carved from wood. Many masks were stylized. Some of them and some of the costumes looked like they were more than a hundred years old.

We were disappointed in the actual dancing, which consisted of repetitious sequences. Many seemed to consist of shuffling of feet by disinterested performers, several of whom were young children. There was no energy in those performances. We had the impression that there were few if any performers who were not very old or very young. Could the recent wars and persecution almost have succeeded in eliminating the local traditions?

As always, there were several kiosks and pushcarts on the streets offering tasty snacks, iced drinks and candied sweets. Nobody was aggressively peddling their wares, except a few children. When we wanted something, we had to go and get it, which was a most pleasant change.

Firecrackers were constantly exploding throughout the festivities. These were not simple little toys. They were hand made, humungous explosives. Some were the size of a 14 oz. jar of jam. They were stuffed into a thick steel tube about a metre long, a flaming match was pressed next to the fuse, then the pyrotechnic-man would run away with his hands over his ears. Thththwoooommmb. A stream of blue grey smoke would streak upwards, climbing for several seconds before exploding with a flash of light, a tiny amount of smoke, and a horrendous **Bwram** that temporarily deafened many.

The used pipes were really hot and couldn't be used again for several minutes. They reminded me of home-made mortars.

Once a fuse instantly ignited the explosive and one poor fellow was surrounded in smoke, slightly singed and deafened. Fortunately there was no permanent damage — to him or his clothes or to the front of the church — and he and his friends were soon laughing and loading other launchers.

I and most others never knew when an explosive would be set off. The men in charge seemed to pick their own times. If I had been one to jump out of my skin at unexpected noises, I'd probably still be floating around somewhere in Totonicapán.

At the close of this day, we watched as a long rope was tied to a high church steeple then lowered and tied to a telephone pole. A considerable amount of seemingly disorganized time was necessary to get it just right.

A shaman or layman priest came by and blessed the performers, the rope and the knot with incense and several chants in an unknown language. He was old, wrinkled and stooped over.

He wore an old and dusty black suit. He used grubby melted-down candles and incense in battered and blackened tin cans. But nobody was going to do anything until he was finished, nobody. His blessing was essential.

For the next half hour, individually, men in costume crawled out of the church steeple and slid partway down the taut but swaying rope. With nothing but 14 m (45') of air between them and aconcrete courtyard below, they swung and twisted and hung by one hand and clambered about and hung by their heels and twisted some more and did things most people wouldn't or couldn't do. They did all of this while wearing masks which limited their vision considerably. These were brave men, very brave men.

All in all, it was a most enjoyable day. We were fortunate to be in the right place at the right time.

Turicentro Auto Mariscos

It is the best campground in Central America. Maybe. Probably. Absolutely! It is a mere 34 km south of Guatemala City and cost us only Q 175.00 for a full week of full hookups.

This safe, very clean, well-maintained RV park and balneario offers a heated swimming pool, a Jacuzzi, a wet sauna, two long slides, two kiddie pools with marine creatures to climb on, a restaurant, two large grassy areas for soccer games, a concrete outdoor basketball court, many picnic tables, and twelve level trailer sites.

All this is surrounded by lush green hills, dormant volcanic cones, and one hidden active volcano that spurts steam and smoke every ten to fifteen minutes. These volcanos provide the thermal energy that heats all the pools and the sauna, without releasing minerals and aromas to assault the sinuses.

There are, unfortunately, a nearby highway and a set of railroad tracks which do seem to be used mainly in the early morning. But at least they are not as noisy as roosters and burros. And you'll never have to complain about vacation days being too short. Little English is spoken by the staff, so guests have a chance to practise their español. But if Eduardo is still a waiter there, he'll be glad of any opportunity to improve his English. German is spoken by the owners.

Once here, it was hard to leave, even the fourth time.

There is another, albeit of slightly less quality, RV park adjacent to Auto Mariscos. It might be able to take an overflow of trailers and campers if a caravan is visiting. Both are extremely popular resorts. There are several other swimming complexes nearby which can provide limited camping facilities, as well as an interesting miniature golf course without divots.

If you are going to drive, fly or boat to Guatemala, you owe it to yourself to visit this tidy and relaxing resort.

Turicentro Auto Mariscos awaits you.

Antigua Guatemala

Antigua Guatemala (Old Guatemala) is a beautiful tourist town that is well worth visiting. If you desperately need an official reason for going (income tax, business, etc.), it is also a centre for many schools that teach Spanish.

It is much warmer than Xela.

There are many language schools; therefore there are some excellent ones, some good ones, some adequate ones, and some bad ones. Talk with your potential teacher or instructor. Select the best you can afford. Don't get suckered in by advertising that states that they are non-profit and are committed to educating and helping poor natives. All those I talked to told me that. Probably it is true, but no school is unique in that regard.

Antigua is big enough to have anything you need, including computer supplies and repairs. It is big enough to have or to get almost everything you want, such as a jet for a gas lamp, repairs to a scratched lens, or duct tape. Yet it is small enough that you can walk through and around the entire town in one day, if you don't stop to gaze at too many sights.

Traffic can be extremely heavy, especially during political rallies. During one such rally our rig had to squeeze past three blocks of cars parked on both sides of a narrow main street, many with wheels forced upon a sidewalk. Some cars had to move over a few inches more, other times we could creep by if they folded in their external mirrors. A couple of cars were low enough that our mirrors passed over them. None of the drivers were angry. In fact they were just the opposite: they were very courteous and helpful, and smiled with us for even trying to get by in a wide motorhome.

This city is clean. It is the "San Miguel de Allende of Guatemala" without the artistic overtones. It's a fun place.

There are many sights to see in and very near to Antigua. Visit the staff in the tourist office next to the cathedral; they speak reasonable English and have lots of information. Of course, there are many churches. Some such as Ruinas de Santa Clara and Ruinas de la Recoleccion were destroyed by earthquakes centuries ago. There are also the Popenoe House, La Casa de M'ajom (Mayan music) and a Colonial Museum to visit. The grounds of historic Hotel Casa Santo Domingo should be on every visitor's list. Marimba music was played every night in Hotel San Rodrigo, only a couple of blocks from City Park.

There are many restaurants of varied cuisines of varying quality at various prices. The Rainbow was a vegetarian restaurant where we exchanged and bought paperbacks and hardcover books.

Liz had some pictures developed at a Kodak colour Lab, and the colours were excellent.

A local dentist filled two of my teeth for less than Can$ 30.00.

When not sightseeing, we studied español for four weeks at almost half the regular price because we were there in the off-season for tourists.

"Ruinas Santa Clara" in Antigua Guatemala, Guatemala

Do take time to sit in City Park. People-watching is always interesting. It is also a great way to meet other tourists who are people watching, and to barter with street vendors who speak sufficient English, German or French to convince you to buy, buy, buy. Buy from one and you'll be surrounded by many. But that's okay, it's all a game and enjoyable to play.

If you are not going to buy, say so at the very beginning. They won't believe you, but at least they were warned. When bartering, offer 1/3 or 1/4 of what they ask, then you might pay half or less than the initial asking price. It is still more than you should pay, but what the heck. By the way, they will never sell at a loss, never.

When grocery shopping, make sure you check out the building behind the downtown Texaco station for some bargains. It's also a good place to get bottled water.

Cramped RV camping was possible at Hotel Jorge. Or, if conferences or rallies had not been scheduled, we could have rented the lovely landscaped parking lot at a Lutheran church on the edge of town.

The parqueo of Hotel Santa Lucia, across the street from a terrific little bakery and close to the daily market, was a desirable downtown location for us. Trailers and motorhomes longer than 8 m (25 ft) or high fifth-wheels might be unable to negotiate the off-street entrance. The weekly price was reasonable but that might have changed.

Although essentially a secure parking and storage area for cars and trucks, some facilities were scrounged. Water was available anytime to top up tanks, but not to connect to. With a screw-in light bulb adapter and a long cord, we hooked up our trailer to low amperage 110V AC electricity. Air conditioners could not be used. Our Swiss friend hooked into my external electrical socket, so we had two trailers in series using minimal power. Disposal of grey and black sewage water was not a problem because they were carried in buckets to a small toilet in the back of the hotel.

Would we go back to Antigua, Guatemala? You betcha!

Panajachel

Getting to Panajachel is dangerous, but well worth the small risk.

The new blacktop highway to Panajachel rapidly descends several hundred feet to the bottom of a valley. Chances are, if you do not gear down to Low near the top of the descent, you will lose your brakes due to overheating. Without brakes on a steep and winding road, with rock walls on one side and air on the other, how and where will you stop?

If overheating brakes are a serious problem with your rig, you can stop en route at Sololá and take time to explore this town. There are always food and ice cream vendors who will be pleased to serve you something delicious.

Our 4.5-Kg (5-ton) Class C has a three-speed automatic transmission, rear drum brakes and forward disc brakes. We travelled with a friend whose Mercedes Benz camper van has six manual forward gears, an optional lower range, and drum and disc brakes. We travelled down to Panajachel together. Both of us geared down and used our engines for braking. At the bottom of the hill, we stopped, joked about the steep descent, and discussed where best to park for a day. Then we drove away, without the ability to brake to a stop.

Fortunately, I realized that I couldn't stop almost as soon as I started to drive. Didi, our friend, was going considerably faster when he found out, but he had enough experience to be able to get into double bull low.

Both of us crept along to our destination, not wanting to delay the other and not knowing the other had the same problem. Upon arrival we opted to try to find a better camping site, but neither of us left for forty minutes. Our brakes needed time to cool down. There are few situations more heart-pounding than not being able to stop one's vehicle!

We discovered Dos Mundos, or Two Worlds. It's a lovely hotel near the centre of town that has a small parking area way back from the busy street. For an exceptionally reasonable fee we were allowed to park there. With only one hose, we could top up our water tank. With a bucket, we could spread our grey water over an empty grass field. And with an extension cord and, sshhhh, a socket plug-in extension, we could tap into an outside yard light for 110V AC.

A "Bird of Paradise" flower next to our rig in parqueo Dos Mundos

Thank Heavens for our choice of motorhome. I don't know if a rig longer than 9 m could have manoeuvred in and out, or if one wider than 2.6 m would have left the vines clinging to the wall on our right.

In Panajachel there is a large RV campground with electricity. Near the bottom of the hill turn right, away from the town and toward Hotel Vision Azul. We discovered this place after we were settled, so we didn't move.

Driving downtown past hundreds of temporary sidewalk stalls was like driving through the aisles of a warehouse store. Anything that might attract a tourist's interest was displayed from whatever was available: string, wire, nails, rock walls, shrub branches, boards and tables. One table had two street legs longer than the others which were on a sidewalk. Mixed in with these stalls and tables were wheeled carts with hot food or cold drinks. Beside and often behind these street vendors were stores, stuffed to the rafters with cloth and leather goods. And people were everywhere. What would this place be like at the height of a full tourist season?

We arrived Saturday afternoon, setup our rig, took a couple of hours to wander around town, then had supper. Darkness settled in, and Liz and I left hand-in-hand for a stroll down a main street. Having quickly exhausted that pleasure, we found ourselves in front of lovely Hotel del Lago, so we wandered in.

The lobby displayed some beautiful paintings which extended down a long hall. We strolled ever deeper into the hotel, past a bar, and into a courtyard with an eye-catching, illuminated pool. As we stood there admiring the stars, a full moon and tropical trees, our ears perked up. We heard Marimba music. We rushed back (actually we walked, but by now that was rushing for us ambling meanderers) and asked if we could have coffee served pool-side. ¡Claro! Of course.

What a magical half hour. Behind blue water in a curved concrete pool tropical trees reached up beyond the full moon, trying to sweep pixie dust off twinkling stars. Secrets and shadows shifted between jungle plants bathed in subdued light. A six-piece Marimba band played softly and romantically behind our lounge chairs, where we sat and sipped hot coffee whitened with warm milk and sweetened with amber sugar. A waitress kept silently appearing to ensure that all was well. But eventually the music and then the magic, but not the memories, faded.

We paid our Q 4.50 bill and wandered outside and joined other lovers and families strolling on silver sidewalks. Eventually we sat on a stone wall to watch Jupiter and Venus ever-so-slowly slide behind and between two quiescent volcano cones and disappear before hitting the mirror surface of Lake Atitlan. A third volcano sported its platinum cloud cap that sometimes almost disappeared but was always there, night or day.

On September 15, the day of Guatemalan Independence from Spain, the tranquillity of Panajachel was blasted by a parade of eight schools, or at least eight groups in different colourful uniforms, marching to the beat of drums, drums and more drums. I guess there is money for cloth but none for brass, because there were no trumpets or trombones. Or maybe there were no trained teachers for these instruments. Every band had one or more Moms walking beside their little loved ones.

We took a crowded bus to Chichicastenango (Chichi) but were disappointed in what was supposed to be a thriving, exciting market. There was almost nothing there. Oops, wrong day; Thursdays and Sundays are market days. The city storekeepers weren't selling anything. We saw no other tourists.

Why do American and Canadian television explode small incidents into such monstrous distortions? Tens of people are robbed and killed in these two countries every day and it hardly rates a mention on page 12 of local newspapers. But let a tourist get roughed up or killed in a foreign country and the wrath of the Fifth Estate knows no bounds. I sometimes wonder if some super-nationalistic tourist group pays reporters to broadcast foreign bad news so North Americans will continue to spend money in their own countries. Guatemaltecos are friendly people!

We almost missed our inter-highway bus connection, but we managed to bus back to Panajachel, arriving just after it started to rain, really rain. Our air conditioner leaked like Victoria Falls and next day I had to take it out to find the problem. When it was installed, one screw was left out but the hole was drilled in. Smart thinking, hey?

To celebrate yet another successful repair job, Liz and I took a five-hour boat trip to three smaller villages on the far side of Lake Atitlan. On the outskirts of the first village we saw peanuts being sun-dried on concrete pads. We were shown a peanut plant, whose seeds grow below ground like potatoes, then encouraged to dig up and eat a raw peanut. It tasted like a fresh bean.

We never did get to visit the second village. As we got off the boat, an ex-pilot came up to me and shook my hand and invited us over for a beer. Surprise! We had met Jim months earlier in San Blas, Mexico. With him were Joan and her daughter, but without their beautiful Labrador pup, all of whom we had met in Navojoa, Mexico. It really is a small world after all.

In the third and last village of this tour, San Antonio, the women peddlers were unexpectedly pushy and irritating. However, once they finally realized that we weren't going to buy anything, they left us alone. Returning to our boat in a much better mood, we did buy two colourful scarves. Each village has its own style of dress, for both men and women. The differences are slight, but they are there.

Cloud caps crown these volcanoes, even under clear skies.

During the trip back, el Señor Carlos Romero, with whom Liz had been talking while I was sunning on the deck, presented us with a beautifully hand-carved boatman he had bought in the second village. He is justifiably proud of his country and wanted us to have yet another happy memory. Amazing. Gracias.

The real boats are made from wide, thick planks hammered together and caulked with black pitch. They look ungainly but they can move a good-sized load or family at a fair speed, when used by local fishermen. Tourists seem to rent boats that move more slowly while randomly twisting and turning.

We spent a week in Panajachel, and could easily have spent several more relaxing days there. But it was back to Antigua and more lessons in español. Ah well, there will always be a next time.

A 90 Day Extension: Was it Worth it?

I think we might have been smarter to leave Guatemala after thirty days, stay in Mexico for three or four days, then return to Guatemala. The paperwork to get a vehicular extension was horrific.

But we didn't leave. We braved downtown, diesel-sooted Guatemala City on our motorcycle. We almost had an accident. We barely avoided it by locking the brakes, quickly turning to the right, sliding sideways, and coming to rest beside a car. That car acted like it wanted us to hit it. Maybe the driver didn't like tourists, or maybe he wanted insurance money.

Driving to where we were told to go, which turned out to be wrong and several kilometres from where we really had to go, almost cost us a ticket. We ended up driving the wrong way on a one way street (on purpose, we could see our destination) and a policeman was hidden there behind some cars. He hauled out his ticket book and waved it menacingly. We shrugged our shoulders, smiled, uttered "Canadiense" in español and said everything else in English. Looking disgusted while wagging his finger, he put his book back in his pocket. Then he helped us to make an illegal left turn against the traffic.

Next day when we finally got to the "Ministerio de Finanzas Publicos", at 8th Avenue and 21st Street Zone 10, it was a madhouse. Government bureaucracy is so bad that street vendors can make a living preparing various forms, and delivering them to hard-to-find offices. Everybody uses them, not just tourists. Of course, bartering about how much to pay for this service is an essential game. I enjoyed it. Liz didn't.

Processing forms takes time, for everybody.

After getting over the shock of having paperwork for two vehicles done on an ancient manual typewriter on a wobbly desk by a man standing on a littered sidewalk, after our passports and vehicle papers were photocopied in a below-street stationery store, after these copies were signed by a Notary Public on the second floor of a nondescript building around another corner, only then were we taken into the Centro Civico building, past hundreds of people waiting in lines in front of several wickets, up one flight of stairs to the elevator lobby, up an elevator to the 14th floor, over to another elevator and down to the 11th or 10th floor, around one corner, through an exit door and into a narrow corridor. Only then did we stop at the end of a line of five persons in front of a tiny wicket. When our turn finally came, our papers disappeared behind a glass window, accompanied by much unintelligible-to-us vocalization by our guide and shrugs by the woman who took the papers. As we walked back through the maze of places and people, we were told that it would take five days to process the forms, and to return next week. I maintained self-control.

Hopping on our motorcycle we left to look for a tourism office, found it and five friendly staff-members, one of whom spoke English. We bought a detailed map of Guatemala City. Now we could go anywhere, if the map didn't blow out of Liz's hands as we scooted past people, cars, trucks, more people, and buses.

Five days later we challenged Guate again, found our guide, but had to wait for him to finish his work with another person. (We had a tasty lunch from a mobile canteen parked in a dirt parking lot behind an almost closed gate.) Once again we followed our guide through the bowels of Civico Publico, arrived at the right wicket, and discovered that the forms were not finished. More vocalizations, more shrugs, and once again we were back on city streets without necessary papers. No, I would not pay to speed up the process. I maintained self-control.

Two days later, after biking past an eight-kilometre traffic jam on CA-9, we zipped through Guate and found our guide. We followed him to the wicket, got our papers, and descended into sunshine. I was about to pay the remainder of our contracted fee, when I was told that now we had to drive to somewhere else and get the stickers for our motorhome and motorcycle.

Liz agreed to stay behind while we two men drove away. I married a courageous woman.

We almost hit another car that ran a red light, but swerved around it and several pedestrians and kept on going. We hadn't hit anything or anybody, so why worry? Eventually, after only one wrong turn, we arrived, somewhere, beside unused railway tracks.

Would I give him some money so he could get the paperwork done quickly? I lost self-control.

I grabbed the papers from our guide and made like I was going to tear them in half. He grabbed them back as I was saying that this wasn't worth the time and trouble, that I was going back to get my wife, and that I would leave Guatemala tomorrow, that I . . . As he hurriedly disappeared into a building, he tactfully suggested that I should stay outside.

Several minutes later he returned, and we both went inside. Inside to an office where the man he had talked to was leaving his chair to walk down a hall, and from which he didn't return for many long minutes. Okay, I can play that game. I found an unused comfortable secretarial chair, leaned back and waited. And waited. Our guide got up from his metal chair and talked to someone. He returned, looked at me imploringly, and I shook my head. We waited. Eventually our man came back, shook his head, went into his office, and closed the door. We waited.

We won. He opened his door and invited us in. He read our papers, gave us another one which he signed, and we went to another office to get the stickers.

We had to wait there because a young man, who had married a Guatemalteca and was now living in this country, was also trying to get his papers. He was extremely frustrated, but so was the agent, who eventually asked us in while ignoring his other client. More vocalization, more papers almost ready, no transferring of money, more waiting, more discussion. Eventually, I was told that I could have a motorcycle sticker but that I couldn't have the motorhome sticker because he had to put it on the windshield himself.

A mental light came on. I explained to him that I couldn't bring our rig here because it was in a garage having the front wheels realigned after falling into another giant pothole. I was sorry, but I would have to leave his beautiful country without the sticker. My visa would expire tomorrow. That was too bad, because I wouldn't be able to take any more Spanish lessons.

The agent shrugged. He seemed to have grown shorter. He and my guide left, then returned a few moments later. My guide motioned me to leave, and we did. The young man was still there.

As we walked to my motorcycle, secretively I was given both stickers.

We managed to find our way back to where Liz was enthusiastically chatting with a local woman. I paid the guide the remainder of our agreed-upon fee, plus a bit more, and we parted company. He had worked hard for his money, I had kept most of mine, and I had all papers and stickers I needed.

Was it worth the hassle? Sure. Once. I played their prolonged and protracted time and money game, and I won. It was challenging, and fun some of the time.

The Caves of Languín and the Pools of Semuc Champay

If you want to be the second person in recent history to drive your motorhome to the caves of Languín and the naturally terraced jungle pools of Semuc Champay, then I suggest that you might also want to visit a psychiatrist.

The 210 km drive north of Guatemala City to Cobán is a pleasure. This highway is probably the second best stretch of blacktop in the country.

En route to Cobán, visit the Biotopo Quetzal Reserve and cloud forest near Purulhá. Early morning bird-watching will probably reward you with a view of the beautiful and rare Quetzal. This tiny but colourful bird, a bird of freedom that allegedly dies in captivity, is the national symbol of Guatemala.

Myths just aren't what they used to be. Months later in an aviary in that superb zoo in Tuxtla Gutiérrez, Mexico we saw a Quetzal bird fly from limb to shelf to branch. There is no mistaking its long tail-feathers and reddish breast.

RVers can camp overnight in a fenced area inside the Biotopo, but not in the parking lot by the entrance. The fee was very small and the security was good. Not having to drive to the Biotopo left us time to walk slowly up the side of a mountain along a well maintained trail with some fantastic views and pastoral solitude.

A little farther along the highway, you might forfeit a few minutes to visit Pozo Vivo, or Living Well. This is an artesian spring that is a 200-m leg-stretch beyond a dead end alley, across from the highway Esso station outside of Tactic.

Once through Cobán and past the next small village, the blacktop abruptly changes into an uneven cobblestone and dirt road with innumerable potholes. At kilometres 16 and 22 there are sideroads where it is easy to turn around and go back. Three to five hours—depending how often your brakes become ineffective and your engine overheats—and 46 km of teeth-rattling vibration, squeaks and creaks, steep hills, steeper valleys, sharp curves, occasional sharp stones, and really narrow sections where you will invariably meet trucks and buses will get you to Languín and the nearby caves.

Gasoline, via a five-gallon container and siphon, is available at the back of a Roman Catholic church. #30 oil is available in at least one shop.

Another 9 km of even rougher and narrower roadway and even steeper hills will get you near the Semuc Champay pools, assuming you can get your rig under the cables of a suspension bridge as you make a sharp right-angle degree turn. Most vehicles can. Because it is very difficult to get turned around farther on, it is a good idea to park by the bridge and walk a couple of hundred metres uphill to the entrance. The pools are another kilometre or so away, and accessible only by foot.

Within a narrow high-walled gorge covered by thick jungle vegetation, naturally terraced dams of limestone create natural pools of clear aquamarine water, which are a pleasure to behold and to swim in. The bottoms often appear to be so near, and yet they can be two to three metres (6-10') deep. Amazingly, these pools are part of a huge natural limestone bridge, which covers the white water of a river as it roars out of sight then reappears hundreds of metres downstream.

Floating on our backs amidst small fish, with straw hats protecting our noses from the tropical sun, while listening to the sawing chitter of insects overpower the silence, and knowing there wasn't another tourist within shouting distance, was a most pleasant experience.

But because there is no level land anywhere close by, it is suggested that you leave before 5:00 p.m. and return to the campsite near the caves of Languín for a good night's sleep. There is a very good hotel, with a level parking lot and excellent breakfast, only one kilometre (0.6 mi) before that campsite.

The campsite is made for backpackers but is level enough for rigs. Nighttime is so quiet that even whispers seem to rape the tranquillity. And because there is only natural light in this steep-walled valley, thousands of twinkling stars and the Milky

Way are exceedingly bright, while hundreds of fireflies look like silent fireworks. A full moon can be almost blinding.

Gunshots at night were merely avocados falling on a tin roof.

The caves of Lanquín were impressive. One and a half to two hours sped by while we explored the many twists and turns. Mythology has it that these caves extended all the way to Quezaltenango (Xela), and they were used by the Mayans to avoid conquering Spaniards. However, over the centuries there have been many earthquakes and now that route is blocked.

We camped next to and swam in this river.

There were several large high-domed caverns and many huge, but not long, stalagmites and stalactites. The floor and pathways were fairly rough and rocky, but some pipe ladders and bridges were provided. Hiking boots or running shoes with good treads were essential because there were numerous muddy slopes.

Unless you have explored several caves, it is recommended that you hire a guide, with a good gas lantern and waterproof, high-intensity flashlight. We hired one at the police detachment, located in the end room of the Palacio Municipal in Lanquín.

At dusk or early nighttime, it is sometimes possible to wait outside the cave entrance and watch hundreds of bats pour out looking for their evening meal. Unlike birds, their flight is without noise. About the only way you can tell if a bat is nearby is when you momentarily see a grey flash cross in front of you.

Immediately next to the cave entrance, tons of white water roar out of the rocky mountain side and create an instant river of green water. This river is safe for swimming and bathing, about 100 m further down river.

The caves were interesting, although we enjoyed the caves in Juxtlahuaca, Mexico more, and the pools were beautiful. But the 46 and 9 km cobblestone roadways were daunting and potentially harmful to any motorhome. And then, of course, you have to travel those 55 km back to the highway and Cobán. Don't bother. Prepare a backpack, leave your rig in Cobán, take a bus almost to Languín, and stay in the Hotel El Recreo. Organize a ride or hitchhike to the nearby caves and to Semuc Champay's limestone pools, and back.

Enjoy the thrill of an exciting road, some truly spectacular scenery, those cool clear waters of Semuc Champay and the dark caves of Languín. But let someone else drive.

Castillo De San Felipe

What a pleasant surprise.

All that was missing from artfully restored Castillo de San Felipe, guarding Rio Dulce while hidden amid tropical coconut and banana trees, was Errol Flynn at his pirate best. We forgot to bring along a candle or matches. Perhaps a kerosene wick lamp would have been all right, but a modern flashlight would not be acceptable to the mood and ambience. And so we were unable to fully explore all the nooks and crannies and twisting tunnels and some windowless rooms where, possibly, rested bones of *ye pirates of olde*.

We drove to this fabulous Castillo-on-the-Caribbean after visiting the Mayan ruins of Quirigua and its intricately carved estelae. Quirigua is a mere four kilometres of gravel road from the highway, almost all of it through a banana plantation. Any fruit on the road is yours. These ruins are well worth the hour or so it takes to see several amazing carvings. We think those carvings are even more detailed than in Copán, Honduras and worth much more than a Q 1.00 entrance fee.

To get to the castillo, we drove 30 km past Quirigua and turned left onto CA-13, the road to Tikal. We enjoyed good blacktop all the way to Rio Dulce. After paying a toll of Q 4.00, we crossed a bridge and turned left at the very first cobblestone street. It changed to 5.3 km of dirt road, an inconvenience that was quickly forgotten after experiencing the Castillo.

Castillo de San Felipe was a great Spanish fort to visit, but it definitely is not wheelchair-accessible. When we finished sneaking through the maze of passageways, rooms and tunnels, we enjoyed a cool and relaxing swim in Lago Izabel then spent more time just hanging out in the clean grassy park grounds. Unfortunately the swimming pool at a nearby restaurant hadn't been cleaned so we couldn't swim there, and thus we chose not to eat there either.

It cost us Q10.00 to park that night in dusty parqueo Glindy at the edge of the relaxing park that surrounds the fort. Next day we travelled to Puerto Barrios and Livingston.

Tikal

As usual, reports indicated all roads to Tikal were rough but passable.

There is no car ferry from Puerto Barrios, Guatemala to Punta Gorda, Belize. If there had been, Liz and I would have visited southern Belize, then driven to Tikal, Guatemala.

In April 1995 highway CA-13 from Frontera to Flores was reported to be extremely bad. One couple from Alaska broke the front struts of their motorhome driving from Tikal to Rio Dulce. Because of their time constraints, I suspect they drove too fast for road conditions. Another couple in a small compact car took eight hours to travel the same road, but suffered no damage.

Having seen Tikal three years earlier and because of road conditions, Liz and I decided not to go again, even though we had fabulous memories! However, if we hadn't had that particular experience, we would have gone by bus from Rio Dulce or flown from Guate.

Tikal is a must-see.

Puerto Barrios and Livingston

The wonderfully smooth highway to Puerto Barrios, which is the best in Guatemala, would be worth a drive in itself even if the scenery didn't vary from mountainous to level agricultural lands to lush tropical green on the Caribbean coast.

Puerto Barrios was disappointing. It is a port town, not a tourist town. So too is Santo Tomas de Castillo. Both have a lot of big trucks travelling to and from their wharves.

But we did manage to find an excellent place to drycamp. We parked in a roomy, shaded, paved parking lot in front of a large, public sports complex—Centro Deportivo—on the outskirts of Puerto Barrios.

We used their spotless, Olympic-sized swimming pool often. With temperatures hovering around 38^{0}C (100^{0}F) and humidity so high that laundry took a long time to dry, that pool was a godsend. Our skins got so wrinkled and white that we feared we might lose our tan. We didn't.

For a small daily fee the custodian-guard agreed to let us park inside a fenced area. This was a blessing. We expected to have to leave our home empty for three days and nights while we toured Livingston, which can be reached only by passenger boat.

Originally, we had booked a private boat to take us to Livingston, but after exploring more of the town and asking around, we went back and cancelled. Next morning we took one of the many scheduled taxi boats for less than a fifth of the original price. Not that the first price was unfair, it wasn't.

Livingston, like Tikal, is a must-see. This is one pleasant, laid back, Caribbean village. The majority of the population is Black, and everyone is friendly. There were only one or two hawkers about; if we wanted something, we had to find a store that had it.

We investigated the huge hotel which was visible as we approached Livingston, but it was too pricey for us. Mind you, quality costs, and we would have enjoyed a day of luxury, but we just didn't have the free cash. Nevertheless we were made welcome as we wandered about.

Leaving by a side door and walking along a side street, we came across a small hotel-restaurant that served delicious frozen custard on a stick. I had to have seconds. I wonder how many tourists have stayed on main streets and missed that special treat?

Liz and I spent the day walking all around this secluded, comfortable town. We wandered through stores, along beaches, and checked out several hospedajes and hotels.

A tailor sits in the door of his house, with all windows closed.

One of my rare attacks of "I need to be alone" surfaced, and I wandered down to a beach-side palapa which served beer or small bottles of a potent white rum. The latter are normally ingested straight, preceded by some salt and lime juice. And followed by a beer by a wimp like me. A big bottle would probably have killed me, I got the smallest there was. I talked with a couple of fishermen, and listened to nonsense from two grey-haired North American expatriates who chain smoked sweet smelling hand-rolleds.

Once back with Liz, we walked down to the wharf and organized a boat ride for next day for ourselves and three young Canadians we had met during our wanderings.

Our supper was a mouth-watering and stomach-satisfying meal of fish in sauce and lots of rice at Restaurante El Viajero.

Next day's breakfast of pancakes in a mainstreet eatery was neither filling nor as highly rated as in our guide book.

The boat trip up Rio Dulce to Castillo San Felipe was satisfying, if not exciting. Some of the advertised attractions en route were a bust—especially Agua Caliente—but our companions were informed, talkative and pleasant. They, and the lush greenery, many colourful birds, natives paddling tiny home-made canoes, occasional sunny breakthroughs, and the Biotopo Chacon Machacas made the trip worthwhile.

To be able to see the Manatee, or Sea Cows, we should have been at the Biotopo in early morning or at sunset. We weren't and we didn't. Inside the reserve I tried to learn to paddle up a jungle river in an extremely unstable and leaky cayuco. It won and I got wet. Liz and the others waited on the decking extending into Rio Dulce and saw several dolphins playfully cavorting only a few metres away.

I returned with my mud stained pants—ha ha—and we set off for and reached the Castillo about an hour later. We sailed under the bridge we had driven over only a couple of days earlier. Liz and I read or walked while the others explored the scenic fort.

Restaurante Los Palafitos on Rio Dulce.

On the return trip, we stopped at a riverside restaurant called Los Palafitos for supper. I was surprised at the eating preferences of our companions; they didn't want to try anything too exciting.

After our superb meals, I asked them to walk over to some palm trees so I could show them a secret. Our boat driver, with a machete and no safety gear, climbed up, up, up a palm tree and cut down four or five coconuts, which fell to the soft earth without splitting open. Our companions were surprised to discover how good the jelly from fresh green coconuts can be. They, and two locals who had come to watch, were exceedingly surprised to learn about that flavourful coconut sponge that comes from fallen coconuts which are beginning to sprout. I was surprised that the locals were surprised.

Daylight was threatening to disappear so we headed back to Livingston, happy and satisfied.

As we docked at the wharf, Liz and I saw a taxi getting ready to disembark, so we rushed over and asked if they were going to Puerto Barrios. They were, we jumped in, and then paid what they asked.

Livingston was a great place to visit. We would have liked to stay another day, just to do nothing, but we didn't have the time. Why did we have to get that letter telling us our son was getting married on such and such a date, and have to hurry back?

La Democracia and Santa Lucia

As we drove through Esquintla en route to La Democracia, Santa Lucia and the Mexican frontier, Liz and I drove past a huge, bi-level shopping mall. It seemed much too big for this city, so probably we missed a lot of it. Maybe we should have explored more in Esquintla. But we do know where excellent ice cream can be found and enjoyed.

La Democracia is a small town, with a small museum of pre-Spanish artifacts and a central plaza with a dozen huge rocks carved into faces or in the shape of rotund men (or women). These faces definitely are not Mayan.

As we drove into La Democracia, we followed directions from one sign by INGUAT (Information Guatemala) and eventually realized that we had driven completely through the village.

Back to the highway, back to the INGUAT sign, and we tried again. This time, after driving four blocks, our increased scrutiny revealed a cross on a pedestal one block to our left. We turned down the street then right to avoid running over that pedestal, and lo and behold, there was a plaza to our left and the museum to our right.

As often happened during our return trip, we arrived just as the museum was closing for a two-hour lunch break. But for once, we were allowed to enter anyway. There were hundreds of artifacts lying on shelves but, this being a small museum and our having seen several others, we were not overly impressed. Except for a fabulous jade mask which rested in solitary honour against the far wall.

Outside, those huge stone heads were something else. They are replicas of the original carvings, but unless you knew that, I doubt you would realize it. These should be visited, if for no other reason than to see the different facial and racial(?) features. In centuries past, I think there must have been many more distinct societies than there are now. I suppose today's Ruta Maya should be called Ruta Maya-Oltec-Olmec-Toltec-?

Then we drove to Santa Lucia, which also displays a multifaceted history of carvings. A few excellent reproductions are displayed in the central plaza.

Outside this town, on private land behind a gas station, were some more carvings, one authentic. We got our instructions mixed up and had to drive through a

A very realistic genuine imitation.

small garbage dump and over an interesting "pathway" to get to the road leading into Finca Soluciones. The people there were most pleasant and cooperative. Without them we would have missed one sculpture located in the middle of a nearby meadow.

These small diversions of ours as we drove along the Pacific coast were short but interesting. If we'd had more time and less brake problems, we would have stayed longer and visited some beaches. Can you believe it? Sixteen months of travelling and we still want more time to see more things.

Final Impressions of Guatemala

If you visit Mexico, you should visit southern Mexico. If you visit southern Mexico and Chiapas, you should visit Guatemala. If you don't visit Mexico, you should visit Guatemala anyway.

Guatemala City is a great training ground for professional Smash-em-up Derby drivers. If you can drive safely in downtown Guate, you can drive safely anywhere in Central America, and Mexico City should be a snap.

If you want to keep your vehicle in Guatemala for more than thirty days, then you are going to have to drive in downtown Guate to get an extension. It can be done.

I wish the government would legislate a minimum truck speed on the highways near the capital. It would certainly improve traffic flow; overloaded and underpowered trucks would have to lighten up. They probably wouldn't break down as often either.

Spanish schools in Antigua are significantly cheaper than similar schools in other countries. There are equal quality schools in Xela, which is not nearly so overrun with tourists, but Xela is much cooler.

We're glad we left some sights to be seen on our return trip. Livingston was worth the drive.

Turicentro Auto Mariscos is an excellent full-services campground, and very cost-effective for a week or a month visit.

Belize

Belize City
Belmopan
Punta Gorda

Central Bank of Belize
ISSUED UNDER AUTHORITY OF THE CENTRAL BANK OF BELIZE ACT, 1982
TEN
DOLLARS
LEGAL TENDER FOR THE PAYMENT
IN BELIZE OF ANY AMOUNT
GOVERNOR FINANCIAL SECRETARY DIRECTOR
BELIZE 1st MAY 1990
$10
AA375764
AA375764
$10
$10

Belize

Belize

Liz and I visited Belize, for 43 seconds!

We had hoped to travel to the Yucatan Peninsula via Belize from Puerto Barrios, Honduras or Petén, Guatemala. Unfortunately, there were no car-truck ferries, and all roads to and from Petén, or Tikal, were rumoured to be very bad. So we drove the long way around, via the Pacific Coast.

But darn it all, I wanted to be able to say (and write) that we had driven in every country in Central America. So when we left Chetumal, Mexico I drove to the Belize border while Liz shook her pretty head, fluttered her Gallic-ancestral hands, and muttered to herself.

While Liz waited in our rig, I chatted with border guards and immigration people, explaining what I wanted. 'No, we don't have multiple-entry tourist cards. No, gracias, we don't want new tourist cards. Por favor, all I want to do is drive over the bridge, turn around on Belizean soil, drive back over the bridge, and come back into Mexico. No, I would not be going to see Belizean immigration. No, we don't want a new tourist cards. Yes... no.... no.... yes... OK? OK!'

Followed by bewildered stares and shrugged shoulders, I rushed back to our motorhome, climbed in, started it up, and drove past the check points and over the bridge into Belize.

There we drove twenty metres to a place that was wide enough that we could turn around, and did so. Well, it wasn't quite wide enough so I had to manoeuvre back and forth a couple of times until we were facing Mexico. I knew Liz's thoughts, but what were the drivers of those three cars who had to wait for us thinking?

Back over the bridge, back into Mexico, past the check points (waving without stopping), past incredulous Immigration personnel, and we were on a Mexican highway heading west.

We have driven in every country in Central America.

El Salvador

Sorry, we spent all of our money.

El Salvador

Border Crossing: Guatemala to El Salvador

Contrary to guidebook comments such as "The crossing is quick and easy." or "El Salvador has the most modern system of all of Central America.", our passing through Hachadura on CA-2 has been our longest and most protracted border crossing. Eventually resorting to using a guide, it took almost an hour and Can$25 to clear out of Guatemala. With another bilingual guide-moneychanger—guides work in only one country—it took another three hours and Can$40 to get into El Salvador. I suspect it would have taken longer, but we arrived in the early afternoon and finished just before the offices closed. We parked there overnight.

Without asking, we were given 90-day visas for both ourselves and our vehicles.

At all border crossings, propina (tip) or mordida (bite) is expected and demanded. A friend of ours, travelling from Switzerland with a Guatemalteco, had his passport grabbed from his hand and stashed away in a drawer until, extremely frustrated, he paid over Can$80 to get into the country.

Money changers at the border give a fair rate when changing money from one country for another. You must have U$10.00 per person to enter El Salvador; the moneychangers will have US dollars.

Expect to be asked to empty out most of your cupboards and storage spaces for customs inspection and narcotics searches, and curiosity. Liz and I got by with less by acting as if we didn't have enough money for the crossing and might have to go back to Guatemala, by being relaxed and cheerful and sharing coffee in our rig, and by refusing a couple of times to pay without a receipt. The guide was essential and saved us three to four times what he cost, which was 15 Colones, or ¢15.

When we travel back north, we will bypass El Salvador because we will have seen most of it. It is a small country and a second visit is probably not worth the time, the border hassles and the expense.

Fuel and Propane

There has just been a price change at the pumps, upwards of course. Prices are really in flux. It amazes me to see cars getting gas at a station where the price is 10% higher than at the one across the street.

El Salvadorean diesel seems to produce much less smoke and soot than diesel in Guatemala.

The following values have been used to calculate equivalent prices in Canada. The exchange rate was US$ 1.00 = Can$ 1.35 = Colones ¢8.72 and 1 US gallon = 3.76 Litres.

As of November 2, 1994, representative prices were:

	El Salvador	Canada
Unleaded/Premium	¢14.40/USgal	Can$ 0.59/L
Leaded/Regular	¢13.10/USgal	Can$ 0.54/L
Diesel	¢8.05/USgal	Can$ 0.33/L
Propane	¢8.65/USgal	Can$ 0.35/L

You might have trouble filling your propane bottles, even though you can get full bottles almost anywhere. I don't know if they'll make exchanges because the connectors will probably be different.

There is a Shell propane plant south of San Salvador, on the left at the turnoff from La Libertad to Santa Tecla. They would not serve us, and I got the impression that they serve only the Army.

There is a Tropigas plant in San Miguel, but it is used only for filling bottles. They had the correct connection for our permanent tank, but because we couldn't drive up on their platform none of their hoses were long enough to reach our vehicle.

There is a Tropigas plant on the east side of San Salvador, 4-5 km from the city on CA-1 toward Turicentro Apulo. You'll need your passport to get in. The plant is hidden behind the almost invisible Coca Cola manufacturing plant, but there is a Shell station on the corner. Both plants are close to the Eastern or Oriente bus terminal. Driving through and from the city, the turnoff to the right is 0.4 km after the Good Year truck repair-facility. Driving west from San Miguel or Apulo Turicentro, the turnoff is 0.4 km from the overpass (rampa) but on the other side of the road.

First Impressions of El Salvador

The people, Los Salvadoreños, are very friendly, helpful and pleasant, waving and smiling as we drive past, but not as often as the Guatemaltecos. Those who have their own vehicle give reasonable highway directions to nearby places.

English-speaking Salvadoreños pop up anywhere, and many have been in or want to go to America. To me, an amazingly large number have been to Canada. Many times we'd fumble along in español and they'd reply in reasonable English. Nevertheless, knowing basic español is essential.

It has been difficult to buy Salvadorean T-shirts because most designs are from USA. The American influence on shopping is very pervasive.

Unlike in Guatemala, there is no obvious indigenous costume. Everyone dresses the same, allowing for differences in financial ability. A sense of history and culture is missing. Women's waist-long hair, so prevalent in Guatemala, is seldom seen here. We miss the many and varied colourful costumes.

Guatemalans have dark skin and straight black hair. Salvadoreños have dark skin and black hair and light sunburnt skin and blonde hair and curly hair. The overwhelming Spanish and indigenous influences so prevalent in Guatemala are not evident here.

The cities and buildings appear old and tired. As in Mexico and Guatemala, many buildings are allowed to run down, but here there is a subtle and disquieting difference of profound neglect. Graffiti is fairly common. Some are merely sprays of paint, but others appear to be in a script other than español.

The overt presence of police and army is almost nonexistent on streets and highways. However, there are military bases which can be found if you look for them. Banks and some other businesses have armed guards, but they are dressed in an appropriate civilian-security uniform.

Vegetation is very thick and very green, like jungle images in the movies of my youth. I finally realized that Tarzan couldn't have used vines to swing from tree to tree to tree because there just wasn't enough room. Sometimes the roadside growth is so thick and so close that we had the feeling we were driving in a tunnel of vegetation, like mice moving through runs in a hay field.

The northern beaches are black volcanic sand; we've been told to expect golden beaches farther south. Unfortunately, the black/grey beaches look dirty even when they are not.

Random Thoughts While in El Salvador

There are relatively few cars driving around, but buses, vans, mini-vans, and trucks are everywhere and almost always full or near full with passengers. Trucks of any description can be and are used to haul people and families around, especially on weekends. Family members are often comfortably seated in chairs or rockers.

Overall, vehicles in El Salvador look better and are better maintained than in Mexico or Guatemala. We have seen only one vehicle broken down on the highways.

Great brakes but rusty bolts. Fortunately nobody was hurt.

There are Japanese, French, American, Russian, German and Mexican cars, but the vast majority of newer ones are Japanese. El Salvadorean diesel produces some black smoke, especially from older buses, but not nearly as badly as in Guatemala.

In Guatemala, there were many many scooters. Motorcycles tended to be 2-cycle, knobby-tired, off-road types from 100 - 180 cc. Not so in El Salvador. Quiet, 4-cycle, city street motorcycles are the norm, and usually 400 cc or bigger.

Cities in El Salvador look almost like those in North America because there are so many signs and advertisements for products which I recognize. We haven't found any really big stores yet, but lots and lots of little ones which specialize in furniture, electronics, electrical appliances, automotive parts and brakes, but which almost always conduct some other sideline, such as selling pop or groceries.

Motorhomes, rigs, trailers and fifth wheels (or fivers) are unexpected in El Salvador and naturally subject to intense scrutiny and curiosity. Expect to be openly stared at and stared at and talked about.

Pupusas, a local dish, are so good that they alone are almost enough reason to visit EL Salvador. Pupusas are thick, handmade corn tortillas filled with beans, or cheese or a little meat, which are cooked over a wood fire then served hot with pickled coleslaw and sour cream. Delicioso!

We experienced a 4.4 magnitude earthquake followed by a half hour delayed aftershock. The moderate shaking only lasted about 3 - 5 seconds. I understand that its epicentre was about 60 km at sea, but coincidently, Volcan Pacaya in nearby Guatemala experienced a large ejection of steam, smoke and lava.

Turicentros of El Salvador

There are 14 government-run Turicentros established in some of the most picturesque parts of the country. Most have pools and beaches. Many have flower gardens or special forests, picnic sites, restaurants and snackeries (merenderos), playgrounds for kids, and bathrooms without seats. Except for Joya de Ceren, a couple of Pacific beaches, and the Teatro Nacional, these are probably the best tourist attractions in the country for RVers.

An inexpensive visit to a Turicentro is usually worthwhile, if only for a quick swim or a shady spot for lunch. A list of turicentros should be available from tourist information offices at each border crossing, and at the downtown San Salvador tourist office.

Of the ten we visited in November, only Apulo, Los Chorros and Agua Fria were clean and free of litter. We stayed at and returned to Apulo for several days and nights. We would have stayed longer than two days at Aqua Fria, but we discovered it just as we were heading toward the Honduras border.

Turicentros are expected to be used during the day. None have camping facilities and many will not allow overnight parking. But if they do – sometimes that will depend upon when and to whom you talk – additional overnight charges vary from nothing to double the daily rate.

Use of a granular chloride in the water, and patches of raw concrete on the bottoms, of several swimming pools make them look green and murky even though they are sanitary.

All turicentros are fenced and gated, but there is no security at these parks, day or night. Of course, they are not responsible for anything that happens to your vehicle if you park there. Anything left on the ground or clotheslines is fair game to passersby and sneak thieves (los ladrones). Whatever you want to keep, keep locked up when you are not around. I forgot about a pair of shorts and wet runners and they disappeared overnight.

Agua Fria is a gem you should visit. En route to western Honduras, it is at the end of 28 km of excellent highway leading to Chalatenango. The turnoff is 3 - 4 km after crossing over Embalse Cerrón Grande. This turicentro is very clean and quiet, and its beautifully maintained and well laid-out grounds and three pools are not overly crowded by local tourists. A shaded paved parking lot behind locked gates provides good dry camping. There is one nearby tap of potable water that can be used for topping up trailer tanks.

A 5:35 sun rising over the volcanic lake at Turicentro Apulo.

Amapulapa is not on CA-1, but about 4 km south of San Vincente on the road to the coast. We arrived just before dusk and stayed the night in a large parking lot. In the morning, we walked around a large pool and through some picnic areas but the litter was so bad, we quickly left.

Apastepeque is situated just 2 km of dirt road off CA-1, 53 km east of San Salvador. The faded sign was almost completely hidden by political posters. It is situated on a lovely lagoon, but there is no parking available except on the narrow dirt road in front of the gates. We didn't have time to go in as dusk was imminent, but many local people have suggested we go there.

Apulo is a clean large turicentro you should visit; it puts many North American daytime parks to shame. It is located adjacent to a clear lake (bright green or blue depending on the sun) inside the caldera of an extinct volcano, and merely 4 km off the CA-1 and 16 km east from San Salvador. You can drycamp in a paved parking lot in the shade of many leafy trees. Potable tap water is available, electricity can be borrowed from a merendero, and black and grey water can be carried to nearby baños (toilets). Only a few metres away, a chlorinated pool is flushed nightly and closed every Monday and Friday for cleaning. The merenderos are so clean we had no qualms whatsoever about eating in them; the pupusas were fabulous. Beer and pop trucks come by at least twice a week, and they will sell their wares at wholesale.

Balboa Park is just south of the zoo and above the smog in San Salvador, and a pleasant place for a picnic. We were allowed to park overnight in the driveway to the local police detachment. Pass through this park and spend a few moments in Acoustic Cave, look through La Puerta del Diablo (the Devil's Door), then climb 262 steps for a fantastic view of the surrounding valleys. Beware of clouds obscuring the view.

Volcan Izalco is eyeball distance from Cerro Verde.

Cerro Verde is a should-see. Its mountaintop hotel provides a reasonably priced, Salvadorean breakfast in its glass-walled restaurant. Some of the views as you drive up the mountain are stunning. You can drycamp in an unlighted parking lot, and you might have to if you want to enjoy the fabulous views before morning clouds enshroud you with mist. Walk out the gate and you can look down into Izalco Volcano! Take the paths to the lookout points throughout the cloud forest and you'll be amazed to see hundreds of orchids. In season, this colourful 'weed' and look-alike but drab bromeliads are everywhere.

Costa Del Sol can be reached by leaving CA-2 and driving some 20 km toward the beach of the same name. It has limited parking, fair merenderos (specialty meals and soups from the sea), much litter, but a beautiful beach and warm swimming. Although there are supposed to be swimming pools, we didn't see any; they might be across the street. No overnight parking there, but on the way back one or two smaller rigs might be able to drycamp at the private and pleasant "Bar de Ostras".

Los Chorros, 18 km west of San Salvador, right beside CA-1, is another must-see. It is probably the prettiest turicentro of them all, and is built to complement the natural beauty of a gorge. Four swimming pools use fresh, untreated, clear, clean and cool subterranean water, some of it coming from a waterfall. It is clean but not quite litter free, and quite busy. You might be able to park overnight in their unguarded parking lot.

Sihuatehuacan is on the eastern edge of Santa Ana. (Do visit the theatre which was under restoration.) Drive to the central plaza, turn right, then take the one-way road to its end. This turicentro has four large pools, tennis courts, an open-air theatre, merenderos and hundreds of large black birds. This location has been used by RV caravans, and you can drycamp overnight in a paved lot for extra money. A water tap can be used for topping up tanks and at least one merendero will let you use their electricity (long cord needed, and no air conditioner please). Unfortunately unswept paths, untended gardens and littered grounds gave us the impression of neglect.

Toma De Quezaltepeque is a quiet pleasant turicentro only 20 minutes from Joya de Ceren archaeological site, and a pleasant spot for a picnic or a swim in either of its two manmade swimming pools. It has a large parking lot; maybe you could stay overnight but we forgot to ask.

I wish we had known about Complejo Turicentro de Libertad on CA-2; we might have enjoyed the western beaches more. Based on people's comments and postcards we've seen, we're sorry to have missed Altos de La Cueva.

In conclusion, RV campgrounds are definitely in short supply in El Salvador. We know of only one, adjacent to a beautiful Pacific beach, 4 km from El Cuco in southeast El Salvador. If it weren't for those pleasant turicentros, our visit to El Salvador would definitely have been much shorter.

Driving in El Salvador

In Mexico, we learned to ignore instructions that began with "Drive two blocks and turn right". We've also learned that "directo" in El Salvador invariably means a road quickly forks left and right, or there is a traffic circle or a detour ahead. I think "directo" means that if we were to travel by bus, regardless of the number of turns it makes, we wouldn't have to transfer to another bus. Maybe so , maybe not, but I do know that 'directo' does *not* mean keep going straight ahead until you reach your destination.

I have also deduced an amazingly obvious fact of driving in cities: drivers do not have eyes in the back of their heads. Logically therefore, the driver whose body is ahead of your nose has the right of way. If a driver wants to cut in front of you he automatically has the right to do so, provided that he sticks his hand out of a window, and particularly if he waves it energetically up and down. Also, a driver can cut in if his passenger puts out his or her hand.

A truck with a full load of very colourful baskets.

Nobody watches tail and brake lights because most of them don't work. The only way you might prevent his cutting in front of you is to honk your horn (if it works) but you'll have to be quick.

Frustrating Directions

I would like to strangle that tourist agent! Which one? The young enthusiastic gentleman at Amatilla on the eastern El Salvador-Honduras border.

He was particularly enthusiastic about the "Museo de la Revolución" so Liz and I decided to drive a little out of our way. What he didn't tell us, is that it would take three hours of driving 59 km on a potholed something laughingly called a blacktop highway. He also forgot to mention that there was no gas station in Perquín. Of course, we forgot to ask about those conditions; therefore, he was under no obligation to tell us.

This was like many other times we've asked directions on how to get somewhere. Even with conflicting answers, by using advice that agrees most closely we have always managed to find our destination. But sometimes it's like a blindfolded man being tied to a tree; if he walks far enough in circles, and wraps enough rope around the tree, eventually he will get to the tree.

Of course, when you do get to where you want to go, sometimes the place is closed, or under repair, or the hours were changed to accommodate a politician, or the brilliantly coloured poster advertising a festival was printed last year.

It seems to me that the people of Centro America are very guarded, even secretive. They will answer any question you ask but seldom will they provide additional information. The fact that such information is important is obviously of no concern since you didn't ask. Or perhaps they think you know already, and they don't want to embarrass you by implying that you don't know.

Sometimes a person won't know the directions, but he would look bad if he admitted it, so he makes them up. We have learned to ask at least two people the same question.

Short answers are great, long and involved answers merely mean that we listen to the first twelve words and ignore the rest.

To be fair, our español still isn't very good and we have no trouble misunderstanding some of the answers. What RVers like us need is a language course or cassette tape that deals only with asking and listening to directions.

And the obvious isn't.

The only propane plant in El Salvador that can fill our permanently-affixed tank is located immediately behind a Coca Cola plant. As you know, Coca Cola and Pepsi are in an all-out war and there are huge signs, big signs, small signs, wall painted signs and entire restaurants painted with their logos. But the Coca Cola plant is unmarked and indistinguishable from other nearby buildings and security walls. We drove through and across San Salvador twice before we found the plant, passing it at least four times.

In small towns and pueblos and subdivisions (colonias), when you miss a turn (and you will) back up. Do not drive around the block. Many times the block isn't square, or has five corners, or some streets dead-end and you have to drive around another block which probably isn't square either. Many times 'driving around the block' made me think that I was a rat in a maze.

Mexico has good highway signs, Guatemala has reasonable highway signs. In El Salvador, most of the few road and highway signs that do exist are so rusted that they are illegible or they are obliterated by rival political posters. In all three countries, city and pueblo street signs either don't exist or are hidden behind trees, vines, or stain.

Getting maps — large detailed maps — is a great idea. Unfortunately you'll have to ask directions to get to tourist centres or to stores that might sell them. Good luck.

Never, well almost never, show a map to a person from whom you want directions. You will spend a lot of time explaining how to read a map, showing where you are and where you want to go, and then you'll still have to listen to the answers which are completely unrelated to your map because they don't understand it.

Because you will have to ask directions, learn to ask lots of questions of lots of people. And ask people who are driving cars, taxis or buses because they've driven there. Even so, remind yourself that "Do you promise to tell the truth, the whole truth, and nothing but the truth?" is a television cliché, and a myth in Central America.

But I digress. How do I get back to that tourist guide in his office on the east border of El Salvador? "Señor, por favor, ¿como vamos a San Miguel? "Directo a la esquina, entonces a la izquierda y maneje cuatro kílometros a la carretera, entonces a la izquierda a la triángulo y ira a San Salvador occidente. (Straight ahead to the corner, then left and drive 4 km to the highway, then left at the triangle and you will go west to San Salvador.) "Muchas gracias. Adiós."

Our destination was to be San Miguel, 60 km to the east, then back to Amatilla. Ah, the heck with it. Forget about that travel agent. The trip to Perquín wasn't really all that bad. At least I should be able to get back to a highway.

Hasta Luego, if ever we meet.

Santa Ana

Santa Ana is a comfortable city. It is prosperous and obviously takes pride in civic planning, reconstruction and restoration. For example, in two to three years the Municipal Palacio (City Hall) and kitty-corner City Theatre are once again going to be truly beautiful buildings.

Traffic is not exceptionally heavy for a city of 250,000, and the drivers are quite courteous and not constantly trying to beat out the vehicle in front of them. (Drivers in San Salvador are just the opposite types, but still not as bad as those in Guatemala City.) I doubt that there are more than a dozen stop lights in this city.

The main streets and avenues of Santa Ana (pronounced Santaana) are paved, with fairly high curbs. There is little dust, except on streets where storm water and sand can't get into the sewers. Built into many of these curbs are hinges for metal plates which can be laid flat on top of the sidewalks or flipped down to provide ramps for cars and trucks as they drive into driveways or through gates.

The bottom of ALTO (STOP) signs indicate which way traffic can travel, which is extremely useful considering that most of the streets and avenues are one way.

An electrician's nightmare

An RV can drycamp overnight in the Turicentro Sihuatehuacan in east Santa Ana. Unofficially, there is water available to top up tanks and electrical outlets can be found in some merenderos (eating stalls). Enjoying the nighttime solitude of your own swimming pools is fantastic. The gate is locked at 6 p.m., but with only one person who patrols the park and sleeps in the nearby admin building, security is minimal.

Liz had got complacent about wearing jewellery (not that she has much) but was jolted back to awareness when a young thief ripped a 10K gold necklace off her neck and quickly disappeared among hundreds of people in the main mercado. It is not wise, and definitely foolish, to walk about wearing flashy rings, bracelets, earrings and the like. Even rich Central Americans know better than to advertise one's wealth in public places.

If I were to live in El Salvador, I think I would choose Santa Ana. It is a pleasant, unhurried city. And I have the feeling there are several cultural organizations and events available to someone who can fluently read and speak español.

Joya de Ceren

About midway between San Salvador and Santa Ana, Joya de Ceren is one archaeological site that should be visited. Both Liz and I enjoyed it much more than Tazumal.

It is a recent discovery and is still being excavated and studied. Actual diggings are protected by fences but open to public viewing. If you ever thought of being an adventurer in history, this site will show you how much work can be involved in meticulously removing volcanic ash, and what treasures can be found.

Take the turn off the CA-1 to San Juan Opico and turn immediately on the first road to your left, past the Joya de Ceren restaurant, and drive on reasonable blacktop for 12+ kilometres. As you cross a bridge, on your left you'll see metal silos whose construction lead to the discovery of this buried village, which in importance is comparable to Pompeii. Almost immediately the entrance will be on your left.

You do not need any kind of pass, so drive in and park. Then shoo away the sellers of knickknacks and souvenirs; you can buy later while having one or two pupusas and a drink at the cafeteria at the end of your visit.

Walk slowly through the small but very interesting museum, then follow the stone pathway to the various archaeological digs. We saw three, there may be more when you arrive.

I have tried to write about what we saw, but it read like a dull text book, like the kind I remember from long-ago high-school days. But to actually see those digs and to marvel at slowly re-emerging buildings and gardens as layer after layer of ash is slowly brushed away, ah, that is so much better than reading about it. Hasta la vista.

Costa del Sol

The Costa del Sol beach area of El Salvador caters to wealth, with luxurious hotels, private clubs, and many private shore-front properties hidden behind contiguous high walls that block both view and access to the beautiful grey beaches. There may be some open beach but we got tired of seeing an unending 5 km strip of concrete and brick, with only occasional openings that hinted at what lay beyond.

We got as far as the government maintained public turicentro, which we visited briefly and learned we could not stay overnight, then left immediately for Playa El Cuco. Well, almost immediately.

Driving back, we passed "Bar de Ostras" which had an open gate showing a clean and freshly swept parking lot among palms and pines. We stopped, backed up, noticed a small pool in front of a restaurant-bar, and drove in. Following a brief discussion in which we said we would leave next morning well before the Sunday crowd arrived, we paid a reasonable off-season price for one night's parking then moved our vehicle to one side to allow other customers access to the parking spaces.

Within minutes, Liz and I changed into swimming suits and plunged into the warm, salty Pacific Ocean. The beach is shallow and we had to swim/walk 25 m to get to where the breakers were forming, but that is where the fun is. Half an hour later we showered in luxuriously cool water to remove salt and sand, then plunged and paddled in the pool's clear blue water, showered again, and towelled our hair. Then we had beer, lime and salt served to our table in the shade of a red-roofed ramada as we looked out over an endless, clean, flat beach washed by white breakers and dark green ocean.

Part of our conversation seriously joked about how long we would stay in Canada before returning to Central America. We even had the audacity to complain about our meagre monthly financial situation which didn't allow us to taste more delicacies from the varied and inexpensive menu. It didn't mention Oysters! But mainly, we chatted about nothing and just enjoyed the sun, the breeze, the beach, the ocean, and the fact that we were here!

Here, beneath a hot tropical sun, swimming in warm Pacific waters.

Here, at 5:30, watching the golden sun transform into a pumpkin as it slowly slipped below the horizon and beneath the grey-turquoise sea, ending as a brilliant green flash.

Here, watching three layers of clouds, one by one, transform from the orange-red colours of fireplace embers into the blue-grey of faraway hills and finally into black shadows in an ever-darkening sky.

Here, under the jet black of a moonless tropical night, on the Playa Costa Del Sol, in a secure parking lot of the tiny, tranquil Bar de Ostras. Buenas noches.

Medical Help in El Salvador

I write this with my left leg up on our motorhome's dinette seat, swathed in bandages covering five internal stitches and nine external stitches. There is no pain because the nurse at the clinic in the nearby village gave me numerous pills for pain, infection and general healing.

Why?

Liz and I are camping at "El Tortugas", a pleasant North American style trailer park 4 km from El Cuco in southeastern El Salvador. It has ample space, grass, shade, and access to a clean beach the colour of unburnished pewter and warm Pacific Ocean water. It also has full hookups, but water pressure is very low and its electrical system needs repairs to prevent it varying from 220V AC to 10V AC under load.

But I digress. I'm inside because I wanted to drive my motorcycle on the hard packed beach just above the water line, racing through river deltas, shallow salt water, and among the tire track marks left by occasional cars and trucks. There was no problem, even at 80+ km/hr, until I drove on that part of the beach where the sand had dried.

I'm not ignorant, but sometimes I'm foolish. I know that a 305-cc street bike has little traction in dry sand; it's like driving on oil if you don't bog down. But after revving past the red line then locking both back and front wheels, I wanted to find out how quickly I could turn around. Five times I tried, with two complete successes.

But the sixth time the bike dug in, tipped way over and laid on its side. My leg was stuck underneath.

No big deal! I lifted it a little, pulled my leg free, stood up, then wrenched the bike up so fast that it fell over on its other side.

I recovered, stood the bike on its two wheels, climbed aboard and released the throttle while slowly applying power, and I was off for another high speed run. But my left foot felt wet, so I looked down and saw dark blood spurting out above the ankle.

I was concerned (panicked?) because spurting blood meant I'd cut an artery. Immediately I headed back to where my wife, a registered nurse, was building sand castles or watching hermit crabs when she wasn't diving into the breakers. A long kilometre later, when I finally got her attention, she noticed my foot was completely red, tore off our temporary cloth seat cover and made it into a tourniquet with a knot pressing on the gash.

Liz hates driving on anything besides blacktop, but she gritted her teeth and hung on as we sped 4 km down the beach toward the pueblo of El Cuco. One, two, three tiendas and a pharmacia later we finally understand that the nearest clinic is 7 km away in the hamlet of Chirilagua.

Liz was embarrassed because she was inappropriately dressed in the village in only a swim suit. I hadn't given her time to change outfits before our looking for medical help.

Away we went. Fourth, fifth, sixth and last gear, then I put my leg up high on the handle bars to reduce bleeding. The entire bandage was red. Liz hung on as I wove between the potholes, read the highway signs, and told me to turn left. Once in the village, we turned right, avoided several wandering pigs, then turned left, left again, then right and we scooted up the driveway into the clinic.

In broken Spanish we made them understand what happened. Once they cut off the tourniquet (they couldn't untie it) the problem became obvious. Quickly, I was lying on a bed and taking deep breaths every time the nurse injected me with freezing. Four times.

A doctor arrived, left, returned a few minutes later. A nurse poured a lot of pale yellow liquid over the gash while the doctor used swabs to clean out any sand, then they used a couple of litres of distilled water and more swabs to make sure it really was clean. The strange thing is that as I was watching all this, it was as if I were watching television. There was no pain, and I was curious; I wanted to see it all.

I sat up—"Don't move your leg!"— and saw a 8 cm (3 1/2") gash with a sliced small white tube at the bottom. It reminded me of lean meat in a supermarket.

They poured something else over it. The doctor got some curved needles and started to sew, stitch by stitch using fishermen's knots. He stitched the inside flesh and muscle, then the outside skin. Real-time television was great, but I was talking a mile a minute and Liz said I was in shock.

Once the emergency was over, they cleaned out a small hole near the anklebone and covered it with a Band-Aid. Then they put lots of Mercurochrome on a smaller cut on the other leg, but left a shallow scrape and minor burn alone. Good thing. The sight of all that red Mercurochrome was enough to turn anyone's stomach upside-down.

Throughout the entire procedure, the nurse was talking to Liz, two professionals comparing notes. "Do you use these sanitized packages?" "Penicillin or something else?" "Read this label." "What do you use in Canadá?" To me it seemed that the nurse was apologizing for services in El Salvador.

There was certainly no need to do so. The doctor and the nurse were doing a professional job of surgery, and doing it quickly but not hurriedly, and using sterile dressings and thread taken from boiled sealed packages.

I enjoyed the conversation and camaraderie between doctor, nurses and patient. Another nurse even came in to watch and learn. I was a real person being fixed up by real people, not some slab of meat on an operating table. It felt great, strange as that may sound.

Tomorrow I have to go back for further inspections. Infection? Bleeding? Who knows what? But I'm not too concerned. The tiny clinic, far from the major cities and in a village of dirty streets and free roaming pigs and garbage on the outskirts, does what it has to do, and does it well.

Time passed slowly, bringing with it some rain during the night. Today we drove on our motorcycle more than 4 km of muddy, bumpy, potholed dirt road to get to the blacktop. I lost a sandal in a ditch we slid into, so I left the other one there too. We should've driven on the beach, it would have been faster and safer.

At the clinic, a different group of nurses welcomed us in, sat me down and put my leg on the only bed, which was already occupied by a man receiving an IV. They removed the bandages, washed down the cut, looked at it, then put on new sterile bandages.

As we left, we asked how much we owed. ¢ 3.50, or sixty-seven cents Canadian! We didn't have anything that small so we asked them to keep the change.

Now, I don't recommend your having an accident just to find out how good or bad medical care is in different countries. But in El Salvador, if you do have an accident, don't worry. Just go to the nearest rural clinic. You should be well and competently treated there. I was.

Herida Update

I was pleased with the services provided by Dr. Hernandez and the nurses in that clinic in Chirilagua. I still am, but now for the rest of the story.

Five days after the accident, five days with no pain, I had used up my penicillin and anti-inflammatory pills and all was well. However, the suspicion of the sixth day was confirmed on the seventh when the wound (la herida) definitely showed signs of infection. It took only two days to go from nothing to bright red, inflamed and swollen skin that was tearing away from those nine external stitches.

Maybe I shouldn't have been so macho and maybe I should have listened to that lovely nurse I married. Maybe I shouldn't have gone for one more bike ride in the sand, maybe I shouldn't have walked so much, maybe I shouldn't have got my bandage wet with salt water and mud, maybe I shouldn't have put cough syrup on the wound thinking it was hydrogen peroxide, maybe I should have kept my leg elevated more often, maybe . . .

Who needs traffic lights? Drivers can always untangle a mess.

Whatever the cause, the rapid onslaught of infection was scary. We had to pack up our motorhome just two days after we had decided to stay at Turicentro Apulo for a week or more and had set down roots (they looked suspiciously like electrical cords and rubber hoses) and drive into San Salvador. Oh how we hate congested traffic and soot-fuming buses in big cities!

We visited the Canadian Consulate but, because it was closed, we had to ask a local pharmacy for the location of the nearest clinic. Due to our lack of language ability, we ended up in the office of a specialist in internal medicine. But we waited and he finally did look at my festering wound. He also spoke English very well and, in very few words, I was told to fill this prescription, take my pills, sit down, keep my leg raised, and don't move for three days. Sheepishly, under Liz's I-told-you-so glare, I agreed. Fortunately, I am not allergic to any medication so my prescription was for a new and very powerful antibiotic. And very expensive. The original pharmacist misread the typed prescription (maybe they weren't used to being able to read prescriptions) and gave me only half of the necessary pills. Of course we didn't notice that oversight until we had comfortably settled back into Apulo, so next day Liz, for the first time, had to drive us back into the city once again. We went to a different pharmacy and had to pay even more for those potent pills, so we mentally apologised to the first pharmacy for all our "ripoff" thoughts.

Two and a half days and six changed bandages later, we were back in the doctor's office. The infection was gone and the swelling was down, so the doctor took out the stitches. While so doing, he told us that he had been very worried that he would have to cut open the wound to clean it out, because that meant that the re-traumatized wound would take weeks, possibly months, to heal properly. There seems to be a code of silence amongst medical professionals; later Liz told me she'd had the same concern.

Once again I write this with raised leg inside our motorhome, and being limited to hopping outside to sit in a chair and prop my leg up on a stool. Every shower means having a plastic bag tightly taped, yea doubly taped, to the hairs and skin of my leg, and then of course, having to rip it off. Strangely, Liz exhibits no compassion whatsoever.

Total cost for visits, medication and travel was ¢856.00. Of course, in Canada it would have been much more than Can$142.50, but nevertheless our travel budget has suffered a minor cut too. Hah well, we weren't going anywhere for awhile anyway.

Six days later the wound finally stopped seeping and scabbed over, thus protecting itself from outside infection. Propping my foot up in the sun to get as many germ-killing ultraviolet rays probably helped.

Nevertheless, two days later we began to worry about the redness of the skin near the centre of the scar. We relaxed only after we realized that the traumatized skin was, yes it was, sunburnt.

Hopefully there will not be a third article about the results of my stupidity (That's Liz's word, I prefer to call it 'testing the limits'). Soon, the sooner the better, I'll be able to go for another swim. Then we'll be on our way to Metépan, and Honduras.

Across the Waves, Eventually

We arrived on the beach as prearranged, but the outboard motor was in pieces.

Selbin Alberto, a young man to whom we had occasionally given English lessons during the last ten days in Apulo, had finally convinced us to take an hour's trip on Lago de Ilopango, an 11-km wide, 250 m deep volcanic lake. We had agreed to start the trip at 5:00 p.m., which would put us well out on the water when the sunset was expected to be at its brightest and most colourful.

And so we were surprised and annoyed to see a disassembled motor. "Is there a problem?" I innocently asked. "No, of course not" was the unexpected and obviously untrue reply. Maybe I had heard and/or translated his reply incorrectly, but as I was trying to formulate another question, the boat was turned around and we were being pantomimed to get in.

Obviously Selbin wasn't worried (or he was bound and determined to get our money) so we scrambled over the bow and took our seats amidships. All this time, the repairman was putting pieces back together and tightening screws and bolts.

We're settled, Selbin pushes, the boat breaks free from the sand, drifts out into the lake, and Selbin clambers in with dripping feet. He grabs an oar and continues to move us into deeper water, then rests. A breeze blows us back to shore, so we're poled out again. And again. Finally the motor is reassembled, except for one wire hanging down the left side and, surprisingly, it starts on the first pull of a cord then idles like a purring kitten. Unfortunately, it can't go any faster; so, off comes the cover, the man pushes his finger against something, and the motor revs up. Back to idle, change from neutral into reverse, push something, and we are circling away from shore. Back to idle, change gears again, apply pressure, and this time we're moving forward into the breeze and the tiny waves.

Our speed varied constantly and considerably, as did our direction (I think his finger kept getting tired from constant pressure) but generally we were heading toward a faraway island. There was a short stop while something was adjusted or reassembled.

Any attempts at coherent conversation were quickly doomed to failure because of our lack of español, Selbin's quick soft voice, and the noise of the motor. But that was all right because the scenery was impressive and Liz and I weren't too talkative.

It amazed me how quickly the shape of cliffs, peninsulas and bays could change. And the sky was starting to change into that ethereal golden colour that precedes dusk.

Almost the entire island was surrounded by white Styrofoam buoys supporting hundreds of metres of fine fishnet. Lacking precise directional control we almost drove through one net. Although there are reasonably large fish in the lake— it was restocked after constant dynamiting (CIL lures?) destroyed the fish population— these nets are used to ensnare fingerlings. Slightly larger than minnows, these are used for bait and food. As food they can be salted and sun-dried, or deep-fried for toppings on pupusas.

Having circled around the island, we were heading back when somehow we convinced the driver to head to a nearby semi-submerged island that was completely covered with leaves and surrounded by reeds and weeds. Slowly we wove our way over there, and were surprised to see one Ceiba tree on a small hill above the water line. We had just completed our tour when the engine quit.

It wouldn't restart, and Selbin was concerned that we had to be back on shore by a certain time. We didn't, he smiled, and the motor was taken apart, reassembled, tried, taken apart again, reassembled, and worked. Total time, about twenty minutes.

We'd had twenty minutes of quiet, with only the lapping of tiny waves making any kind of noise. The motor had come apart noiselessly and, even though the boat rocked in the waves and swells, not once did we hear a screw plunk into the water or hear a nut or a wrench rattle down to the bottom of the boat. I was wondering how many pieces I would have sent to the bottom. Like the sky, the silence was golden. Fantastic.

Sunset came. Clouds turned pink and hills turned blue. Each succeeding hill was darker than the one in front, except the last where the sun continued to shine. On the other side of lake Ilopango, a gigantic silver full-moon began its swift ascent. The higher it got, the smaller it became. Slowly the sunset disappeared, stars began to appear, and the moon got brighter and brighter.

I can't think of anything better than having enough time to bob above undulating waves, listen to silence, watch a moon shrink to half size, and have all of this while my wife relaxes in my left arm. Even with money, I couldn't get much richer than that.

Darn it, the motor sputtered to life again, and we drove back to the weedy shore of Turicentro Apulo.

We had got off to a slow start and finished in darkness, but what the heck, motor or no motor, we weren't going anywhere anyway.

Forty-eighth Street, San Salvador

In San Salvador, 48th (or 49A) street is directly accessible from the Alameda Roosevelt portion of CA-1 (or PanAmerican Highway) that passes through that city.

Coming from the south or west on CA-1, past Colonia La Sultana then the beautiful "Monumento a El Salvador del Mundo", stop at a stoplight and there on the right is Leon Money Changer and Express Mail. Turn left and go one block for Shell gasoline or diesel. Travel another block to get to a three-level shopping centre, or turn right onto 'Tercera Septiembre' and drive through the city while bypassing the old downtown and mercado area. If you don't know which streets go where, driving among cars, buses and vans through a crowded, aromatic, nose-affronting mercado during a hot afternoon is not recommended.

Coming from the south or west on CA-1, turn right at the stoplight at 48th Street and go two short blocks and turn right on Olympic Avenue and a couple more blocks for Credomatic (Visa/MC cash advances) on the right. Park around the corner in a private but abandoned parking space if your rig is less than 7 m long.

Continuing on Olympic for another block or two, but before a roundabout, brings you to two large food stores, one with ample street parking and a parqueo (parking lot).

When you find 48th Street in San Salvador, you don't have to drive much farther to get anything you need. But if that is all of that city you see, you wouldn't have the frustration of getting lost and the fun of exploring, would you? Drive on, oh intrepid one.

Perquín and its El Museo De La Revolución

The tourist agent on the eastern border was obviously proud and particularly eloquent and enthusiastic about the "Museo de la Revolución" (sometimes called "Museo de las Armas") in Perquín. Impressed, Liz and I were convinced that we should take time to visit this out-of-the way village in the northeast corner of El Salvador.

We're glad we did.

We're also glad that we have a big motor in our older and sturdily built Vanguard-Security motorhome, because of what the agent (a politician in the making?) didn't tell us.

This was the worst, a months-old rockslide waiting to be cleared.

Liz and I suffered through three gas-guzzling hours of climbing, descending and turning in mountain valleys while braking, bumping, and swaying over 50 km of potholes amidst some cracked blacktop. At times we drove on well-used but rough gravel shoulders that were smoother than the road.

Perquín is close to the site of the last battle in the civil war that ended two years ago. All bridges blown down during the war have been replaced by narrow, squeaky and noisy 'temporary' Army constructions. A final and additional 9 km has seemingly remained untouched since the bombings and convoy battles, with the exception that enough of the boulders of last year's large rockslide have been pushed aside to provide passage for single lane traffic.

We hadn't quite reached Perquín and both fuel needles were hovering on 'E' — 'E'stupido, 'E'diot and 'E'mpty — when we met and stopped a United Nation's vehicle. (There are lots of them in El Salvador.) After a brief discussion with Spanish and Columbian officers — the tourist agent also forgot to mention that there was no electricity, and therefore no gas pumps, in Perquín — we turned around and followed them for 11 km to a large garage that pumped gas and diesel. It was hidden behind trees and a cantina. Of course, there was no sign on the highway; after all, everyone knows where it is.

Because of the road we didn't want any extra weight, so we got just enough for the trip to the Museo and back to these pumps. It was so comforting to see both needles next to the 1/4 marker. Surprisingly, the price of gas was less than at the main highway junction 45 km away.

A night's sleep, knowing what to expect, a cool morning, and lots more gasoline helped to reduce the frustration of our return trip on the Road from Hell. But most of next day I spent checking fluid levels, tire-wear and pressures, putting wires back on my horns, replacing burnt-out signal lights, and rebuilding one of my badly shaken and disintegrating storage compartments. Several of those problems could have been in the making before this particular side-trip, but they were evident now. All roads, with the exception of CA-1 from Guatemala to Santa Ana to San Salvador, are bad and CA-7 might be the worst.

Having made it to Perquín and back safely, albeit slowly, we are still glad we went. The small Museo de la Revolución is sobering. And surprising.

Surprising because our Canadian flag is proudly displayed, along with a few others of course. Salvadoreños always seemed to be asking us about their friends, acquaintances and Salavdorean nationals in Canada. I thought they were trying to be nice, or setting us up to offer a gift, but now I know that Canada did open its immigration doors to many Salvadoreños and political refugees. Politics is necessary, but humanitarianism is good.

Sobering because the museum has mainly to do with people, although there are some military equipment and weaponry on display in the various buildings and on and under the grounds. There are tributes to generations of people who were leaders and heroes, people who were tortured, people who went missing, people who were assassinated, and people who died fighting for what they believed. Although the words were in español, it's not hard to figure out what they and those pictures are saying.

Even though I am a cynic about history—his story is biased but mine isn't, history is written by the victors, all victors are nice guys and gals but the losers were dirty rotten cruel devils, both claimed God was on their side, etc.—this museum touched both Liz and me. Not because of who won, but because of the obvious misery of any war.

And it reminded us that Canada and Canadian politics have shielded us from a lot of misery, wounds and death. Maybe it struck us particularly hard because for the last few months we've been on vacation and happily ignoring the world.

Nevertheless, when you are in El Salvador, I suggest you brave that last 9 km of almost-road to Perquín, visit its museum and then, free of the hum of electricity and under a clear sky unhindered by lights, thank your lucky stars that you live in Canada.

Why is it that most people have to leave their country of birth to really appreciate it, both bad and good since nothing is perfect? But of course, that is one of the reasons we travel, isn't it?

Balboa Park and the Devil's Doorway

Coming into San Salvador from the south or west on CA-1, you have two ways to get to Turicentro Balboa Park, the Devil's Doorway and Acoustic Cave. As you come into the city and pass by Colonia La Sultana turn right onto the Autopista and turn right at 48th then travel 10 km or so to get to the park. If you miss the turnoff (we did, twice) visit the "Monumento a El Salvador del Mundo (Monument of the Saviour of the World)" then drive toward the city centre and turn right on 49A(48)th street and keep going until you get to a modern Autopista by driving under the bridge.

Now that you finally made it to Turicentro Balboa Park and paid your ¢5.00, drive around and find a picnic site. Or perhaps you could head immediately for the Devil's Doorway and the Acoustic Cave, and stay long enough for the clouds to temporarily clear so you can enjoy the view. It takes 262 steps to get to the top of a special lookout, but the view is awesome.

Even though the sky was overcast and some rain fell, we enjoyed the afternoon and darkness came too quickly. After a considerable length of time and, I suspect, several levels of bureaucracy, finally we were given permission to park next to the driveway in front of a police detachment. We invited two policemen in for coffee, and a curiosity-satisfying look around inside our motorhome.

One returned later and gave us a bunch of delicious bananas. Unfortunately, I dripped some white sap from the stem on our sofa seat and it won't wash out. Looks like it might be there forever.

Balboa Park with its Devil's Doorway was a relaxing break from driving and touring around a crowded city.

Final Impressions of El Salvador

The border crossings from Guatemala took a long time. Use of a guide is mandatory for those who can't speak español.

El Salvador is a small country, and still recovering from its civil war.

The highways are full of potholes and badly in need of repairs, excepting those highways from western Honduras to Metepán to San Salvador and the 28 km to Chalatenango. It is difficult to achieve an average speed in excess of 40 km/hr, and this greatly reduces gas mileage due to constant braking and accelerating and using the engine at much less than its optimum RPM. A damage-resistant front wheel alignment and very good brakes are absolutely essential.

Contrary to expectations, drivers seldom use their vehicle's horn, even in heavy, snarled traffic.

Cities are amazingly Americanized in their advertising and in what you can buy in shopping malls.

Question: How many Salvadoreños does it take to sell one greeting card? Answer: Four. One clerk helps you choose; one helps you pay; one checks that you have only what you paid for, then carries to another. One wraps it for you.

Propane can be obtained only in the capital city.

Civilian armed guards are everywhere; these people seem paranoid about security. The military is almost invisible. The Policia Nacional Civil are clearly visible, and just as clearly not going to bother an RV.

Contrary to what we had been led to believe, English is spoken by a great number of Salvadoreños. Almost everybody of any financial standing and recent education speaks English. However, when Liz and I tried to speak español they would let us practise murdering their language, if they weren't really busy or until they could stand it no longer.

Like Guatemala and Mexico, this country is dirty. Plastic litter is almost everywhere.

Men relieve themselves whenever and wherever they want. It was a long time before I realized that "No Pise la Grama" meant "Don't walk on the grass."

A must-see is Cerro Verde and from there the adjacent volcano crater and Lake Coatepeque. (Don't drive around the lake. The dusty road is bad and there are so many walls that you won't see the lake anyway. Just look at this lake from up high.) At the beginning of the rainy season, I would expect to see a cacophony of riotous colours.

We've seen very few brightly coloured birds other than in zoos or in cages in hotels and restaurants, and we've seen almost no animals except woebegone dogs, skinny cows, and beautiful luminescent green iguanas.

The people are very friendly and will go out of their way to help a stranger in trouble. For example, when our motorcycle suddenly refused to run, we and it were delivered 20 km to our motorhome.

El Salvador is a country that should be explored, at least once.

Honduras

La Cieba
Trujillo
San Pedro Sula
Masca
Copan
Valle de Angeles
Gracias
Tegucigalpa
Jicaro Galan

REPUBLICA DE HONDURAS, C.A.
BANCO CENTRAL DE HONDURAS
D3690432
14 DE ENERO DE 1993
MARCO AURELIO SOTO
REFORMADOR DE LA REPUBLICA
1876
DOS LEMPIRAS
D3690432
PRESIDENTE
GERENTE
MINISTRO DE HACIENDA Y CREDITO PUBLICO

Honduras

Border Crossing: El Salvador to Honduras

We drove north from San Salvador on CA-4, after spending two nights at lovely Turicentro Agua Fria, then crossed into western Honduras just a few kilometres from Nuevo Ocotepeque. We were dreading the border, wondering if it could be worse than our entrance into El Salvador. It wasn't. It was a pleasure.

We really didn't need a guide to clear through the four offices of El Salvador, but we had a few extra Colones to get rid of, and the young man was clean and pleasant. The border personnel were friendly and efficient. (Maybe that Can$ 0.75 for our guide helped after all.) Of course, doing everything by handwriting takes time, but we exited El Salvador in less than thirty minutes for less than C$7.00.

Using moneychangers, we managed to get a rate of 1.06 Lempira (L1.06) for 1 Colon, which was 2% better than predicted.

Clearing into Honduras took about an hour, including a 15 minute wait to get started. If the bill of sale for our motorhome had been done correctly in Canada, we could have saved some time. We hired a Honduran guide for less than two dollars.

Officially, it cost US$ 20.00 (L184.85 or C$27) per vehicle. In actuality it came to Can$ 44, what with mordida and other unreceipted "expenses". I figure we paid about Can$ 6-7.00 more than what we observed the local travellers paying.

Everyone was friendly, and it was a relaxed crossing. The little extra 'grease' money was worth it. And besides, I managed to convince them that the motorcycle was nonfunctional and undriveable, and so I didn't have to pay US $20 for it as well. Maybe I'll take up acting as a new career. As I get used to playing the Frontera Game, lying is getting easier with each frontier we pass through.

{At subsequent frontiers, our dirty motorcycle was always "decompuesta y no corre" (broken and not running), once truthfully. Later, in this and any country, whenever we were stopped while riding our motorcycle, we never had a problem with police as long as I could show them where the motorcycle was listed on our motorhome permit. They usually checked both the serial number and licence plate.}

We went to the Texaco gas station in Nuevo Ocotepeque and bought a map of Honduras; it cost us about Can$ 3.00. The country map is big and it also has four useful city maps on the other side. All in all, this map was a good buy.

Nine Days After the Border Crossing

At the border, the Policia de Transito issued us with only an eight-day temporary pass for our vehicle. Day one was the day of issue. Subsequently we were forced to go to San Pedro Sula or Tegucigalpa to get it extended for a month. (Coming into Honduras from Nicaragua via Chinandega and Somotillo, the permit was good for thirty days. Go figure!)

We miscounted the days, got stopped on the ninth day just outside of San Pedro Sula, and were ideal victims for police mordida. Mordida translates as "bite", which means "bribe". Twenty minutes of discussions in limited español, many attempts at clarifying the location and address where my driver's licence would be stored if they took it from me, our adamant refusal to pay any small amount on the side of the road, and a very hot afternoon sun finally resulted in our being asked for "un refresco frio". This translates as "a cold drink" but which can also mean money for a cold drink, or a bribe. We gave them each a glass of cola and ice cubes. Then, exasperated and reluctant, they permitted us to leave with our wallets intact.

Five kilometres later we were stopped again. Because our RV has only lap belts and no shoulder straps were visible from the road, the police thought that they had us. But when they realized that (a) our seat belts were on and (b) many motorhomes don't have connections or hardware for shoulder straps, they let us go on our way. We thought it wise not to mention that our vehicle permit was outdated!

When we finally got to the transit office, our permit was quickly extended at no cost. The grey, two storey office building was in the NW part of San Pedro Sula, accessible from and within a block of the Avenida Circunavegación, near 12th and 12th. Refer to a Texaco map if you have one.

By the way, the transit office was closed from 12 - 1:30 p.m. A mere one block south along the avenue, a small restaurant served excellent and inexpensive lunch hour meals and snacks. We had two baleadas, an enchilada, and a tojado. I don't know how they were made, but they were delicious. Hopefully, the handwritten menu-board will be considerably more legible sometime in the future.

Fuel

Prices had just surged upward at the pumps. Of course the government said price changes were due to international market prices. Prices varied between stations and cities.

The following values were used to calculate equivalent prices in Canada. The exchange rate was US$1.00 = Can$ 1.39 = L9.13, and 1 US gallon = 3.76 Litres.

	Honduras	Canada
Unleaded/Premium	L13.83/USgal	Can$ 0.560/L
Leaded/Regular	L13.43/USgal	Can$ 0.545/L
Diesel	L 8.99/USgal	Can$ 0.364/L

Propane

It is possible to buy propane in the following places.

La Ceiba Driving from Tela, on the left of the highway about 2 km before La Ceiba, Tropigas can and will fill a fixed tank or removable bottles. Because they do not have a meter, you must know how many pounds of propane that your tank will need. Propane here is expensive. Driving from La Ceiba to Trujillo, about 3 km from the city, on the left side of the highway, there is a Texaco propane plant which I didn't check out.

San Pedro Sula There is a propane plant on the left side of the highway, at kílometro 7.6 from San Pedro Sula en route to La Lima, El Progresso and Tela. We didn't stop because traffic was heavy and it was difficult to drive across the highway.

Tegucigalpa There are at least two propane plants, both located several kilometres outside of the city. Tropigas is located on the right at kílometro 6.3 on highway CA-4 (Honduras 15) en route to Juticalpa and its pine forests. We had no trouble getting gas in there, after lunch break was over. En route to Comayagua and San Pedro Sula on CA-1, on our left a few kilometres outside of the city, we drove past another propane plant without stopping.

First Hour's Impressions of Honduras

Spaciousness! It is hard to imagine that crossing an imaginary line called a border can affect countryside so much, but in this case it did. It was as if we had been transported suddenly from downtown Toronto onto the Banff Jasper highway.

Cleanliness! The streets of the pueblo of Nuevo Ocotepeque were wide and clean. There was no litter in front of any of the houses or businesses. Except for one spot, the new highways were free of garbage. The air was fresh and a treat to breathe. We've not passed or met any diesel buses or trucks spewing black smoke.

Quiet! This was the first time in almost two months that we have been able to listen to our stereo without the volume set to distortion. I had to explain to Liz that that hiss we heard was the sound of tires on new blacktop. I think we might have a pinprick of a hole in our exhaust manifold, but a deep-throated roar only occurred when our 7.5L engine was working hard.

Solitude! Where are the trucks and cars? Where are the pueblos, the towns and villages? I felt as if I were driving in prairie country after midnight.

Fun! Western Honduras has a market garden economy. Roadside vendors had fresh beets, onions, potatoes, cabbages, carrots, and a delicious local fruit whose inside is like that of a grape, but with a subtly richer flavour. I finally had to stop stopping, our fridge was full.

Comfortable! The three-lane highway was in excellent condition. There were no potholes. One stretch of road was under construction, but gravelled portions were smoother than El Salvadorean asphalt. What a pleasure it was to set cruise control at 70 km/hr, then keep my foot off the gas pedal for five minutes or more! This was remarkable because we were travelling in rugged mountains on an up and down road with several switchbacks.

Open! With respect to housing, Honduras is the most North Americanized Central American country we've seen. The block-long walled courtyards of Mexico, Guatemala and El Salvador are almost nonexistent here. Many houses are surrounded by a yard, often grassed, but few have any type of wall or fence. Any fences are see-through.

We like Honduras!

Consulates You Will Need

In the twin city of Comayagüela-Tegucigalpa, Honduras, the Canadian Consulate is situated strategically close to many services, including other consulates. It is close to the United States Embassy.

Because of many hills, Tegucigalpa can be an extremely confusing, sprawling city in which to drive. Some of the streets are very narrow. All of them are filled with cars, trucks and buses. Most drivers were kind to us often-lost tourists.

The Canadian Consulate is directly across from Credomatic and American Express banking outlets. It is on the sixth floor of tall Edificio Los Castaños, on the corner of Avenida Morazán (a boulevard easily accessible from the city's prominent central stadium) and Calle Ramon E. Cruz. Access to the consulate is from the backside of the tower building through an unmarked doorway and past a guard to two elevators. As you walk through the doorway, you will see a bi-level mall on your right.

At the far end of the mall is a well-stocked grocery store, SUCASA. You can park behind the mall for free in the store's parqueo, one block off Morazán. Chances are that is the only place you will be able to park.

On the second level of the mall, the Book Village has a good selection of reasonably priced English books and magazines. Its selection of monthly computer magazines is excellent. It might even have the latest issue of the guidebook "Handbook of Mexico and Central America".

Also in the mall building, but with access only from Avenida Morazán, is a Fuji Colorlab that can take visa and passport pictures—Nicaragua requires them—and can, of course, develop films in a couple of hours.

Within two blocks of the SUCASA parqueo, and behind the Japanese Embassy and an empty parking lot, is an excellent restaurant called La Cerca. Liz and I had two cocktails, and two full meals and delicious deserts in pleasant ambience for less than Can$ 35.00. This restaurant had a large parking lot in front of it and, when asked, the owner let us stay there overnight. Unfortunately, on our return trip the parking lot was being converted into yet another mini-mall. We safely parked in the street overnight, across from two businesses that posted 24-hour armed guards.

Behind the Canadian Consulate, and two short blocks along Calle Ramon E. Cruz, you will find a Honduran tourist office on the third floor in the same building as Lloyd's Bank. You probably guessed it; go through another unmarked door and past another armed guard. We got excellent information but no maps.

The Nicaraguan Consulate is within five minutes driving time of the Canadian Consulate, and surprisingly easy to drive to. From the corner of Ramon E. Cruz, drive three blocks westerly along Boulevard Morazán and turn left at the lights. Continue straight ahead, then around a roundabout. Another few blocks and up a hill will bring you to the Nicaraguan Consulate.

Visa hours were from 8 - 12 a.m. If you arrive early, your visa can be processed in a relatively short time. But if you arrive late you will have to pick up your 30-day visa in mid-afternoon. Make sure you bring one picture and US $25.00 (not Lempira or Cordoba) for each visa.

Note: Even though we got an official-looking receipt for US$ 25.00/person, a travel agent in Granada checked in his book and told us that Canadians are only expected to pay US$ 5.00, and another US$ 20.00 at the border if driving a vehicle. That is what we had been told before leaving Canada. Another time we were told that visas cost only $5.00 at airports. Once again, it looks like tourists pay for ignorance.

The Guatemala Consulate is en route to the Nicaraguan consulate. Take the very first right turn after the roundabout, traffic circle, and the consulate is about 2 1/2 blocks more, on the left side of a narrow street. It cost us US$ 10.00 per person for one of their visas.

When in Tegucigalpa, if you can find the Canadian Consulate, you can find everything else you will need nearby, including the desire to escape from this confusing labyrinth of busy streets.

Credomatic

In Honduras, there are at least three Credomatic centres where you can use both VISA and MC for cash withdrawals. There may be others.

Tegucigalpa Credomatic and American Express are located near the corner of Avenida Morazán and Calle Ramon E. Cruz, in the north-northeast part of the capital city. It is directly across the street from the Canadian Consulate. There is also a Credomatico Cambio next door where we converted Lempira into US dollars for the Nicaragua and Guatemala consulates.

San Pedro Sula Credomatic is located in a very small passageway behind a bank, near the centre of town, at Avenida 5a and Calle 2a, Norte Occidente (NE). The town centre—plaza and church—is located on Calle 1 and Avenida 3, both of which are reasonably wide streets. Parking is always a problem (so are the one-way streets) but you can park at a Shell gas station on Calle 1, a hundred metres or so from Credomatic.

La Ceiba Although advertised as being on Avenida San Isidro, opposite Hotel Iberia, we didn't have to look for it. Check with the tourist kiosk inside the central park for directions and times.

Random Thoughts While in Honduras

Honduras has the best new roads in Central America. The country is undergoing a massive update in transportation facilities, but there are still some bad ones left.

In Honduras we were stopped so often that I was tempted to build easily-visible imitation shoulder straps. Occasionally the police checked all our signal and brake lights. Just because a lot of lights on locals' vehicles don't work, does not mean that lights on tourist vehicles don't have to work. Be safe and save money. In Honduras always wear seatbelts, and replace any blown fuses or light bulbs.

Local drivers seldom pay any attention to signal lights, but they are always aware of hand signals. When making a right turn, have your co-pilot stick his or her hand straight out of the window.

When contractors lay new blacktop, they first lay down a layer of blue or white plastic which entirely covers the old blacktop. Is that to keep water from getting into the gravel base, and therefore prevent new potholes? I hope the plastic adheres to the old asphalt; I'd hate to be on the highway when the entire top layer slides into a ditch.

The two dirt roads from the north coast (La Ceiba, Olanchito, and Trujillo) over and through mountain ranges to Highway CA-3 to Juticalpa or Tegucigalpa were disastrous. Eventually they'll be paved. They were very wide, but continuously rutted, potholed and full of washboard. Trying to make up some time, we sped along the westerly, shorter dirt road. As a result, one storage compartment shook apart and spilled half its contents into the dust and ditches before I could stop. We would have made equal time by backtracking to San Pedro Sula and driven from there to Tegucigalpa.

I now know whence cometh the expression 'defacing a statue'. In Copán, the expression is literally true. All of the stelae, which are beautifully carved and annotated rock statues of important persons, have been defaced. Every face has had the nose, and sometime more, chiselled away. Possibly this was done by victorious invaders to remove a person's face from memory, and thus commit that person to oblivion.

Juticalpa houses administrative buildings for a large, Canadian-sponsored and assisted water-

project in this area. The Canadian International Development Agency (CIDA) has several water and electrical projects in Central America.

These cities are often extremely noisy. It took us a while to realize that almost all businesses would go onto generator power whenever the electrical power was cut off due to rationing. Occasionally the noise level from hundreds of those tiny gas motors was so high that Liz and I had trouble chatting, unless we faced each other and yelled.

One local story relates that the reservoir was full but, due to concerns about the integrity of construction of the huge hydroelectric dam subjected to severe cost-cuts, it was emptied of most of its water before more rains came. The expected heavy storms never occurred, the water level never rose, and it became necessary to ration electricity. Uh huh, government bureaucracy and expert opinions are the same everywhere.

If we hadn't heard the clanging of a spade as it bounced along a dirt road, we might have lost the entire lower compartment.

Anything to save a centavo. Most kiosk and food stalls tear their single-ply napkins in half.

In the fields, we often saw leafless cornstalks that were broken and bent such that the cobs were hanging upside-down. We understand that this keeps the corn dry all year and there is no need to put it in storage, where bugs and rats will eat it. Because locals seldom eat corn as a vegetable, this technique works well for overripe corn that will be ground into masa and made into tortillas.

Many of the peasant houses have thatched roofs with no chimneys. Smoke from inside fires just seeps through the roof and drifts away. I wonder if this technique helps to control the number of bugs and insects that would like to live in those roofs?

Some things never change. We just saw a man separating chaff from beans by filling a scoop with beans, then dropping them onto a plastic sheet. A slight breeze blew some of the chaff away and onto the ground. This was followed by another scoop, then another, then others. After awhile, the man and his son piled all those beans together and scooped and dropped them onto another sheet. How many hours does it take to clean a 50-kg bag of beans? And how many big pieces of chaff remain? No wonder Liz has to hand-sort through every package of beans and rice she buys.

There is a Pizza Hut in La Ceiba that is renowned for its weekday lunch special. You get all you can eat plus salad bar for a very reasonable price.

In La Ceiba, we bought four large grapefruit from a street vendor for Can $0.25. They were absolutely superb, sweet and juicy!

At Lancetilla Botanical Gardens, we picked a grapefruit right from a tree. A visitor told us that originally grapefruit grew in clusters, like grapes, but over the years that feature was bred out of them. If true, and we have our doubts, that explains their name.

The dollar-to-Lempira exchange rate must be even more fantastic than I thought. Liz just returned with several packages, and was heard to mutter "It was hard work, but I managed to spend it all."

We hear so many locals who are concerned about our safety and who warn us of as-yet unseen dangers, that even I am getting paranoid. Now I've added a lock to prevent persons from opening up the hood over the truck engine.

In the town of Danli, we could've drycamped in the fenced parqueo of El Gran Hotel. And it was only L.50.00 per person per night, for nothing. Maybe next time. Not!

However, there was a clean, inexpensive laundromat which we did use. Two women did all our washing and folding while we walked about.

In Danli we bought a short wave radio; I needed to listen to some Canadian and World news. The Jewish owner of the store had immigrated to Honduras. When we found this out, we lent him Liz's cassette of Hebrew music. His teenage daughter, born in Honduras, couldn't understand why he was so excited. Within six minutes, her father left his store, had that tape high-speed duplicated, and gave us back our cassette. When one knows where to go, anything is possible in Central America.

Copán Ruinas

Our one-day drive from El Salvador to Copán, via Nuevo Ocotepeque and Santa Rosa and El Entrada (turn left at the Texaco station), was on 200 km of good blacktop plus several more kilometres which were under construction.

We have been told that the road from Guatemala via Florida to Copán Ruinas—both the town and archaeological park have the same name—is very bad and very slow. It might be better to travel from Esquipulas to Nuevo Ocotepeque.

There should be ample parking available on the road next to the Copán Ruinas archaeological park. Break and entry into your vehicle is extremely unlikely, but do not leave anything outside overnight. We were told that some days there were two kilometres of vehicles parked end-to-end. In the close-by town, Hotel Paty—on the right just after you cross the bridge—allows secure parking for L.20.00 (C$3.50) if its parqueo is not filled with vehicles from paying guests.

When you are in Copán Ruinas, immediately get a copy of the newsletter "COPAN Tips". The tourist information desk in the souvenir shop in the entrance of the archaeological park should have some. If necessary, go into town and to its publishing office which was adjacent to Lavanderia Justo a Tiempo. (Although a laundromat, it also had a large selection of books for exchange.)

You should also get "HONDURAS Tips" if you can. If, unlike us, you are the type of person who plans well ahead, you can buy the latest copy for US$ 5.00 plus US$ 2.00 S&H from Aventuras Centroamerica, S.A., PO Box 3450, San Pedro Sula, Honduras, C.A.

Depending on which day rationed electricity is available, you might want to visit the excellent museum in the town first, saving the archaeological ruins for next day, or vice versa. When you visit that small museum, some of the displays are difficult to see without lights. There is one exquisitely carved stelae, and a special incensario. These make this side trip worthwhile, even if you could see nothing else. An incensario is fired pottery used for burning incense, often during a funeral.

Liz and I have seen Tikal, Palenque, Joya de Ceren, Iximche, El Puente and other Mayan-Oltec-etc. ruins. Our imaginations were unable to turn piles of rock and rubble into picturesque ancient palaces and glorious temples. We were "ruined out". For those of you who aren't, there is much to see in Copán. Plan on at least three hours of walking, seeing and sitting. Carved stones, intricately carved stelae, and the grand staircase are the most striking features of Copán Ruinas. Unfortunately, several rooms and areas with carvings were fenced off and we were unable to get close enough to focus our poor old eyes properly. Opera glasses would have been useful.

"Dig these specs!"

I wish we could be back there when construction of the Museum of Culture (and Maya Sculpture) is completed in September 1995. It promises to house some amazing displays. It will cover more than 70,000 ft^2 in nine buildings, and is expected to require two hours just for a 'quick' visit.

The town museum and archaeological park being first and second, our L.30.00 entrance ticket also allowed us to visit a third site, Las Sepulturas, which had been the living area of the elite of Copán. Bases of many structures and houses provide some idea of how that town was laid out. It was and still is a great source of artifacts, tombs and information for archaeologists, and a quiet place for tourists to commune with history.

There is a building whose base points in one direction and, having been built several years later, its walls were offset ten degrees. The Mayas were extremely accurate astronomers, and had great concern about geographical directions, as evidenced by stelae 13 and 19 which are used to mark East and West cardinal points as seen from Copán. All of the archaeological sites we've seen show a group of buildings with one alignment, then a later group with a different alignment, then possibly a third group with yet another alignment. Why? Was Immanuel Velikovsky right? Did the cardinal compass points change?

And why, like the astronomers of ancient Middle East, did the Mayas develop a calendar of only 360 days, which they later changed to 365.23+ days?

But enough questions. When you've seen all you can absorb in one day, or you have to go into town to buy some more film or a gift of leather, pop by the comfortable and clean Llama del Bosque for a unique taste sensation that I won't even begin to describe. Tasty hot appetizers called Las Anafres are served in a large unglazed bowl above a glowing brazier. For those with larger appetites, more substantial offerings are available and all are reasonably priced. Tunkul Restaurant & Bar served us a delicious giant burrito and a flour baleada which, in normal size, is the Honduran equivalent of El Salvadorean Pupusas and Guatemalan Quesodillas. For good beef, visit Uruguayan or Argentinean restaurants.

Copán was the place for us to meet several travelling Canadians. Two were young backpackers whom we met separately in the ruins, a young lady from Ontario and a young man from British Columbia. An ex-Bulgarian lady from Richmond, BC recounted some very interesting stories; I wish I'd had a tape recorder while she dramatized her misadventurous canoe-crossing from northern Guatemala. Another unaccompanied lady tourist was visiting a Canadian family who were living in El Salvador before moving on into Nicaragua. The mother was teaching English and studying natural medicine in the same village where my leg was stitched up. She had heard about us.

Copán Ruinas displays several huge, detailed and richly-carved stone trees. Even if you have seen a couple of other archaeological sites, you should visit this one. Maybe the next time we meet a Canadian in Honduras, it will be you.

A Day to Forget

We should've stayed in bed.

We woke up scratching, scratching in places that we've never scratched before. Overnight, it seemed both of us had broken out in chicken pox and measles from the waist down. Hey, wait a minute, that's not possible. What happened?

Yesterday we visited El Puente, the newest archaeological park in Honduras. In a couple of years many of the buildings will be completely restored; now it is a lovely picnic site. Next to it are two small pyramids each with a tunnel, from inside of which we could see a pyramid within a pyramid.

Late yesterday afternoon, after brewing a pot of coffee and slipping into shorts and sandals, we set up our chairs, footstools and TV table to watch the sun slip behind the mountains. Thereafter, ignoring millions of bright and twinkling lights, we scanned the cloudless, jet-black sky for falling stars. In a couple of hours, mas o menos, more or less, we saw seven. We thought we'd seen many more, until we realized that fireflies can fly high overhead as well as close to the grass.

And we also learned that other creatures lived close to the grass. Small, invisible insects that climbed up chair legs, or hopped up from a blade of grass, or flew and landed undetected on our bare legs. Unbeknownst to us, many could crawl inside our comfortable, loose-legged shorts. Bummer!

But that was last night.

This morning, out came creamy 'Dermoxido' which Liz had bought in El Salvador, and a tube of 'Andantol' which she had bought in Mexico. Dermoxido is slightly better for eliminating stings and itches, but it stays oily for a long time. Both worked. Aah, relief.

Then it was time for a long leisurely breakfast of cantaloupe, watermelon, cucumbers sprinkled with chili salt, oranges, pineapple soaked in lime juice, and bread toasted over propane flame. And perked coffee for me. Unexpectedly, breakfast was interrupted while I washed the kitchen floor. He who knocks a dozen pieces of melon off the counter while pouring a second cup of coffee also gets to clean up.

Later, Liz washed the dishes and tidied up inside, pausing only long enough to bang her head on the overhead beam as she reached into the cab for something.

Meanwhile, hubby stored away the furniture, checked the motorcycle, awning, windows, vents and compartment doors, and kicked the tires. This took longer than usual because the right front tire had gone flat. It was changed using a tiny hydraulic jack, two scissor jacks, four wooden blocks, a potato brush to clean off mud-encrusted studs, and fifty minutes of lost travelling time. A T-shirt was ripped by a spinning tire iron.

We topped up our water tank from a tap in the information building in El Puente; sadly I ran over one rose bush trying to get close enough. Having forgotten to light the hot water heater's pilot light, we were treated to cold showers. But they seemed no worse than when I jumped into Okanagan Lake on January 1, 1991, with three British exchange students and other crazy friends of our daughter. At least this time my hair didn't freeze.

Finally we were on our way. Those seven kilometres of dirt road back to the highway weren't too bad. After all, we were also forced to go slowly on the blacktop. The unbalanced bias-ply snowtire on the right and the summer radial tire on the left were in constant conflict; the right tire was shaking in fear.

While waiting for the tire to be repaired, we shopped in poorly stocked stores and the small central mercado in El Entrada. An hour and a half later, we were off to San Pedro Sula. And constantly on the right edge of the road. Liz finally threatened to close her window if I hit any more branches. After I'd dropped the right wheels into a third pothole, she asked if the frames of my glasses had become bent, or were my old eyes just going bad.

I must admit, I was beginning to wonder what was happening. Today I just couldn't judge sideways distances. Liz inspected and cleaned my glasses. I stopped and checked both front tires and the back four. Pressures were good, nuts were tight, nothing was wrong.

A few kilometres later, some old highway construction narrowed the blacktop to a wedge before it disappeared into a well used and bumpy gravelled road. Trying to stay on the blacktop as long as possible, I slammed into one of several metal markers on the right side, neatly severing the lower anchor bolts of the awning.

I thought it best to stop.

Amazingly, there was no structural damage and only a small gash in the aluminum door panel. That was repaired with duct tape, just one more bandage on our poor mistreated rig. Most of the blow had been taken by the forward fibreglass corner, and yet it was barely marked. My estimation of Vanguard-Security design and quality control went way up.

Of course, the now freely swinging awning arm had to be securely tied down. I carry a roll of wire, which I suppose could be used in baling machines, and Liz had stashed away some gum, so that repair was quick and easy to do.

Within minutes we were on our way. Whatever had been my problem disappeared—maybe it was frightened to death—and the rest of the day passed normally.

Well, almost. There was another brief terrifying moment. In a gradual curve, an 18-wheeler cut into our lane just before we came abreast of a young man on my side of the two-lane, shoulderless highway. When I got my breath back and looked in my rearview mirror, the man was still standing. But he had a startled look on his face and was fighting to remain upright after almost being blown off his feet by the wind from our RV. Liz hadn't made a sound, which confirmed that we had been millimetres away from a serious accident.

Driving during this trip has been fairly uneventful. Unfortunately, statistical odds have a way of averaging out over time. But why did it all have to catch up on one day?

Maybe it is a good thing we got out of bed after all. In all probability, tomorrow will be a better day.

The Fishing Village of Masca

The tiny hamlet of Masca is 34 km past the enjoyable, restored fortress of San Fernando de Omoa near Puerto Cortes in the NW corner of Honduras. There is nothing there worth seeing, except a single dirt road with houses, huts and hovels on both sides.

Ah, but Masca is close to a quiet public beach, where we spent two days and nights secluded from the rest of the world. Sometimes Liz thinks our motto should be "We go where no RV has gone before."

When we arrived, several people were crowded about one area of the beach, so we wandered over and watched them sorting and selecting fish, shrimp and crabs from a large net lying on the sand. One type of eel-like fish reminded me of a barber's strop because it was so long and thin, but of course its shiny silver scaleless skin and many sharp predator teeth made it look much more threatening. This fish is called "Machete", for obvious reasons.

These villagers were picking through a newly-beached net.

Later on, getting our sandals wet and full of sand, we wandered along the beach to a small river where one of three boys was cleaning their fish. A blade sharpened on stones and jammed into a hand-carved wooden handle and held in place by nylon fishing line could have been a surgeon's scalpel. That lad wasted no strokes. In seconds the head, tail and guts were gone—thrown into the river to float into the Caribbean—and another fish thrown onto the pile. Soon all would be fried and eaten. Although these Machetes seemed awfully skinny to me, the boys claimed that they had a full, rich flavour.

The 'surgeon' would gut a much fatter and shorter fish, scrape off its scales, slash both sides four or five times, then string it on a vine with others. These were to be salted and saved for later.

Around noon (sometime between 11 and 2; I had stored my watch while still in Canada) we strolled over to a palapa with a couple of tables and ordered two platters of Machete with vegetables and beer, all for the exorbitant cost of Can$ 7.75. Sometime later the cook came by and let us know everything was ready. We sat down on handmade wooden chairs sunk into beige sand beside a painted wooden table, whose top of warped boards was painted marine grey. The fish were not Machete but they, bananas fried in batter, cabbage salad, and flavourful rice were very good.

A rooster, two chickens, and three dogs joined us for lunch as they fearlessly wandered between our legs and those of the table. The dogs stayed until we left. Because of an offshore wind, there were no flies or other flying creatures. Or if there were, they blew by too fast to be seen or to land.

Without thinking, which isn't hard after ten months of vacation, I discovered once again that one should not chew tiny whole red chili-pods. It took a bottle and a half of beer to stop tears from flowing, and another three minutes for my hiccups to stop.

Just before dark, two young boys came by our motorhome and sold us some coconut bread (pan coco). Warmed in our oven—very few Central American stoves have ovens—and covered with melted butter or cheese, these heavy, full-bodied biscuits, with a trace of coconut flavour, were delicious. We bought several more next day.

Without electricity, when a quarter moon has yet to rise, and when thick clouds hide the stars, it is dark in Masca! Because we had the only light in the area—we were reading on battery power—bugs and other horribly small night creatures could easily find us through several invisible holes in our window screens. We were forced to turn off the lights and go to bed at 7:14, according to the brilliant green digits of our seldom used built-in RV clock.

We awoke to a rooster's crowing, only to discover we had slept 11 hours and had missed yet another sunrise. Although hidden behind blue and white cumulus clouds, we did manage to see pink tendrils just before they disappeared.

We also spotted a couple of men hauling on a rope while standing waist-deep in the sea. Nothing else was visible in the water. Finally we realized that they were hauling in a net. Shortly thereafter, more men and one dugout canoe came by to help and eventually the nylon net was dragged ashore, with hundreds of wriggling fish fighting to escape. A few had already drowned and moved not.

Once again, people sorted through the net picking out what they wanted, discarding the smaller fish and leaving them for the seagulls and pelicans. A few kids took the rejects and threw them high into the air, whereupon pelicans and kites swooped down and caught them in their beaks. Two fishermen seemingly got nothing; I wonder how this system really works?

One fellow collected only shrimp, and a small, semi-opaque squid. Being curious, I pantomimed I would like to hold it, and he placed it on my palm. Surprisingly, it was not the least bit slimy; it felt like wet brown paper. It wasn't dead because its tentacles began to move. And because it bit me and drew blood. The sting, like that of a fire ant, lasted only a few minutes but three hours later the red pinprick was still visible.

As people continued to pick through the catch, one long rope was being looped onto a pile in the bottom of the dugout, followed by some of the net. When everyone was finished, the rest of the net and the other end of the rope were loaded into a metre high heap in the middle of the canoe.

Five men paddled three or four hundred metres down the beach. Two men climbed out and hung unto one end of a rope while the others paddled a couple of hundred metres further out into the sea. When the net started to play out, the canoe turned parallel to the beach. The canoe continued in a curved path until all the net had disappeared below the surface, then back to shore it came. Two more men jumped out and all four began to haul on both ends of the rope, slowly, ever so slowly, dragging in the net. That has got to be hard work. It's no wonder there are no obese fishermen.

And once again, men and women took what they wanted from the catch. Once again the seagulls, kites and cautious pelicans came looking and fighting for scraps. But this time when the ropes and net were loaded, six men including myself used two-metre-long pieces of coconut palm trunk under the boat and rolled the dugout over the sand and stowed it above the high water line.

Far away from the world of television and faxes and phones and automated credit machines and banks and stores and cars and trucks and buses and fumes and noise and towns and cities, we found Masca. Except for the presence of one dirty battered RV in a scene of palm-thatched palapas near a sandy beach where men, women and children were sorting fish in front of wooden huts partially hidden in a jungle forest, Liz and I might have been transported backwards along the river of Time. Like Rip Van Winkle, we decided to stay another day.

Centros Turisticos in Northern Honduras

Unlike El Salvador, there do not appear to be any government-sponsored tourist centres. However, there are many privately-owned Centros Turisticos where one can park an RV for a small fee.

Trujillo 1 km before this town, take the turn off to the airport and the Christopher Columbus Beach Resort and the Bahia Bar & Restaurant. The latter provided a couple of parking spaces, with a night watchman, water, electricity and cable TV for Can$ 12.00 per day. In December 1994, electricity was rationed on a three-day schedule. Because we needed only 12V DC and because we don't like to watch much TV, Liz and I decided to dry camp about 200 m past the end of the runway, on an access road to one of the best beaches in Honduras.

Silin is a tiny pueblo 4-5 km before Trujillo. As you approach you will see a "Hotel" sign. It is advertising Hotel Agua Caliente, which is a clean and pleasant tourist centre and balneario with several swimming pools fed by hot geothermal water. There is level space available for drycamping, cost unknown; this resort could accommodate a caravan of several RVs. On a nearby hill-top, a replica of the Church of Medjugorje overlooks a beautiful bay. Close by is a well-equipped machine shop run by the owner(s) of Hotel Agua Caliente. Between that shop and the resort, someday there will be various sports fields and a miniature golf course.

La Ceiba There were some turicentros advertised, but they weren't acceptable to us. However, one small, unnamed turicentro 18 km west of this town, on the right of the highway, was OK. It would have been better but its empty swimming pool was being repaired. The bar had an adequate variety of various coloured liquids, and the quiet music was enjoyable. So too was our inexpensive chicken supper, which was cooked on a wood stove. The parking area was level but hookups were not available. We managed to get electricity by using our socket extender in one of the lamps in a nearby palapa where we sat to read and eat supper. We also topped up our water tank and, because Honduran water is NOT potable, we added a capful of bleach to kill a few thousand germs.

Parque Nacional Pico Bonito

"Parque Pico Bonito (Pretty Peak) is a unique and largely uninhabited virgin rainforest on the north shore of Honduras, only a few kilometres from La Ceiba. Mountains of tropical rainforest rise steeply from the Caribbean coast to Pico Bonito, which is 2435 m above sea level. It is the largest national park in the country, with 500 km^2 of unexplored core area.

" In 1987 the Honduran National Congress passed a law that protects all cloud forests above 1800 m from deforestation. Being bathed in clouds for most of the year turns these forests into a very wet, dripping and ethereal environment, with little light. Some frogs spend their entire lifetime in the upper reaches of the rainforest, laying their eggs in pools of water formed by plants. Pico Bonito was enlarged in 1992."

Doesn't that excerpt from a tourist brochure sound great? It sure does, so rather than visit another marshy ecological reserve, slim Liz and overweight I opted for the rain forest of Pico Bonito.

The only problem was that we weren't allowed to drive in a protected zone. To see such beauty, we had to scrabble several kilometres uphill along narrow footpaths before getting into the rain forest.

Notice the word 'foot'path. Some paths were so narrow that we had to put one foot in front of the other because there was no room beside it.

When one climbs higher and higher (several hours usually, or perhaps even days and nights of camping) in rubberized raingear (which captures one's bodily heat and perspiration to form a private sauna) and one finally reaches the rain forest (or cloud forest, or some other interesting public relations name for a bunch of leafy trees that drip water onto stringy hair and down one's neck) where footpaths turn into mudpaths (where three slogs forward is immediately followed by two muscle-straining slides backwards or one zip sideways) and soggy running shoes (obviously a misnomer) disappear below the brown surface of puddles (filled with invisible creatures of nature), one has to wonder at least once about one's sanity. I mean, really, is that rambling sentence the logically incisive thoughts of a sane person?!

Having contracted a guide from a nearby forestry school for an extravagant fee, Liz and I scrambled upwards for three hours, finally said the he-- with it even though the misty clouds did look a little bit closer, and limped back to soak our blisters in clean warm water in our home on wheels.

Mind you, en route we did see a peanut bug (it really does look like a huge peanut shell with wings), many, many tree trunks (so many we couldn't see the forest), and we swam in a cold mountain stream (we both got colds and sniffles). Although we spent almost a full day on a damp mountainside, we never did make it to the rain forest of Pico Bonito.

Oh, yes, we did see a couple of ordinary, everyday-type frogs.

We should have gone to the salt marsh and ridden in a boat!

Trujillo

Trujillo is at the end of the coastal road of northern Honduras. Except during Christmas and Easter holidays, this is not a heavily visited tourist area. Which is just as well, as Liz and I prefer to be by ourselves as we swim in clear Caribbean waters and sunbathe on clean white beaches.

Trujillo has the nicest beach on mainland Honduras.

And it has grocery stores (there is no need to starve), hardware stores (so we men can buy important stuff), souvenir stores and tiendas (so women and wives can buy frivolous gifts for friends, family and self), hotels (Glyndia offers the best price on takeout beer), and beach-side palm-thatched champas (so someone else can do the dishes after an excellent repast).

Up the hill, along a concrete, then potholed, dirt road the majestic Hotel Brinkley provides an awesome view of the town and bay. Inside, an ever-present breeze keeps the bugs away from expanses of beautifully hand-carved wood. This hotel offers a daily scrumptious breakfast buffet which even we, penny pinchers that we are, thoroughly enjoyed. Peggy, the owner, is one of the very few persons who are truly 65+ years young, a dynamo of dreams, construction and conversation.

Down on the beach, immediately at the end of the road that wanders down the hillside behind the central plaza and beside Forteleza Santa Barbara, El Rincon de Los Amigos serves excellent daily luncheon specials. The Spanish owners of this champa, or seaside restaurant, have obviously influenced both menu and music.

When you come here to Trujillo, maybe you will be able to discover the secret location where Pan de Coco is made; the champa owners refused to tell us. A warm thick slice of that special bread with butter and Mango jelly is a mouth-watering treat with which to start another day of swimming and sunning.

A typical Caribbean adobe dwelling.

Trujillo's worst feature is sand fleas, especially at dusk. Some days, Liz and I had to wear shoes and socks as we strolled along the beaches. One evening we had to sit in chairs atop our RV roof to watch a silvery moon and sparkling stars slip behind black silhouettes of coconut palms rising out of an ethereal sandy peninsula.

Trujillo's best is its beach. Not that portion that is part of downtown, because it is dirty and littered, but that kilometres-long portion that encircles the blue waters of the bay. Most bayside properties do not have houses, and thus very few residents. These beaches are as pristine and natural as you will find anywhere except Nicaragua.

We drycamped on a beach access road that ended one metre from the sandy beach. To our left was a small murky river, where occasionally children would come to fish or play. To our right was a newly built two-storey house, with fence, large dog, and a guard. The owners were very friendly and we exchanged daily visits. Within an hour of our arrival, a young man came by and asked us if we had any work for him. Being pleasantly surprised that we hadn't been asked for money, we did find something for him to do each day we were there.

Although we toured the countryside and town on our motorcycle, although we visited museums and banana ships alongside commercial wharfs, and although we ate in restaurants and champas, our favourite place was the beautiful curving beach just outside of Trujillo. Oh, we might have stubbed our toes on an occasional coconut husk, palm stem, or one or more of hundreds of pink sea shells, but eventually we learned to avoid these annoyances while leaving behind wet footprints that disappeared beneath beach-washing waves.

And eventually we disappeared too, to reappear on different highways and roads and paths in search of other beaches and mercados in this and other Central American countries. It feels so good to be able to travel while we're healthy and old enough to enjoy being youthfully audacious.

More Impressions of Honduras

The Nicaragua to Honduras border (Guasaule en route to Choluteca) does indeed close at 5:00 p.m. But until approximately 5:20 it is possible to pay a couple of dollars—much less than the original request—to have someone open the gate then drive a few tens of metres to a level parking lot. After 5:20, the only options are to park on the bridge, which shouldn't be any problem, or drive back to the highway.

The frontier crossing was a real pain, and expensive. If I had been feeling better instead of reacting badly to some medication, I might have won some reduction in the unreceipted expenses. But Liz had to do all the bargaining and she wasn't used to it. Of all the things that most affect our desire to return to Central America in a motorhome, border crossings are absolutely the most negative.

Money changers began at L9.00 for US$ 1.00; the official rate was L9.13/$. Not too bad.

Compared to Nicaragua, this country gave the impression of being much wealthier. The people here seemed more energetic too. But interestingly enough, we didn't feel as comfortable or safe as we did in Nicaragua.

Cedeño was a crowded, dusty and dirty Pacific beach village. It might be OK for backpackers, but RVers will have a hard time finding a place to park. The dirty sand was grey and powdery-fine. At high tide, the beach disappeared as the ocean lapped against stilts holding restaurants above the water.

Shortly after passing through Jícaro Galán, we noticed Turicentro Oasis Colonial offered an excellent opportunity to relax. For L10.00 (Can$ 1.60) per person, Liz and I were able to use their hotel facilities—billiard tables, pool, and mini zoo, plus bar and restaurant of course—for all day and part of a night. There might be a little extra charge to drycamp in their parking lot overnight, depending how the security guard feels. Except perhaps on Sunday when it could be very busy, this turicentro was a great place to swim, sun and read for a few hours.

There were very few gas stations between Choluteca and Tegucigalpa, and a lot of steep, curving and shoulderless highway to climb. Of course you could be as fortunate as we were. Just as I switched over to our second, getting-pretty-low tank, Liz's oft-repeated prayers were answered when a gas station magically appeared out of the side of a hill. A miracle? Maybe.

Tegucigalpa was an easy city to get lost in. Because of hills and rivers, I doubt any street or avenue is straight for more than six blocks. Pedestrian-only and one-way downtown streets added to our confusion. There were a few street signs but that didn't help much because we couldn't buy a map with street names.

As in the rest of Central America, we could park anywhere. The drivers were very considerate of us haggard tourists.

Valle de Angeles

Valle de Angeles is a small, four-street town—all named and signed!—which has a few artisan shops and co-ops specializing in wood carvings. By 1996, construction on the last half of the 22-km road east from Tegucigalpa should be completed. The paved highway will be in great shape but, of course, it will still be steep and curvy.

Being high up in the mountains, this town is a tranquil area which is refreshingly cool and quiet at night. The probability of theft is small, and maybe even less inside a fence which surrounds the main co-op where we parked for four nights.

One night, at 9:30 p.m., this two metre high fence posed an almost insurmountable problem. Returning from a moonlight stroll, we discovered that the gate had been locked and the guard had retired for the night. Gracefully, we pawed and clawed our way up and over and down the chain links, with only one scratch to remind us of our escapade. But the highlight occurred next morning when we found out that the lock wasn't locked. It only needed to be twisted to open it.

Until we returned to Honduras, we hadn't realized how few locally typical foods there were in Costa Rica and Panamá. Many restaurants there have converted to North American food styles. Here Liz and I stuffed ourselves on Anafres (crispy chips with refried beans and melted cheese served over a flame), Pupusas (corn tortillas stuffed with cheese and/or beans and topped with a pickled salad), Baleadas (flour tortillas filled with cheese and butter), and Dulce de Leche (handmade fudges). They tasted wonderful!

This street leads to an excellent restaurant just around the corner and up a hill . . . try the Paella.

Valle de Angeles had postal service three times a week which, although slow, was better than having to drive into hot, smelly, busy Centro Tegucigalpa and eventually having to park on some crowded, narrow, one-way street near Calle Peatonal. The convenient local post office was accessible from inside a court yard which could be entered only from the central park. It took a while for us to find it.

We thought the park was filled with purple crocuses until I realized that the ground was completely covered with hundreds of blossoms, which fell from two large trees.

Nearby, several workers were manually digging a deep, two-block-long trench to hold water pipes and telephone lines. They were breaking large imbedded stones into smaller pieces by burning day-long wood fires next to the stones until they were very hot, then pouring copious amounts of cold water on the rocks. Some rocks split in two, others would break apart in three or more pieces.

Valle de Angeles had an excellent selection of locally mass-produced, handmade wood carvings, paintings and pottery. Some stores even had imports from Guatemala, El Salvador and Nicaragua. There were also several one-of-a-kind art pieces and treasures. The weekday we were there we saw at least eight Honduran couples-families-tourists arrive to buy something. All in all, this was a pleasant place to do some souvenir shopping for friends and relatives.

I bought a 1966 Honduran licence plate from Miguel Nuñez—down Calle Los Angeles—who also makes lamps and chandeliers from soft steel and aluminum. Since I have my real Canadian licence plate inside a rear window, I'm going to put the outdated Honduran plate in the regular spot when I leave this country. I wonder what la policia will do?

At Restaurant Anafres, we met a lady from Florida who has been here for a year and a half, living in a three-bedroom house she rents for Can$ 175.00/month. Of course, she also pays for a full-time maid and a gardener. Terry, an exporter with a very interesting background, lives in a slightly smaller house for Can$ 105.00/month. We also met a man from Ontario who visitsCentral America regularly, but always seems to end up in Valle de Angeles. Rather than staying in a very nice hotel, this time he rented a house. He said he'd be back in September for several more months, possibly with his piano. These were our kind of people. They love life and enjoy its challenges and bounties with enthusiasm.

Valle de Angeles was a quiet place for us to shop and snack, and for me to write this article. We stayed an extra two days just to hang around, doing nothing. And thus we discovered Luis' Don Quixote restaurant-on-the-hill and a church with a beautiful marble altar.

When we drove away from our parking spot, we tore down a low hanging telephone line that got snagged in our unused air-conditioner. Two locals and I fixed it. Liz and I left.

Gracias

Gracias, the first and ancient capital of Honduras, is 45 minutes from Santa Rosa de Copán on a good highway. It is also accessible from Tegucigalpa via the Siguatepeque turnoff to La

Esperanza. This mountainous route is a pleasant four-hour drive, except for a 40-km stretch of rough, rocky, dirt road.

When paved in a few years, this road will be an excellent alternative route to and from the capital city. By then it is unlikely you will have to pass a slow-moving car by driving on the sloping side of an inside ditch dug next to a sharp downhill curve. Some of the excitement will be gone.

Yet another stop to fix our brakes: metal-to-metal is not good.

Gracias has an empty reconstructed fort overlooking the colonial town, two so-so churches, the relaxing Los Lencas restaurant and cultural centre, and a hospital.

Returning from the nearby swimming hole and hot springs on our motorcycle, my wife and I were struck from behind by a truck rapidly passing us on our right. We think our handlebars hit its left rear fender, because we ploughed into the ground after the truck had sped by. Helmets saved our lives. Within seconds of our bouncing and sliding to a stop on a rutted, rocky dirt highway, locals came to our rescue. Two of them drove us to the hospital, after I chained our motorcycle to a tree, and they didn't even complain about Liz's dripping blood.

Semana Santa and noon-hour is not the best time to be injured in Gracias; we never did see a doctor! Our wounds were cleaned by a nurse and we were released, free to walk to the police station in dirty and tattered clothing. Next day, Liz had to get a local doctor to come to Los Lencas and shoot me full of muscle relaxants to stop muscle spasms in my upper back that were keeping me a prisoner in a chair. He also closed the open wound in Liz's elbow with three stitches.

Froni, who hails from Holland but works in Los Lencas and serves a refreshing drink called Mora, speaks several languages. She helped us to describe the accident to the police. Many thanks, Froni.

Because of the accident, we never did get to see beautiful Celaque National Park and its cloud forest, a mere 9 km away by vehicle and several hundreds of metres up by foot.

Hopefully, our next visit won't be interrupted.

Final Impressions of Honduras

Friendly people, inexpensive living, excellent highways, and lots of space are the first thoughts that come to mind when we think of Honduras. These are followed by thoughts of beautiful Trujillo Beach on the Caribbean, the three distinct geographical areas, numerous pine forests, and a capital city without a single straight street.

Honduraños were gentle, passive people and therefore they did not impose themselves on us, as did the pushy Mexican and El Salvadorean vendors. Of course, it is possible that by now we've become used to a different life style and, therefore, the Honduraños are no worse or no better than other Central Americans. Going downtown or into a mercado was a pleasure because we could take our time shopping amid the great variety available.

This is a great country to fly to, to rent an inexpensive furnished house for a few months, to eat a variety of cheap vegetables and fruits, and to travel by bus to northern beaches or neighbouring Guatemala or Nicaragua. In fact, Liz and I just might do those very things immediately after spending Christmas holidays with our children in Canada.

Nicaragua

Matagalpa
Leon
Lago de Managua
Managua
Lago de Nicaragua
Granada
Juigalpa
Isla de Ometepe
Rivas
Bahia La Flor

5
BANCO
CENTRAL
DE NICARAGUA
CINCO
A22289453
CINCO CORDOBAS

Nicaragua

Border Crossing: Honduras to Nicaragua

Liz lost her passport!

Rather than carry all her papers through customs she thought she would put only her passport in her pants' pocket, and now it was gone. We spent a panicky ten minutes looking for it—in our motorhome, on the ground, offering a reward to locals—but nobody could find it. So we had to head back to the Canadian Consulate and try to get a new one. Would we make it before our visa expired? Could we get a new visa?

The custom house is down at the end of this canyon of trucks.

After five minutes of teary-eyed driving Liz found it under a seat cushion. Rolaids! (My grade four teacher would never approve of that spelling for RELIEF!) Back to the border and a good but sheepish laugh with everyone there.

The border crossing from Honduras to Nicaragua was the most expensive to date. But all of it was receipted, which means that there was no obvious mordida.

Our Nicaraguan guide was a ten-year old who knew what he was doing. He did a great job. At the end I paid him too much money but, what the heck, the Christmas season would be upon us soon. ¡Feliz Navidad!

Fuel and Propane

Nicaraguan prices have been converted at the rate of one Canadian dollar equals 5.00 Cordobas, using US $1.00 = Can$1.40 = ᶜ$7.00. 1 US gallon still equals 3.76 litres.

	Nicaragua	Canada
Regular	ᶜ$ 16.75 /USgal	Can$ 0.89/L
Unleaded	ᶜ$ 18.20/USgal	Can$ 0.97/L
Diesel	ᶜ$ 12.25/USgal	Can$ 0.65/L
Propane	ᶜ$ 7.46/USgal	Can$ 0.40/L

Both times we were in this country, gasoline prices were scheduled to rise 0.20 Cordobas per month for the foreseeable future.

During one of few days of city travelling, while shopping in mini-mall La Fe which is next to a major roundabout in Managua, we noticed a Tropigas propane truck stopped by a kiosk selling snacks. So we drove up behind it and asked the driver if he would fill us up. He would, he did, I paid, we left. A couple of days later we saw the same truck there, once again at noon, so perhaps he'll be there when we come back, and when other RVers drive by.

During transit from Huellas de Acahualinca to Xiloa on the western side of Managua, we drove past a Tropigas plant and several parked propane trucks. It was on the left side of the street, just before the Hotel Xiloa sign.

Before we left Nicaragua the second time, we filled up there. Not from the central storage area, but from one of several parked trucks. The main area did not have a hose with the correct connector that was long enough to reach our motorhome. RVers with detachable bottles should have no problem getting refills.

First Impressions of Nicaragua

This country is tired and poor. Most buildings are very run down, some still have bullet holes in them. Entire city blocks are walled in, with a central court in the good old defensive colonial style.

The highway is in quite good shape, considering all the derogatory comments made by natives and travellers in Honduras.

Highway police checks were more numerous than in Honduras, but they did not seem to be trying to get mordida. The police were friendly and just doing their job. Their primary concern was about our motorcycle and its serial number.

Random Thoughts While in Nicaragua

Now into our second year of travelling, the excitement of seeing palm and coconut trees, swimming in warm water, hearing español, buying in mercados, etc. has begun to pale. Like a good marriage, the intense feelings have become replaced with those of a deeper contentment.

There were no more trains running, which is just as well because the only tracks left are those that cross highways and are buried in the asphalt. All the rest of the rails have disappeared, being used for cattle-guards, bridge supports, telephone or power poles, and whatever else someone could think of.

Platanos Fritos are an excellent chip-like snack. This banana-like fruit is cut in thin lengthwise strips, deep-fried until crunchy-crispy, and packaged in small plastic bags (of course). Street vendors were easily found near bus stops and mercados.

Whenever we found someone who sold fried whole platanos served flattened on wax paper and smothered in sour cream and jam, we bought some. They were delicious.

Central Americans prefer platanos to bananos , we didn't. Besides, bananas (los bananos) are much cheaper.

"Yoplait" yogurt has the best flavours in Central America, and actually contains small chunks of the fruit listed on the front of the container. It has the only Banana flavour that tastes like banana.

Trying to listen to a shortwave radio inside an aluminum-covered motorhome is frustrating. It's like being inside an electrically-isolated Faraday Cage, which isn't too smart. Better reception can be obtained by touching the antenna to the frame of the windows or, better yet, by attaching an alligator clip to 20 or 30 centimetres of flexible wire and fastening the other end to a window frame.

Contrary to what guide books say, no police or border personnel have ever questioned our having a CB radio. Of course because we know so little español, there is almost no one to talk to because there are so few tourists driving their own vehicles.

It took me four mornings, in different weeks and different locales, to figure out what was flapping on our roof. When we park under trees for shade, seeds and seed pods fall onto our roof, then birds peck at them for breakfast. Tap, taptap, taptap.

Why must bus drivers honk and honk and honk their horns between 4:30 and sunrise? And as if that wasn't bad enough, the noise sets off the roosters who take umbrage to competition, which causes barking dogs to wonder what's going on and they want to be part of the excitement too. Sleep-ins in Nicaragua are a myth.

We've come to the conclusion that Nicaragueños are dehydratable, and re-inflate when dipped in beer or water. Nine people plus picnic supplies just exited from a Ford Pinto station wagon, then two more drove away in it.

How can a 125cc motorbike carry two adults, one child, a large cooler, a container of water, and an inner tube without crumbling into a jumble of twisted frame and wheels?

There are several road signs telling people to drive on the right side of the road. One person explained that such signs were necessary to break drivers of the habit of driving over the centre line. During the recent war they drove in the middle to avoid land mines planted under the edges of asphalt. Maybe so, but it is also true that many potholes can be avoided by straddling the yellow line.

Entrepreneurship is everywhere. On highways, men will fill in potholes with dirt, then as you drive by they ask for money for doing you a favour. Sometimes their work really was useful, then we paid them.

In the city of Managua, I almost lost the front end of our motorhome. Fortunately, I managed to avoid an accident by driving around an open manhole, like all the other vehicles must have done. I wouldn't be surprised if the cover had been missing for weeks. Defensive driving is essential.

Which reminds me, Central American drivers are very alert drivers; they have to be to survive. Being in an easily seen motorhome was great. All drivers knew we were tourists who probably didn't know where we were going, so they were especially careful of us.

Where to this time?

Besides, we were much bigger than they were.

Next time I park our motorhome on the side of a city street, I'm tempted to erect a post beside the passengers' door. Then when people walk by and stare in the open door, they'll smack into the post. Sometimes the intense direct stares of Central Americans just gets to be too much.

Technology wins again. We've just seen our first oxcart with rubber strips nailed onto its wooden wheels.

Nicaragua is a country of cities filled with murals, many of them depicting heroes of the war. Some are beautiful and all are well done. What a pity that the government doesn't have enough money to repair damage done by both man and nature.

Generally speaking, supermarkets in this country are very poorly stocked. There is little variety, and cans of North American foods are expensive. Mercados and street vendors provide better quality fruits and vegetables, particularly if one shops in the morning and buys half-green-half-ripe fruits.

Hotel Camino Real

Hotel Camino Real, a mere 1.5 km from Managua's international airport, was a five star surprise!

We were encouraged to camp in their guarded parking lot. Electricity and water could be made available if we needed any. We were also invited to stroll through their manicured garden, and use their laundry service, beauty parlour, taxis and car rentals. In addition, their shuttle bus would take us to and from the airport.

This was an ideal situation for us. We planned on flying to the Islas de Maiz (Corn Islands), but couldn't do so until we had three nights of secure parking for our motorhome. We found that and much more at Hotel Camino Real, which has never had a vehicular break-in in all of its years of operation.

It seems nobody told all the security people that we would be parking in their lower lot. Just before dark of our first night there, three burly men came by and stood in a large triangle that surrounded us and our motorhome. I recognized their positioning; if one man were shot, the other two would finish us off before they could be attacked. Only one fellow came up to us and, after we explained that we had permission to park here and after he checked our story on his walkie-talkie, he wished us a pleasant stay. A quick signal and all three melted away. These guys were professionals; I wonder who was staying in the hotel?

This hotel is accessible from the PanAmerican highway, from either direction, and is probably indicated on some tourist city maps. Driving into Managua from Estelí or Tipitapa, it is on the right 2.3 km after the huge University sign, or 1.5 km past the airport. Driving from Managua to Tipitapa, take the second turn immediately after passing a Texaco station on your left.

Its friendly and personable Resident Manager, el Señor Joel David Velásquez, described some of their expansion plans. These include large parking spaces for five campers, complete with water and electrical hookups and access to all hotel amenities. Use of these spaces will be free—they'll accept no responsibility for unlikely damage or robberies—but I'm sure that a tip for the security guard, hiring someone to wash your vehicle, or eating an excellent meal in their restaurant would be appreciated.

For RVers tiring of Nicaragua's pristine sandy beaches and congested mercados, Hotel Camino Real provides a rare opportunity. You can get all dressed up, dine in elegance, taxi to El Teatro Ruben Darió in style, and still return to sleep in your own bed. Try it, you'll be glad you did.

Playa Poneloya

18 km from Leon, on the north Pacific coast of Nicaragua, is a beautiful, kilometres-long white beach without sand fleas, ideal for swimming and sunning. Playa Poneloya is also a small village with two hotels—one cheap, one not so inexpensive— and a large flat parking lot with all day shade for one RV, ours.

As we drove into town, on the left we noticed rows of tiny concrete buildings, some with people living in them. These were erected immediately after the 1992 tidal-wave disaster as temporary housing for the victims.

All of Playa Poneloya is rebuilding slowly from that tragic marine disaster. There are still empty lots and concrete skeletons of houses along the single main street, but there are also several beautiful new ones, and more under construction. I'm still dumbfounded by lack of zoning regulations. I do not understand why people will put up 250,000 cordoba houses next to ramshackle huts and garbage infested lots.

Hotel La Cayo had been highly recommended in one of our guide books. The author must have seen it before the bottom floor was washed away by the tidal wave which had been generated by an earthquake near faraway Japan. Now the hotel is a dilapidated building with cheap accommodation on the second floor and an open-air restaurant below.

Hotel Lacayo .. note the missing lower floor

But it serves the best repochetas we've ever had. Every afternoon we would sit on rusty metal chairs—the two wooden rockers were always taken when we arrived—next to metal tables advertising one beer or another, beneath a sagging wooden ceiling held up by concrete columns and a wobbly staircase, on a tile floor divided into nonexistent rooms, and enjoy yet another plate of tasty repochetas.

At one end of the white sand beach, a fishing community harbours their boats in the mouth of a fresh water river. Although the local restaurants look like (and are) shacks, some of the fish dinners they served were delicious.

In the middle of town, along a dirt road, in a house so smoke-blackened and dirty that the road looked clean, was a panaderia that made and sold excellent bread and buns. They were made daily. Once I saw a man in a grubby chef's hat milking a cow in the front yard; now that's a really fresh ingredient!

At the other end of town was a liquor store that had a mini-zoo in its back yard. The zoo's inhabitants were a cow, a deer, a monkey, a couple of iguanas, two geese and several chickens.

Playa Poneloya is a good beach, as well as a little town, close to Leon. It's a great spot to swim, sun and relax for three or four days.

Christmas in Nicaragua

We drove into Playa Poneloya on December 18, planning to spend the Christmas season away from large cities. Liz and I were a little down. After sending off Christmas letters and cards (my organized wife had brought her updated Christmas List from Canada), even the adventure and beauty in Central America couldn't keep thoughts of home from intruding upon us. We really missed the kids; it was the first time we hadn't spent Christmas together.

We were lucky enough to be able to park in the one spot in a dusty parking lot where the sun was hidden behind buildings or trees for most of the day. Our rig never got scorching hot and we could sleep at night, if we didn't use our propane stove to cook supper.

As it turned out, we had an excellent Christmas and New Year's Day.

In the second day during a stroll along a clean, white beach that extended kilometres in either direction, we saw two white-skinned 'snow-birds'. Wandering close by we asked where they were from and, lo and behold, they were from Ontario, Canada, down here visiting Canadian friends who were working on an electrification project sponsored by CIDA (Canadian International Development Agency). Eventually six of us got together over Tonya beer and delicious snacks in Hotel La Cayo.

As the blazing sun moved close to the cloudless horizon, we were asked if we would like to join them for Christmas Day. We accepted. Cliff and Marj were renting a large house, complete with a maid-cook and a gardener-guard. It looked like a mansion. Our motorhome was half the size of their kitchen, and it was one of the smaller rooms! When we weren't at the beach, our Christmas holiday was spent parked in front of their walled home.

What time is Midnight Mass? "Midnight" replied the maid.

¡Claro! Of course! But when we arrived at the biggest cathedral in Central America at 11:30, Mass was over. Christmas Eve midnight was spent with hundreds of others walking the festive streets of Leon. Grandparents, parents, children and babies were everywhere. And so were coloured lights, vendors and sidewalk sellers. But the night was surprisingly quiet, there was little music and no dancing.

Liz had the feeling of watching desperation: this was just a longer day for vendors to make money; there was no family time. The only real excitement surfaced when a four-metre high effigy —

The largest old cathedral in Central America is beautiful inside.

La Estrella Azul — wandered and spun and cavorted through the narrow, crowded streets. We hoped to see other "nose-thumbing" historical reminders of Spanish conquests, but didn't.

Christmas Day dinner was enjoyed by six Canadians, three Americans, one Ecuadoran, and one Nicaraguan. We all ate too much, particularly of shrimp and ripe pineapple, but otherwise we had a fabulous time. We sang a couple of Christmas carols but just couldn't get into the mood. It was 28°C+ and we sat next to flowering bushes under minuscule shade of palm trees.

The morning of December 27 was spent eating, drinking drip coffee, and chatting while Liz and Marj worked in the kitchen. I've seldom seen Liz more contented. She got to use a full-sized oven. And a microwave oven. And a breadmaker!

A couple of days later, we celebrated someone's third (?) 29th birthday. Cliff had arranged for a four-piece band — two guitars, a tenor guitar and a huge bass guitar — to come by and play and sing for an hour. Their lively music and witty lyrics were a treat.

Liz and I spent New Year's Eve and Day alone in the house. Our hosts and another Canadian couple went to a New Year's Ball in the biggest and brightest hotel in Managua, and stayed for two nights. The maid and guard had been given time off to visit their families, and so we had the place to ourselves. I had almost forgotten how to drown in unlimited shower water and when to chase my fleet-footed Love through several spacious rooms!

But all things must come to an end. January second saw Liz and me sadly packing up and moving on, carrying cherished memories but leaving behind new found friends.

Thank you, Cliff and Marj.

Volcan Masaya

Almost immediately after leaving Masaya for Managua, off to the right is a huge forteleza (fort) on the top of a hill. If you have lots of power, and can turn around in a small area, turn and drive past the arch and numerous potholes and up to the fort. That's what it was called by the tourist office, but in reality the fort is a not-so-old prison.

Prisoners in North American jails and penitentiaries should be incarcerated here after a strike for better living conditions; they'd think twice about striking again. Often 15-25 people were locked up in unpainted concrete cells, with a hole in the floor for a bathroom and a high slit-window for light and air. Liz and I used our Coleman gas lamp because flashlights were almost useless in this dark, underground prison.

The steel doors will be locked, but someone will open them for you, invite you inside, then lock them again. Although entrance to this complex is free, we played the game (that's all it is) and paid for our freedom when we left.

Having "escaped from jail", we travelled a short distance to Parque Nacional Volcan Masaya. It was not very well marked so we had to make a U-turn to drive in. Unless you've seen lots of volcanos before, this is a must visit. It requires only a couple of hours and a 30-km round trip on excellent asphalt.

The park information centre is excellent, even though all information is in español. We asked for and began a tape-recorded slide show but the projector's light bulb blew out. They didn't have a spare because of insufficient funds. Even though I said they could keep the price of admission, they insisted on returning it. I think they were embarrassed.

The drive to the mildly active volcanic cone was easy. At the first stop, we parked beyond the yellow line so we could look over a stone wall. The guard was upset because we might have caused the side to give way and slide into the volcano. Our second stop was on the other side where you can breathe sulphur fumes and, with binoculars, see red-hot stone. There is no bubbling lava. The geological layers and structures of an adjacent caldera are quite surprising. It was hard for us to realize that this is a small volcano.

After driving about 100 m away from the second parking lot, we stopped and took a path that let us explore an intriguing lava tunnel. It was only a couple-hundred-metre walk to the first of several entrances. I still cannot imagine how such a geological formation can exist. What was flowing inside hot lava when liquid rock hardened to form this tunnel?

When travelling from Managua to Granada, or vice versa, plan on taking a full day and take some side trips. We travelled that route three times and always saw something new.

Isla de Ometepe

If you ever wanted to travel in a banana boat, a trip to Isla de Ometepe gives you that chance.

You can depart from Granada and enjoy several hours reliving life on a salvaged and refitted African Queen.

A manually-operated bilge pump on a ferry to Isla de Ometepe.

Isla de Ometepe, formed from two adjacent volcanos, is the largest island in any fresh water lake in the world.

Or you can drive south along the PanAmerican highway to Rivas, turn left at a Shell station then left and through San Jorge and onto the ferry terminal, where you can get a boat. Trips left at 8 a.m., 11 a.m. and 4 p.m. Time of day determined which type of boat—banana or speed—was available. Fares were very reasonable.

Motorhomes and recreational vehicles can be parked inside a protected area of the terminal for C$5.00 per day, although the guard exercised his right of entrepreneurship and tried to charge us C$10 per day.

Motorcycles cost the same as people, but a tip for extra work was expected. The banana boats load motorcycles after all persons are boarded and all seats are taken. I was nervous watching them struggle down a wobbly gangplank with my heavy bike, but they did fine. Then they lashed the bike so tight with a one inch rope that I thought they would bend the frame.

Good thing, too. Our ancient boat wallowed and twisted and thumped through metre high waves. One woman was sick several times. There were others who were the colour of unripe bananas. One crewman, then another, was continually pumping out the bilge. It seemed like an awful lot of water was pouring out of the pump onto the deck, sloshing beneath the boards below our feet, then flowing overboard. But since the deckhands didn't use both hand pumps, I surmised there was no real danger.

On our return trip, our ferry had to tie up next to and outside of another boat that had engine troubles. Because our ferry was a smaller boat than the one we had on our trip out, and because the island wharf was higher, I had driven my motorcycle over a gangplank and onto the boat's flat roof, where handlers

CRASH!! . . . Liz. Dang it. Stop laughing and help me up. Don't say it. I know. It's time for me to lose some more weight.

tied it alongside another bike. Now how were they going to get those bikes ashore? No problem. They flung a long narrow gang-plank between the roofs of those two tossing and rolling boats and walked the bikes across. Then they flung the same gang-plank from the close-in boat down to the wharf and walked them down. Simple.

As far as Liz and I are concerned, there is only one beach on the island worth visiting, Santo Domingo. We spent a full day motorbiking along dusty roads looking for and visiting others, but Santo Domingo was the best.

Oh, by the way, if there are four-cornered palapas on the beaches, be careful when stringing a hammock kitty-corner. Those thick vertical logs and smaller overhead logs might look solid, but they're not. Placing my 80 kilos into our hammock was shortly followed by some creaks and groans, falling palm leaves, crashing cross beams, and tumbling corner posts. Liz has a picture of me lying in sand beneath logs and leaves, right arm raised to ward off falling objects. Fortunately, the wood was so old and soft that it was lighter than Balsa wood, and nothing was damaged but my pride.

On a previous day, we had driven over to the second volcano, turned left at a junction—that dual rutted road looked slightly less rocky than the one to the right—and we drove to the end of the road. There we asked a man if he could guide us to some petroglyphs and he said yes. He said a whole lot more, but we didn't understand him. We think there was another group of petroglyphs up the side of the volcano which most tourists visit.

Off we went, slowly walking along a rarely travelled shore line—past a freshly dead monkey—then up into an untrod field full of tall grass, ground vines, and burrs. Eventually we came to a rocky outcropping. Our guide hacked away at the overgrowth with his machete and, ta da, carved rocks began to appear.

Eight carvings were bared to the afternoon sun, and our untrained eyes saw several faint lines traced into black volcanic rocks. By adjusting our line of sight, while trying to enhance shadows without falling into crevasses or thick grass, we did manage to see some recognizable patterns of man and animal figures. A couple of rocks revealed nothing but faint lines; I wished I'd had some soft chalk for tracing and outlining.

(The archaeological museum in Juigalpa, on the east side of Lake Nicaragua, has one example of such carved rocks. It too had many curving lines, but I couldn't determine if it had a pattern either.)

Seeing these petroglyphs forced me to realize just how good a job a professional photographer can do in bringing forth a sharply detailed picture from a barely visible jumble of faint lines. 3D computerized edge enhancement and stress depiction by false colours can do even better. Nevertheless, we were seeing actual petroglyphs, imagining ancient workmen chipping away, and trying to fathom the meaning of those basaltic carvings. We were there. And those petroglyphs were real. Burrs, bugs, thirst and lack of shade didn't seem to matter anymore.

Later, we were talking with backpackers who had seen those other petroglyphs. They were not favourably impressed. Maybe we saw better ones, or maybe we have better imaginations.

These same hikers, obviously experienced and in good physical shape, had climbed through the rain forest to the top of Volcan Concepción. Some even ventured down into the caldera to see a lake. All were exhausted from slogging through calf-high mud. As they collapsed into chairs with hands almost too weary to hold a cool cerveza, they told us if we wanted to go to the top, hire horses and plan on a very long day.

Hospedaje Ramon Castillo used to be the only reasonable restaurant and lodging in Alta Gracia. We suffered through three mornings of cold showers and three nights of almost no sleep on 1" foam mattresses above boards of various thickness. Finally we checked out Hotel Central on the main street, even though it didn't look like much from the outside. Appearances can be so deceiving. Several clean rooms (with real mattresses!) surrounded a lovely garden restaurant. It was slightly more expensive than the hospedaje, but worth every Cordoba!

Isla de Ometepe, formed by two volcanos, accessible by banana boat, skirted by dusty roads, blessed with a good white sandy beach, and hiding two sets of petroglyphs, is worth a three-day visit. And there is at least one establishment with soft mattresses.

Bahia La Flor

Bahia La Flor on the Pacific coast has a clean, quiet, secure beach ideal for dry camping. Unfortunately, to get there you have to travel and return on 22 km of narrow dirt road from San Juan del Sur. (Take the first turn right as you leave the town, splash through two creeks and rumble over one cattle-guard.) Fortunately, that 22-km road keeps a lot of people away, and the curving beach is almost always empty, and seldom crowded.

San Juan Del Sur is a clean town with a pretty, non-polluted small harbour, a great beach, and cool water. There is no gas station. Being a tourist town—La Presidente de Nicaragua has a house there—eating in restaurants can be expensive. There is no mercado but there are several household stores (pulperias) where you can buy foodstuffs, and there are some street vendors that sell vegetables or fish. At the suggestion of the Policia, and being careful of hidden branches, we parked in front of the TelCor building on a wide and treed boulevard that runs next to the bay.

On the third day there, after waiting for our laundry to be returned by one of TelCor's staff, Liz and I left for Bahia La Flor only a few minutes before sunset. With headlights hidden behind our motorcycle we arrived just as dusk turned to dark night. But thanks to light from a full moon, we could see well enough to follow what we hoped was a road through a forest of trees heading in the general direction of hissing and pounding surf. Once past the trees, we turned left on grassy sand and parked parallel to the moonlit snow-white beach and silvery waves. Four 2x8's and ten minutes later, we were level, water was boiling for tea and coffee, and we were outside seated in our chairs enjoying a refreshing off-ocean breeze.

Wish you were it . . . after we're gone, of course.

The contrast between distant black sky and blacker ocean and the repetitious appearance of slow moving, brightly glistening waves and nearby ghostly phosphorescent foam was remarkable. Even the majesty of twinkling stars behind a scarred platinum moon was almost ignored. Being on this beach instead of in our living room reminded me of the difference between watching the seventh playoff game on TV and actually being in the hockey rink when that first overtime puck is dropped.

Late next morning, as we laid down our small indoor-outdoor carpet to keep the sand where it belongs, which is not on our easily swept linoleum floor, we discovered we were parked within centimetres of an old empty turtle nest. If our front wheel had dropped into that 8 cm (5") deep crater of soft sand and dried egg shells, I would have needed a couple of hours to get us out. It would indeed have been a dark night, Coleman gas lamp notwithstanding.

Because Bahia La Flor is a fenced ecological refuge, with an armed guard at the narrow gate and eight army personnel patrolling the area, we expected to have to pay for the pleasure of secure parking in one of the prettiest of Nicaragua's beautiful beaches. Sure enough, it cost us five Cordobas each per day. For three quiet, secure and relaxing days and nights, for a total of Can$ 6.00, we could leave our chairs and tables set up all night while parked under leafy trees next to a half kilometre long beach of white sand, which was washed by cool water without a riptide. And where nobody came by to stare in our windows and open door.

No roosters, no dogs, and a steady cool ocean breeze ensured a good night's sleep. Next morning's dip in refreshingly cold water removed any sleepiness and tenseness that we had brought in. The water must have been 10°C cooler than at Playa Poneloya, which is only a couple hundred kilometres to the north. (It is not freezing cold, as written in one guide book. Unlike myself, maybe the author never jumped into Saskatchewan's Waskesiu Lake or PEI's Mill River on a May 24 weekend, nor Nova Scotia's Zwicker Lake or British Columbia's Lake Okanagan on January 1.)

A relaxing, stress-free day of reading, swimming, wandering, sunning, swimming and sunning came to a satisfying end as we watched the red sun flash into green as it settled below the cloudless pink horizon.

(During that January Saturday afternoon several carloads of intruders 'crashed' our private paradise. Why couldn't they have stopped off at Playa Coco, which is almost as pretty?)

As in the harbour of San Juan del Sur, there is only one wave at a time. Even now I'm still amazed when one wave forms in an arc that stretches from one end of the beach to the other. Far out near the mouth of the bay, a long depression starts to form. Then, as it approaches the shore, it becomes an elongated curving wall of water of ever increasing height, until finally the green water towers so high that the top of the wave overruns the bottom, arcs over, and crashes down in a roiling avalanche of white foam. Very often so much air is trapped that fountains of white water will jet up from the frothing ocean. Occasionally, one end of the wave breaks first and, like a fuse that burns for 5 - 7 seconds, the roaring, hissing white cap races uninterrupted along the crest to the other end. And behind that white churning water and bubbly foam, yet another depression has already begun to form, and the relentless magic continues.

There being no riptide to drag unwary swimmers out to sea, I would go out until those two-metre waves began to break just in front of me, then I'd dive under the turbulent avalanche of white froth. Once it passed, I'd surface and float in thousands of bubbles, in Nature's own Jacuzzi.

Believe it or not, we are actually on a concrete bridge-culvert.

During the second morning, returning from exploring tidal pools hidden among sedimentary cliffs at the end of the beach, we discovered a solitary baby turtle making its way from the direction of our trailer toward the beach. Providing shade, we followed it to the ocean and, after the fourth time of its being washed back up on the beach, we carried it to deep water and released it. Then we backtracked along its distinctive trail, which looks like a long, jagged scar amid closely spaced holes left by stitches. The nest was only 5 m (16') from our trailer. There were no other turtles.

Bahia La Flor is the cleanest, quietest beach we've seen in a year of travelling. Although we have still two more countries to visit before we reach our goal of crossing over the Panama Canal, we will return. Guaranteed!

The Sea Turtles of Bahia La Flor

At full moon in October and January in and near Bahia La Flor, Nature displays another of its wonders.

Tens of female sea turtles leave the cool waters of the bay and scramble over the warm white sands to lay and bury their eggs above the high water mark. A month and a half later the eggs hatch, and hundreds of 5 cm baby turtles try to get back to the water. Most of them do.

Questions.

How many of those rubbery-shelled eggs, buried 10 to 15 cm in solar heated sand, survive onslaughts by ants and crabs who also live beneath the same beach?

How does a newly born turtle manage to break through its shell then wiggle-swim-push itself through centimetres of sand up to the surface? How many minutes or hours do they take? Do they have to breathe, and if so, how? As the turtles escape up and away, the centre of each nest slowly collapses into itself, forming a small crater that challenges those hatchlings that emerge later.

What percentage of turtles die en route to the ocean because of exhaustion, dehydration, or predators? Do large crabs eat those turtles that fall into their holes and die there?

How do they know to head toward the ocean? Is it the sound of the surf?

Liz and I have many other questions, but we'll read about this phenomenon once we get to a good English library.

The first night, we went to investigate several "beach crashers" gathering about 100 m distant. Imagine our surprise when we saw 42 baby turtles which had left their nest and were scrabbling toward the water. When we got there, they were spread out in an area 10 m by 2 m; by the time they had travelled the 25 m to the waves, their path was no wider than 5 m. They knew where they were going, and went there by the most direct route! One or two didn't make it, and a few others wouldn't have made it if the spectators hadn't carried them to the water. All were temporarily blinded by many, many camera flashes.

Thereafter, Liz and I walked the beach, but we saw no more. So it was off to bed after setting the alarm for 1 a.m., the time of high tide. If Liz hadn't insisted on getting me up, I would have thought that alarm was just part of my dream. Later, as we walked the beach we saw so many sets of turtle tracks that we wouldn't have been surprised to see "Turtle Crossing" signs like the ones we had seen in Boissevain, Manitoba many years ago.

Most tracks were traced back to now empty nests, but we did find one nest where a turtle was resting, and a second was halfway out of the sand. So we squatted down and watched. Number two tried harder, and shortly it was out of the nest and on the way to the ocean, easily passing the first turtle. A third, then a fourth, fifth and sixth emerged and they too headed for and completed the trek to the hissing surf. But that was all. There were no more.

Good thing. By now it was 3 a.m. and our bodies were exhausted from excitement and all the encouragement we gave those six newborns. Being parents by proxy is hard work!

When the reset alarm went off at 5 a.m. Liz asked if I really wanted to get up again, so I ignored her. We slept until we woke.

Granada

Granada is a city of past splendour, on the northwest side of Lago Nicaragua. Before Nicaragua's internationally-involved civil war, it was a city where the wealthy lived, worked, played, and built some exceedingly beautiful buildings. A few of those have been refurbished to their past glory. More will be.

The Central Park is starting to regain some of its former tropical beauty, as is the lakeside park. The plaza in front of the restored cathedral will be marvellous. Each concrete block with inlaid stones is hand-made and hand-laid.

Granada is also a city of attractive horse-drawn taxis. These might be a tourist attraction, but I've seen several locals discuss a fare, put their family or their parcels in those buggies, climb in behind them, and clip-clop down a street. Considering the price of gasoline, using these hay-burners makes a lot of sense.

We also saw two black horse-drawn funeral biers. One was part of a sad procession. The other was a solitary wagon plodding along to an unknown destination.

Granada is a city of numerous Russian trucks and buses, a legacy of the war. Most are in bad condition but a few are in excellent state of repair. The shapes of these vehicles are differ-

Tourists and locals alike use these horse-drawn taxis.

ent enough to be unsettling to those of us who are North American.

I was particularly impressed with two churches. Maria Auxiladora of Fr. Bosco has a beautifully carved wood altar, which takes on a completely different appearance when hundreds of tiny lights are turned on. Xaltava Church is fronted by a lovely and cared for park.

Managua

Managua, capital of Nicaragua, is a large city. Thus Liz and I would prefer to ignore it. However, there are several places worth visiting.

The Canadian Consulate is downtown, in front of TELCOR Central, the main TELecommunications centre and post office (CORreos). Fortunately it is very easy to find when coming from the east. Stay on the main streets leading to Centro then, just after you've passed an old cathedral with twin towers, turn right at the lights and proceed toward El Teatro Ruben Darió. (To your left is Parque Central where the left foot of a large statue of a man with an up-raised rifle was slightly damaged by a protest bomb.) Take the first turn left, onto a street that has a tall building covered with a huge but weathered mural, and stop at the first building on your right. Ignore the no parking sign. Everybody else does.

On your left is TELCOR Central supporting several towers and antennae. In front of it is a parking lot full of street kids. They'll see you and rush over to ask for money or food. They'll also delight in touching your rig and opening unlocked compartments. I know of no way to avoid them. They don't seem to be bad kids, just curious and pesky. They'll make food, fruit and nuts disappear so fast you would think they were magicians.

Behind your parked rig are three nearby buildings worth visiting.

El Teatro Ruben Darió can be toured during any weekday for C$5; activities are usually scheduled for weekends. Walking past the theatre toward lake Managua, there is a spacious lakeshore park where one can buy some food, ice cream or drinks.

We couldn't enter the Palacio Nacional (National Palace) because it was being completely restored by Japanese interests, which may be trying to enhance their chances to build a coast-to-coast container railway. The building will be beautiful once again.

The cathedral was severely damaged by a devastating earthquake, and it cannot be entered either. However, lots of open grill work allows one to see inside.

Much further away, hidden amongst dilapidated houses and surrounded by poverty, is Huellas de Acahualinca. It is difficult to find but worth the effort it takes to drive there.

Huellas de Acahualinca is an archaeological treasure, with two excavations showing 6,000-year-old footprints of men, women and children. It is believed that they walked through volcanic mud which solidified quickly thereafter. The prints are so clear that they could have been made an hour ago. I wonder if that family survived the eruption?

To get to this archaeological site, leave the Canadian Consulate and go back to the main street, turn right at the lights, drive to the 'almost-end' then take the narrow street which angles off to your left. Continue driving west. About 2 km later, you'll pass a deep concrete trench; immediately turn right. Three blocks further, make a quick left and right and drive a couple more blocks, keeping the trench on your right. Proud locals will be pleased to direct you to the site. There is parking space for even the biggest rig or fiver.

Back near the Canadian Consulate, driving from El Teatro Ruben Darió to the stop lights, directly ahead two blocks, on the left side, is the Intercontinental Hotel. It is a white truncated triangular building in which you can buy expensive English paperbacks and book a trip to the Corn Islands. (Can $550.00 for two people for two nights and three days including meals was too expensive for us.)

Instead of turning left toward the Intercontinental, we turned right to get to the Office of Tourism, only a block away. It had limited parking, and no information for tourists. We ended up asking some hawkers on a street corner where to buy a map and they went and found one for us. It was expensive, but the service was worth it.

If you come into Managua from Masaya, you'll probably drive down the hill and pass by the Intercontinental without seeing it. But you should notice the damaged statue in Parque Central on your left. The Canadian Consulate is one block beyond the first stop lights and to the left.

As in Liberia, Costa Rica, there is a tree growing in the middle of a street, supposedly close to a little shop called Artesanias Salvadoreños. We didn't find them. It is known as Arbolita, or little tree. Many years ago, it was small but it grew to maturity and eventually became so large then diseased that the city cut it down and paved over its roots. Because there are no street names, only conspicuous landmarks, in Managua everyone continued to give directions using Arbolita as a reference point. Eventually the city dug up its pavement and planted a new Arbolita.

A nativity scene on the grass in front of the Cathedral.

The "Grand Pooba's Box" — so called by several people — is an example of architectural expression gone berserk. I would be surprised to learn that a Nicaraguan designed it. As you pass by this modern and expensive cathedral on the way to or from Masaya, you should drive over and visit it. This building is a great example of something being useful as a comparison; anything else has to look better.

Managua is probably the cleanest of Central American capital cities, just as Nicaragua is the cleanest of those countries. With even a poor map, it is relatively easy to get around after a couple of days of exploring. That may be so because there is no old downtown, which was destroyed by an earthquake and never rebuilt; much of the rubble was dumped into the nearby lake. If you like driving in larger cities, you'll probably enjoy this one.

Masaya

Masaya is the place to buy hammocks and rocking chairs, and from which to visit Volcan Masaya.

So much stuff ... so little space. What does your heart desire?

Hammocks vary greatly in quality, especially in thread and weaving. Comparative shopping inside the Central Mercado, using fingers to feel the difference, is essential to get a good deal. A new hammock store has opened up on the main highway coming from Granada into Masaya but we didn't check it out because none of their hammocks had NICARAGUA woven into their side panels.

It is best not to park in the cobblestone lot directly in front of the Mercado. You'll be swamped by people trying to get you to hire them to look after your vehicle or to act as guides. If that parking lot is to your right, drive past it, take the first turn left then another left and park beside a quiet little park. Maybe you can hire an old retired policeman to guard your rig. We did.

If you drive toward the baseball stadium and onto the pretty park that overlooks Laguna Masaya, you could pass by artisans actually making the hammocks and you will drive by wholesalers trying to sell them. The latter invited us to come in and look around, but they asked higher prices than in the Mercado. Because we had already bought our hammocks, we declined and didn't even try to barter. However, there were some exceedingly bright colours and we were sorry we hadn't discovered this area first.

The best chairs and furniture are made from red-brown Coyote wood because it is much harder than others. I recommend going to Parque Central, then five blocks south to Parque Chamorro (where the street divides to make a teenie triangular park), then a further 1 1/2 blocks south (and left) to two side-by-side factories: Muebles Egmor and Muebles Lajanca. They look like any other doorways, but they are factories, and worth a visit for their own sake. About five or six blocks still further south there is another muebleria off to your right. We paid high prices even after bargaining, but received excellent and obvious quality from a large selection of rocking chairs.

All furniture is handmade. If we'd had more time, I would have had a chair clear stained rather than buying one that was stained to provide a uniform colour. I like the look of wood which is a mixture of cherry-red and beige.

When in Masaya, after driving around town a while, shop in its huge Mercado for whatever you need or think you might need. It is crowded and hot, but also a lot of fun.

Turicentro Trapiche

Trapiche's well planned and maintained swimming and picnic area is 17 km east of Managua, within 3 km of Tipitapa on the 'old' asphalt road. There is ample day and night parking available at reasonable rates, with four security guards patrolling the unlighted area at night.

It is worth a visit, even on Sundays. Unlike public areas of Panamá, weekend litter and loud music are minimal. Nicaragueños seem to respect their land and their neighbour's privacy.

Trapiche no longer has water flowing from rocks to form natural fountains and pools. Natural underground waters still flow, but they are now captured in one huge, sprawling, and aesthetically pleasing swimming pool, which is completely surrounded by wide walkways, benches and trees. Its water is green but not stagnant because there is continual runoff into the creek at one end of the pool.

Liz and I enjoyed our swims. They reminded me of the days when I swam in muddy Red Creek near my hometown of Prince Albert, Saskatchewan.

Depending upon the day and the time of day, there might be sidewalk vendors or an occasional restaurant open. Trapiche has no stores, potable water or electricity, so it is wise to stock up and charge up before going there. Like us, you might decide to stay more than a couple of days and use this place as base for exploring nearby areas.

Tipitapa was recommended to us for its mud pools, but it doesn't have any. It does have swimming pools heated by steaming hot volcanic water. To get to this balneario, drive through town until reaching the end of a one-way street, then turn right at the T-junction and drive to the end of that street. Pass through the gate next to three white crosses, park under some skinny trees and check out the area.

But there were steaming mud pools near San Jacinto, about 20 km farther along the Carretera Norte (Northern Highway) toward Matagalpa. To get to C. Norte from Trapiche, one must drive through Tipitapa and turn left at the T-junction.

Trapiche, near Tipitapa, is definitely worth a visit. During weekdays, it will seem like one's own private RV resort. And how the stars shinc at night!

Juigalpa's Archaeological Museum

Juigalpa has three redeeming features: an archaeological museum to visit; a green central park in which to rest; and cold Victoria beer to drink.

Juigalpa is about 150 km from Trapiche and Tipitapa along a good asphalt road. Of course, there are always several stretches where potholes abound. En route to Juigalpa it seemed that I was often driving on the left side of the road. I felt the same during the return trip. I guess that means that the number of potholes is not greater on the other side of the road after all.

To reach Juigalpa's museum one should stay on the highway, almost completely bypassing the town until turning left at a small red and white sign high on the right side of the highway.

Drive straight ahead for about six or seven blocks, passing the city park and a huge concrete church on your right.

Supposedly this museum is the best in Nicaragua. If so, the others must be really bad. It was very small and dusty. Inside scarred and cracked display cases were several centuries-old household plates, cups, vases, and many carved stone corn grinding table-ettes. It also had post-Spanish antiques —photographs, weapons, machinery—and stuffed animals. Have you ever seen a Sloth, a Siamese calf, or a leather-scaled Gampar fish? All items came from the Juigalpa area.

These statues are the best reasons to visit Museo Juigalpa.

In its courtyard there are forty or so carved statues of ancient important men and women. Even allowing for artistic interpretation, the number of distinctive facial features is truly amazing. One statue is definitely Oriental, probably even Chinese. I wondered if it were a fake or a joke, but I was told that this very old oriental statue is authentic. Why was there a statue of an oriental in pre-Hispanic Nicaragua? Was he a visitor or did he live there? How I wished I could have spoken better español and got answers to those questions.

Near the end of the dry season, this country is really arid. Interestingly enough, one brown hillside was dabbed with flowering trees of many colours: purple, mustard-brass, olive green, rust, yellow, white and coral pink. I hope Liz's point-and-shoot camera can capture that collage of pastel beauty.

Someone or some group has a project to help the local population control disease. We saw many red-roofed and green-walled outhouses, which are unique in Central America. We also saw a distinctive type of well pump pouring clear water into buckets; the handles seem to be rotating wheels. This is a small but successful humanitarian project.

Where did those really huge tree trunks, probably en route to a local sawmill, come from? Any live trees we've seen are quite small.

Unlike most cemeteries we've seen during our travels, where colour comes from real and plastic flowers, we saw crosses that were painted white, green, blue and red.

En route to Juigalpa, Liz and I were coasting behind an underpowered diesel Land Rover, choking on the huge clouds of black smoke pouring from its exhaust system. Not willing to take it any longer I opted to pass on a slight uphill curve. Imagine my surprise when, after passing the Land Rover and driving into clear air, I saw an approaching yellow car close ahead. It had been obscured by the smoke! I stomped on the brakes, realized that neither of us could stop on time, and turned into the ditch. It was strewn with huge crushed stones, one of which bent an inside tire rim so badly that the tire instantly deflated. There was no other damage and no one was injured. In Juigalpa the wheel had to be removed before it could be hammered back into shape, then the tire and wheel reinstalled. Total cost was 15 Cordobas (Can$ 3.00) and a cool bottle of Victoria.

This side trip wasn't one of our more rewarding adventures but nevertheless we're glad to have done it.

Turicentro Xiloa

Turicentro Xiloa is approximately 18 km to the west of Managua, located atop an extinct volcano that juts into Lake Managua. This spacious turicentro is on the shore of a clean, clear volcanic lake. It has a well laid out and maintained picnic area, with many covered tables and inexpensive restaurant-bars. Usually there will be women walking by selling delicious quesillos – cone-shaped tortillas wrapped around meat and coleslaw and filled with sour cream – and other goodies from baskets carried on their heads.

By luck, while travelling west from historical "Huellas de Acahualinca" and past a Toyota dealer and Flor de Caña distillery, we managed to end up on the correct road – Diagonal/Cuesta de Los Martires – to get to this turicentro.

When we arrived at the turicentro gate, the ticket seller had trouble determining our type of vehicle. We told him that we were a Camion Turista (truck tourist) and he let us in for C$20.00. There was ample space for daytime parking and overnight dry camping, although finding a level area under shade required some exploratory effort.

The water was much clearer than at Trapiche, and we felt that we didn't have to have a shower before going to bed. It was so clear that we suspect it is as clear as some of the waters on the Corn Islands. Liz and I could see down to the bottom, 2 m below.

Outside of marked areas, the large lake quickly becomes exceedingly deep. We saw one person outside of the warning net; most Central Americans do not swim well. Liz and I enjoyed floating on our inner tubes, practising using our mask and snorkel, and chasing little fish.

Locals suggested we stay in the vicinity of the patrolled gate for security because unemployment is high hereabouts and stealing is one way to get what one needs. (True, but we have concluded that all Latin Americans are paranoid and definitely overly concerned with petty thieves.) This area is well lit and some of the restaurants are also homes. There are a surprising number of vehicles, people and animals quietly moving about at night.

Local families voluntarily patrol this area during daylight looking for litter. This park was so clean that we could have eaten off the ground. In fact one horse did. I wonder what was missing in its diet that she nibbled on dirt?

On weekday nights this was one tranquil, but not quiet, location. We couldn't remember the last time we heard so many birds settling down for a night's rest. We couldn't remember being awakened by so many birds either. Where do they go during daylight hours?

Xiloa is our choice of turicentro near Managua. It is a handy base camp from which to visit the city, if one remembers to turn left onto the refinery road when going into town. We enjoyed its cleanliness, neighbourliness and its clear blue water.

In Matagalpa, boys will be boys. They shone my shoes beautifully.

Final Impressions of Nicaragua

Nicaragua has some extremely beautiful Pacific beaches, the best we've seen so far. The fine sand is light beige and therefore doesn't get very hot, even in mid afternoon. There might be some volcanic black beaches, but we didn't visit any.

The people were friendly, and many spoke English quite well. Still, I'm glad that we could speak some español. More important, I'm glad we've started to understand answers to our questions.

Nicaragueños (also called Nicos or Nicas) were very concerned about our safety and the security of our motorhome and motorcycle. After the same attitude in El Salvador and Honduras, even I was getting almost as paranoid as they were. It's really a shame there was unnecessary tension because of fear.

This country, while being the poorest, seemed to be more expensive than Honduras or El Salvador. Gasoline prices were the highest.

Nicaragua is flat, except in the northeast which has very limited roads. Good for mileage, bad for dust.

Nicaragua is the least littered Central American country. In city streets in the afternoon plastic bags are everywhere, but in the morning the streets are clean. Piles of garbage are rare.

I don't know why but, as a people, I liked Nicaragueños more than other Central Americans.

Costa Rica

Volcan Arenal
Puerto Limón
Nicoya
San Jose
Cahuita
Puntarenas
Golfito

100
28 de setiembre de 1993
H09968286
SAN JOSÉ, COSTA RICA
ACUERDO DE LA JUNTA DIRECTIVA
Nº 2
SERIE
H
CIEN COLONES
SERIE
H
H09968286
PRESIDENTE EJECUTIVO
GERENTE
BANCO CENTRAL DE COSTA RICA
100

Costa Rica

Border Crossing: Nicaragua to Costa Rica

This border crossing was relatively easy, but still a guide (un guia) would have been helpful. We were lulled into a sense of complacency by the young Nica at the first wicket. She was extremely friendly and helpful, and gave us a lot of information of what to expect, much of it in English. But we still managed to screw up.

If and when you are here, once you've parked in front of the border buildings, shooed away the moneychangers and young men offering to be a guide, make yourself a cup of coffee or tea and relax as you formulate your battle plans.

You must have some American money, US $2.00 per person. You'll also need ¢$5.00 each. Gather up your passport and vehicle papers, put on your oldest and grubbiest clothes, take a Valium or a deep breath, and step out into the real world of time-consuming inefficiency.

If you need US dollars, you can buy some from the money changers. Ensure that you know the exchange rates. You should be able to get more than the initial offer. The same is true for exchanging Cordobas to Colones. Don't be in a rush. If you're not satisfied, politely walk away. Eventually someone will come by who is willing to dicker seriously.

Next, do ask for an official guide and offer him 10 Cordobas. Finding one that speaks English is unlikely, but it isn't all that important. The guide is there only to lead you to the next wicket and, occasionally, to point to a piece of paper that a clerk might want.

Without a guide, we did all right. Except that we didn't realize that the man with a notepad resting over there under a shady tree had to look inside our vehicle and give us a piece of paper. Four kilometres down the road somebody collects that piece of paper. We didn't have it, so back we went.

That was no big deal, except that we had very little gasoline – it was much much cheaper in Costa Rica – and an unnecessary round trip loomed large in our imaginations.

Passing through Costa Rica customs was a breeze.

Having arrived at the border shortly after noon, we didn't mind the wait for the offices to open. We ate lunch in our motorhome rather than in the cafeteria-store.

All necessary wickets are side by side, in order. If you enter Costa Rica with a vehicle then leave to another country, you cannot revisit Costa Rica for three months. However, we were told that on our return we can get a form so we could zip through to Nicaragua or Panamá in three days or less. Check this out very carefully, the situation might have changed.

Make certain that customs know that you could be coming back by either Sixaola or Peñas Blancas, and that both options are noted on paper.

It is compulsory to buy Personal Liability vehicular insurance. Our motorcycle was classed as recreational equipment and thus its insurance was included in that price. A hand-printed sign indicated that it cost about Can$ 30/month, $55/2 months or $80/3 months. We bought only a month's worth, but we received three-months insurance for $12 and paid some kind of unspecified duty/tax/mordida with the remainder. The sign was not there when we returned two months later as we left the country.

Tourist information and maps were available, many in English. A quick perusal of the paper and brochures made me think that I might as well be in North America. I guess advertising is the same the world over: absolutely superlative.

Before you leave the building, make sure you get your TICKET (pronounced tee-KE-tay). Without it, you will return to customs.

We did, and those alleged 10 km to the next gas station were at least twice that far. But with two tanks, one sucked dry and lots of vapours in the other, we had enough gas to make it to a refuelling station. We didn't even need to drain some gasoline from our motorcycle, which is our true emergency 10L tank.

Fuel and Propane

Costa Rican prices have been calculated at the rate of one Canadian dollar equals 117 Colones (C1.17), based upon US $1.00 = Can$1.42 = ¢166.

	Costa Rica	Canada
Regular	¢ 0.569/L	Can$ 0.49/L
Unleaded	¢ 0.630/L	Can$ 0.54/L
Diesel	¢ 0.439/L	Can$ 0.38/L
Propane	¢ 0.403/L	Can$ 0.35/L

The cost of gasoline appears to be fixed by the government; it was the same price from coast-to-coast and border-to-border.

We bought propane in San José, in the western subdivision of Pavas. We had a difficult time finding this propane plant. Because city streets are not named, the following directions are given assuming that you have a free ICT map of San José in front of you.

Drive from city centre to and around the south side of the large "Parque Metropolitano La Sabana". At its end, turn right and drive about a third of the way up the hill and then left onto a divided highway that angles off to the northwest. Keep going for four to five minutes, until the road branches to the right and a narrower road goes down into a gully. The Tropigas propane plant we used is straight ahead about 200 m, on the left, in the gully.

Tropigas in the city of Cartago fills only propane bottles, both the older and newer North American styles.

There is a Tropigas propane distribution centre just south of the Caribbean port of Limón. Because it was closed both times we drove by, I don't know if they could have filled our permanent tank.

First Impressions of Costa Rica

It's nice to be here. After travelling at least 4 km after getting our Nicaraguan clearance, when we finally found the kiosk for fumigation we had to ask what country we were in.

Almost nobody went out of their way to stare at our rig or in our windows. Quite a pleasant change but, surprisingly, we experienced a haunting sense of loss for a few short minutes.

I don't know why borders make such a difference, but Costa Rican highways are shaded by trees, and the grass and vegetation is much greener than in Nicaragua.

The highway has numerous big rectangular potholes, which reminded me of shallow graves. They forced us to travel below the speed limit.

For one night we did not bother with 'Trailer Park Salinas' at Puerto Soley. We travelled over 9 km of rutted, rocky and dusty dirt road but the trek wasn't worth the effort, or tourist-season rates in off-season. However, it did have full hookups, beach access and lots of trees with low-hanging branches.

If you must park close to the border because of impending darkness, take the second turn into La Cruz (before getting to a highway gas station), go past Central Park, travel 1/2 km on bad dirt road to a beautiful lookout called Mirador de la Vista, dry camp, and enjoy the sunset.

Some of these unmarked potholes were over 20 cm (8") deep.

Random Thoughts

While at Playa Grande, we managed to exchange a few books. Not having our usual selection of novels available, Liz and I have been reading books that we normally wouldn't. Guess what? There are a lot of good authors with different styles and interesting story plots.

We met a couple who had driven their Class A from Ontario to Panamá and were returning to Canadá. They'd been travelling for only six weeks. I wonder what they saw in such a short time? They were really unlucky because they had passed through Costa Rica en route to Panamá and were planning on spending a couple of weeks here on the way back. Unfortunately, they were granted only a three-day transit visa. They didn't even have time to visit Liberia.

I finally realized that road-kill in Central America is different than at home. How often does one see dead anteaters, monkeys or iguanas in Canada?

The fireflies here on the Caribbean coast are exceedingly bright.

When you buy a bunch of bananas, be very careful that you don't let juice from the stem fall onto your clothing or furniture.

It is very difficult to get rid of those stains, unless you cut out the damaged material.

At mercados or from corner vendors, I buy fruit that is not overly ripe, unless we can eat it within hours. Saleswomen use "muy dulce" (very sweet) as an aphorism for almost rotten.

The houses and buildings in Costa Rica are finished. They do not have metal bars sticking out of unfinished second storeys and roofs. Generally, these houses are brightly painted and clean.

When we travelled in Guatemala, Liz and I met a woman who owned a bed-and-breakfast on the southern Caribbean coast of Costa Rica. She asked us to please come and visit her and stay at her place. If she gave us a card, we lost it. All we knew was her name, Pamela. When we got to Costa Rica and after bumping along a dirty coastal road for a while, we stopped to buy some ice cream. For the very first time, we told someone about Pamela. The shop owner smiled and told us that she was his immediate neighbour. What an amazing coincidence!

We walked over to her place. But she had left two days previously to go to her son's wedding in Panamá and wouldn't return until after we were gone. Everything averages out.

Another form of speed control in Liberia's paved streets.

Caribbean sand is of many colours. But most interestingly, it is possible to have a completely black beach transform into an entirely golden beach, within only a few meters.

The black volcanic sand on the Caribbean coast, which resembles dark iron filings, is ferro-metallic. I carried a sample all the way back to Canada, dried it out, and put some on a flat sheet of paper which rested on a bar magnet. Sure enough, it formed the classic pattern of magnetic lines of force. Using the magnet, I could even pick up a short "string" of sand.

I now know where the expression 'pinch of salt' comes from. Uniodized sea salt does not taste as strong or as salty as does commercially purified NaCl. Nor does it harden into one huge lump of salt in a humid climate. But wet or dry, it forms small crystals and cannot be poured through a shaker. Thus it is necessary to reach into a jar and, using forefinger and thumb, pinch a crystal of salt and then sprinkle that onto one's food. We like sea salt.

I lost my reading glasses in Cahuita. Now when I try to read, each line is duplicated like this one. This optical illusion exists when either eye
each line is duplicated like this one. This optical illusion exists when either eye
is closed or both are open. Of course, each line is also quite fuzzy but, in bright sunlight, by squinting really hard I can overcome my astigmatism. I got my glasses back by posting a small reward, in a Canadian-owned tourist services store in Cahuita.

On one beach as we were eating our breakfast of spiced bacon, over-easies, toasted coconut bread and fresh papaya, we were surprised when our tenting neighbours took out two pistols and casually began target practice. They needed it. After several shots the popcan was untouched. But as Liz said, can you imagine this happening in Canadá?

While parked by Volcan Arenal, we had access to tap water under high pressure. It was also time to rid our motorhome of its dusty, oily and grubby appearance, which resulted from our philosophy of "Look rich, get poor; look poor, stay rich." In other words, it was time for our rig's semiannual bath, whether needed or not. It took most of one lightly overcast day to wash, rinse and wax our travel-weary home on wheels. Once again I realized why its colour scheme was listed as white and beige and not grey and brown. It was clean.

For the next three days it rained and misted as we travelled over blacktop and several dirt roads. Ah well, at least the rain beaded on the hood.

When driving around Volcan Arenal, then further northwestward past the Arial Tram site a week later, we came upon two locations where somebody was making a film. No wonder movies cost millions of dollars. In each site there must have been twenty buses, trucks, trailers, flatbeds with humungous generators and, yes, Class C motorhomes. (I almost stopped and hugged them!)

Truth in advertising! We saw a sign that said "Hut for Rent." Of course, some handwritten signs should read "Hovel for Rent."

Panamá Embassy

There is no need to go to the Panama Embassy in Costa Rica unless you want a visa. A 30-day Tourist Card for Panamá can be obtained at the border for US $5.00/person. There are no other charges, even for vehicles.

But if you want to pay a visit, here's how to get there. If street names were used, the directions would be much simpler.

On the ICT city map, the desired street is literally on the eastern edge of the map. It is indicated as an upside down V, where two streets meet.

The embassy is located in San José, in the far eastern subdivision-city of San Pedro. Coming from city centre, after passing under the Periferico (a city or subdivision bypass highway), it is the seventh street from Avenida Central. Immediately prior to this street, on the right, is a Mas X Menos (More or Less) grocery store and a large gas station, Servicentro El Higueron. Turn right on the seventh street and go all the way to the end, about 0.6 km. The embassy building is at the corner of a T-junction, on the right.

(To the left is a micro-mall with a parking lot where we parked overnight. Liz made up some coffee and sandwiches and I took them over to two security guards. One was supposed to be in front of the embassy, but he was curious about us. We had an interesting, struggling-for-words, half-hour chat.)

The embassy was open from 9:00 a.m. to 2:00 p.m., Monday to Friday.

Playa Grande

Playa Grande has two beautiful swimming beaches, which are especially dangerous at high tide when towering surf is present.

At night, between October and March, these beaches are home to gigantic turtles laying eggs and to tiny newborn turtles scrabbling for the salt water. This sanctuary is in Las Baulas de Guanacaste, a protected area adjacent to National Wildlife Refuge Tamarindo, and a few hundred metres north of the small resort town of Tamarindo on the Pacific side of La Peninsula de Nicoya.

We were there just in time. We managed to park two nights for free in a newly levelled lot only 10 m from the high water line. A few months later a bi-level condo would occupy our spot.

Being a sanctuary, there is quite a variety of wildlife. For example, a dark-striped, lime-green iguana just scampered by, pausing to look in our open door. Yesterday, small green parrots roosted and squawked in nearby trees. And of course, pelicans continually dive into the blue and green water of the bay. When they are successful, they float on the surface until they have their meal flipped and turned so that it slides easily down their throat. Only then do they struggle to get airborne again for another attempt.

During daylight hours, access to this beach and water was free. After 11 p.m. there was a ¢200 entrance fee, plus another ¢500 fee for a guide. The beaches were patrolled in an attempt to keep poachers and egg stealers away. A guide was mandatory because you must not be on the beach at night by yourself during the turtle nesting season.

On a wall of a tiny building where fees were paid, we noticed a sign that stated in another two days this National Park would be closed permanently to visitors. I hope it meant only for this season. But if not, then it is another reason we're very glad we did this trip now and not when we thought we might be able to afford it.

One early morning, as we rounded the point to the second beach, we came across hundreds and hundreds of hermit crabs living and moving in the shade of a small cliff. For protection, these crabs live inside the empty shells of snails, nautilus' and such departed creatures.

On close inspection, one crab had grabbed the larger shell of another and was rocking it back and forth. Suddenly, the motion-sick crab extruded itself from its rocking house and stood naked in the sun; how it ever fit in there is a mystery. And how that larger crab, having left its adopted shell, managed to ooze into his victory shell is even more of a mystery. Maybe it was related to Houdini. Quickly the smaller crab squeezed into the recently vacated shell, and both crabs skittered off sideways, minding their own businesses.

A short way down the beach, this scene was repeated, except that the owner of the rocking house wouldn't leave. Finally the bullying pirate left.

Farther along this warm, dry beach, the sand was wet as high as 15 m above the waves. More than half the beach is fed by underground water that slowly seeps out of the sand, flows into rivulets and pools, and eventually makes its way to the ocean. The patterns of dark lines on grey and beige sand were truly beautiful. One area looked like a mermaid's hair trailing behind her as she rested on a giant oyster-shell chair. Another looked like a wood carving of a blazing campfire. Yet another resembled washed roots of an Alder tree.

By the time we finished our walk and I returned with my camera to those special spots, they were under the waves. Ah well, we and they will be there tomorrow.

As we walked the beaches, we saw where one nest had disgorged its baby turtles, leaving dozens of overlapping trails which successfully ended at the high water line. We also saw distinctive tracks and handiwork left by two female turtles which had nested during the night. Another set of tracks was probably made the night before.

Liz and I decided to spend one more night here, hoping a guide could show us at least one nesting leather-backed turtle. No white lights or flash-photography are allowed when turtles are about because it frightens them; some will leave the beach without nesting.

Therefore, I will try to get a picture with my thirty-year-old 35 mm Kodak Pony II camera. You know, the old-fashioned kind without batteries and electronics where, before you can push the release button, you have to manually preset speed, focal length and aperture, then push a lever to cock the shutter spring.

Sun, sea, swimming, sunning, strolling, swimming, tanning, snacking, wading while the sun set, eating and reading. It had been a full, full day; but it wasn't over yet.

At 10:45 p.m. we laid down our books, got dressed for a long coolish night, brought along my ancient camera and an old military flashlight with a red transparency in front of the lens, and headed off toward the ticket wicket. After five minutes of walking beneath a quarter moon, we noticed a large black rock just above the low tide water line. Rock? Could it be . . . ?

Yes it was. A female leather-back turtle was slowly raising itself on its flippers and moving forward about 15 cm with each lurch. Being 5 1/2 feet long (same as Liz) and several hundred pounds (considerably more than Liz), it really seemed to strain. Each breath sounded like a prolonged sigh of resignation. She made about six lunges, stopped for a few seconds, then struggled forward another 6-8 times. She seemed so tired.

Tortuga the turtle took almost half an hour to cross the wet sand. (Why did it leave its watery home at low tide?) A false start at nest digging was followed by another metre or so of labourious travel to where the subsurface sand was warm and dry, and she dug in earnest. Those front flippers could whip sand backwards at least three metres. In forty minutes she dug a hole that was about half as deep as she was high.

She rocked back and forth as she laid her eggs, unseen by us who were staying far away from flying sand. Finished, she moved forward and covered her eggs, which were at least a half metre deep, then she kept on moving more and more sand long after it was needed. We wondered if our being so close made her nervous or if she was trying to misrepresent the location of the nest. We moved back, but she kept on flinging dry sand about.

When the turtle finally headed back to sea, we noticed each rear fin had a silvery tag sparkling in moonlight. Now that the eggs had been laid and buried and there was no danger of an aborted nesting, we got close enough to read the tags: V8924 and V8925. Her warm hide was remarkably soft and supple. Next morning we dropped off a sighting report and our ¢400 park admission at the unattended ticket kiosk.

In the middle of cool night, under a pale moon, we'd spent 2 1/2 hours watching a huge turtle struggle up a beach, dig a hole, fill it back in, and ponderously crawl back to the sea. Was this better than watching a National Geographic special on television? Darn right it was.

An ecological fence of green cacti

Volcan Arenal

Volcan Arenal is split personality. Its east side is covered in lush vegetation from bottom to top whereas its west side is nothing but grey, purple and black rock. This volcano is a silent sleeper and a roaring snorer. It is a daytime wonder and a nighttime spectacle.

When in Costa Rica, plan on spending at least two nights in this area. You might be lucky enough to see everything in one day, but low cloud, obscuring rain and erupting volcanoes have unpredictable schedules.

Volcan Arenal spews forth great jets of steam about once an hour, although a half a day between eruptions is not uncommon. On clear days, these huge vertical clouds can be seen from miles away. Although visible from other directions, we were told these columns of steam were best seen from Highway 4 on the east side of this mountain of fire. There are at least one full-service campground and several hotels, motels, and parking lots nearby.

On the west side, Parque Nacional Arenal was made available to the public in August 1994, was officially opened in November and, with fully trained staff, will start to charge walking or driving visitors US$15.00 / day / person in February 1995. Even with that ridiculously high entrance fee, and for that matter for fees paid to bus tours, there are no guarantees that the volcano will provide a spectacular show.

To get to the park, tourists must travel 2 km of excellent gravel road after leaving the paved highway, turning at the "<— Parqueo 1 km" sign about 12 km west of Fortuna. Alone or in small caravans, motorhomes and trailers can, probably, dry camp in a level gravel lot between the park's administration building and the clean washrooms. There are taps nearby which gush forth refreshing and pure mountain-spring water.

After Liz and I walked to a park observation site that was 1.5 km closer to the volcano, we could hear it breathing. It sounded like an out-of-shape runner who has sprinted 300 m, or the "Little Train That Could", or a distant Australian wobble-board, or a fiery dragon barbecuing its dinner, or a dozen Trolls pounding on anvils in their underground forge.

When several hours pass between eruptions, an explosion can cause the ground, and your knees, to shake. Being anticipated but unexpected, recollections of a buried Pompeii, or visions of roiling clouds of dust from Mount Saint Helens, or fear of being caught in a hail storm of red-hot rocks can erupt as well.

If the entrance fee is too high for some, there are some small parking areas a couple of hundred metres past the park entrance. With these areas being so far away from the volcano, binoculars are useful. By late afternoon these gravel areas will fill very quickly with buses, tour vans and cars.

You have to be at the west side, the park side, of the volcano at night to see luminescent boulders and lava. The red glow of furnace-hot rock starts to become visible shortly after sunset. The first night there, we spent several hours scanning the volcano with our binoculars, seeing many huge pinwheels of sparks and hearing hundreds of crashing boulders roll down from a single horizontal strip of glowing amber. A couple of hours after we went to bed, there was a tremendous eruption and most of the mountainside turned into a river of red. Unbelievably, we slept through it.

During the following day and most of that night, there was almost no activity in the volcano. Many people and tours came and left having seen nothing. A couple of hours after dark, activity increased slightly on the left side, with two, sometime three, small glowing spots and an occasional rock tumbling down and bursting into a cascade of sparks. We almost gave up hope of seeing anything worthwhile.

Then at 10:12 a squadron of jets seemed to start up, and a horrendous garuumphphph was followed by the entire right side of the black mountain suddenly becoming a flood of falling rocks. It was a fireworks fountain on a grand scale that lasted for eight minutes, then quickly faded to black. It seemed much longer.

Volcan Arenal was a marvellous sight. And I'm glad that we had our own free accommodations, our motorhome, because it might have taken three or more days to see flowing lava.

Cahuita

Cahuita is really two places on the Caribbean coast 47 km south of Puerto Limón. Side-by-side, both are extremely friendly, laid-back, and enjoyable.

One is a tourist village where entrepreneurship, restaurants, cabins, hospedajes, souvenirs and usual tourist prices exist. The other is a National Park with nothing in it except jungle, animals and birds.

The locals were truly upset at the government's attempt to empty all national parks of human beings. They are fighting hard to get the price of US$15.00 /day/person reduced to something more reasonable. I hope they do. Perhaps there could be an annual fee, good for all parks, like we have in Canadá.

A restaurant known for its offerings of fresh bounty from the sea.

We drove into Parque Nacional Cahuita after closing, met a ranger, and mentioned that we hoped to stay three or four days. He was apologetic and also very upset by the entrance fee but, being an employee, he was compelled to charge and collect it.

But he was encouragingly enthusiastic when we suggested that we would come back about six in the morning. He said that he wouldn't charge us if we got out before he opened the kiosk at the park entrance at 8:00 a.m. We left and set up camp just outside the park boundaries.

Too bad we hadn't said we would be staying only one night. There is a loophole, say locals such as Rudolfo who lives close by the entrance. There is no charge if you arrive after 4:00 p.m. and leave before 7:30 a.m. Which means we could have camped overnight among the birds and animals when they were most active.

The park promises to be interesting. As I write this, I hear one, sometimes two, "coconut" parrots with a very loud burrrr. Moments of silence are also interspersed with monkey sounds, owl hoots, touch tone dialling from "Telephone" birds, crickets, frogs and an assortment of other unknown vocalizations. This is one of the few times we've found a jungle which seems to be alive.

Unfortunately, mosquitos have successfully adopted stealth technology.

Its 5 a.m. and Liz and I stir. We almost fall back to sssleep, but somehow manage to keep at least one of our four eyes open. Finally we crawl down from our over-the-cab, ever-so-comfortable, high-density-foam, oh-so-soft queen-size bed.

A black sky lightens as we dress in long sleeves and blue jeans. The sun is fully up by the time we finish tea, toast and marmalade. We begin to talk to each other.

As we walk into the park, Liz grabs my arm, asking "Was that a Jaguar? An Ocelot? What was that horrible noise?" Being brave and strong, and having got my own breathing and heartbeat under control after I slipped back inside my skin, I casually said "Oh, it's only a Howler monkey. There's nothing to worry about." No doubt about it, those monkeys do have an effective warning system.

Having localized the screech-cry-bellow (a howl is all of these and more) and noting where a branch moved, we finally managed to find a Howler with our binoculars. But it was too far away to get a good look at its distinctive face and neck.

A sudden, warm rain sent me back for our umbrellas. By the time I rejoined my True Love, it had vanished as quickly as it started.

Farther along the narrow road, another branch moved and we studied three white faced monkeys eating leaves. 20 m more a single white face parted some palm leaves and stared at us, as if we were creatures in a zoo. It kept watching us as it unhurriedly climbed from branch to branch and tree to tree. It passed almost over our heads by stretching from palm frond to palm frond then, looking over its shoulder, ambled back into the trees and slowly, silently disappeared behind too many leaves.

What a change from walking town streets!

Our noses functioned beautifully. Warm odours of freshly turned ground, humidity, sweet molasses, decay, salt spray, acrid animal odours, all of these were present. But not once did we see an animal on or near the ground. I guess city-slickers like us don't become naturalists and trackers overnight. I wonder how many creatures we looked at and didn't see?

Turkey buzzards gliding on a thermal, hummingbirds flitting about, black birds with brilliant red body feathers, several unidentified large birds, all of these were there too.

One bird with a yellow tail sang only when it was upside down. For some time we thought it was doing somersaults—wondering how it managed to keep hold of its branch—but eventually we concluded that it would straighten its legs, flip over, issue its throaty musical chirp then, somehow, snap back to its resting position.

Finding an unused road that disappeared into the jungle, we had to investigate it. Around a curve and 50 m later, it ended in a clearing. Why? Why was it there?

Not knowing but suspecting that it was a lookout for something, we spent tens of silent minutes scanning the jungle. Sure enough, eventually, we saw a tribe of black-faced monkeys moving and snacking in nearby trees. Although they didn't rush, they were in constant motion. Once we learned what to look for, we could see several curved tails hanging below obscuring leaves.

We never did see any of those supposedly numerous sloths. One guide book indicated that their fur can turn green from algae, which reminded us of a camouflaged Cayman we saw in the superb zoo in Tuxtla, Mexico. It moved so sluggishly among lily pads that its back was covered with mud and live vegetation.

Hundreds of birds and animals have left the national park because of dwindling food supplies. At the Puerto Vargas entrance, as opposed to the one closer to Cahuita, El Señor Moé Vega Varelo owns the restaurant-bar Jardin de Cervecero (Beer Garden). Being half Tico and half Indio, he has started his own private park called Jardin de Indios. Besides cutting crude paths through his jungle land, he has planted several trees as food for the animals. A senior government biologist visited his park and offered suggestions.

Supposedly (never trust PR completely) there are more animals in this private park than there are in the national park. This might explain the numerous late night and early morning sounds we heard close behind our trailer.

El Señor Varelo plans to have native guides for hire so that untrained visitors like us can be shown the animals, birds, plants, trees, and be given the Indio names. It cost nothing to walk through his small park but, afterwards, a pop and beer tasted great in the humid tropical heat.

We missed a lot, but we saw plenty. We'll be staying in Cahuita for a couple more days, and we'll see more marvellous sights.

Southeastern Caribbean Coast of Costa Rica

The Caribbean coast, south of Cahuita and all the way to Panamá, is just how we imagined the tropics to be. There were fan palms, African palms, coconuts, banana plantations, beautiful yellow beaches, aquamarine ocean breaking over coral reefs, hot sun, and cool water. And we had to drive 30 km of rocky dirt road to get there!

Unfortunately, all that greenery comes at a small cost. We experienced almost as many wet and overcast days as sunny ones. And this was in the 'dry' season.

Another idyllic setting, with the blue-green Caribbean behind us.

The year we visited saw tourism down to 20% of the previous year. Ouch! Part of the problem was, of course, the US $15 per day fee at national parks.

Willie Burton, a fisherman and guide in Gandoca-Manzanillo Refuge is a real gentleman and, after 40 years in this area, very knowledgeable of the ocean and jungle. His wife Marva makes and sells superb coconut bread. Both speak excellent English and, I suspect, other languages as well. A 2-3 hour boat trip through the mangrove swamps costs 2,000 colones (¢2.000 or Can$20.00) per person, with a three-person minimum charge. Unfortunately, Willie was pre-booked and unavailable.

Fortunately, we could and did hire Jorge Duggan and his extra long dugout canoe for ¢80,000. It would have been the same price with four, six or eight persons. Try as we did, we couldn't find any other tourists who could join us at our prearranged time. Although expensive, we spent a very pleasant and full day with him.

We even got to see a sloth, hanging and eating high up in a tree in Jorge's back yard! Just as the guidebooks predicted, its mousy brown fur was almost green from algae and moss. With that protective colouring and their imperceptibly slow movements, they are well camouflaged and a rare sight indeed.

For the first time during this trip we were unable to go where we wanted; we wanted to park on a golden beach in front of Willie's island home, where a river empties into the ocean. In a sharp curve in an all black sandy road, two palm trees formed a barrier while a third leaned over the road. Low cars could get through, but not our Class C. Still, we managed to camp for several days under some leafy trees within 100 m of our destination. Bread fruit, pipas and coconuts were within walking distance and free for the taking.

After wading through the river, we walked along several sandy beaches, some with coral rocks, and a muddy path past a spectacular lookout point. At one spot, we had to lay down branches and palms to get by without sinking up to our knees. The last beach we visited contained sea life above the waterline that looked like lobster tails buried in or glued to the coral. There was also a blowhole in a rocky outcropping that sounded like Volcan Arenal when it erupted.

Many of the Caribbean beaches are still filled with logs and forest debris resulting from the April 1991 earthquake. Two kilometres north of Las Palmas Resort (so read a faded sign) we turned left onto an overgrown side road and found a beautiful beach about 300 m beyond an inexpensive restaurant and bar. The beach was almost clear of debris, primarily due to the efforts of a seven-year Swiss resident called Angela. It was a fabulous place to park and to swim.

Apparently the ocean in Manzanillo is transparent in Mar/Apr and Sep/Oct; it can seem as if you are floating on blue air above a mixture of coral and sand. However, we swam in reasonably turbid water, a result of storms and winds just a few kilometres offshore and a Chilean earthquake a week earlier. Strange as it may seem, any large Central or South American earthquake affects these waters within days.

Because new national laws ensure that the first 50 m from high water mark is public beach, with severe fines for cutting down ANY plant, there are lots of palms from which you can freely knock down coconuts. Having a motorhome roof that we can climb on allowed us to pick as many coconuts as we wanted, without having to use a long pole to knock them down. Of course, my El Salvadorean machete was really useful in getting past those fibrous husks.

Little green coconuts called pipas contain refreshingly clear, tasteless water. Big green ones have water with a hint of taste and coco jelly which is a treat you'll never find in Canadá. Big brown-gold ones have flavourful milk and hard white coco meat.

Cool, clear 'agua de coco' is a great morning drink. As well, older coconut milk adds a distinctive flavour to coffee. We finally learned to drink coconut water whenever Montezuma's Revenge or the Mexican Two Step threatened. That drink solved all our potential medical problems.

Our sad farewell celebration to Manzanillo consisted of a large meal of Red Snapper at Restaurante Maxi. (We ordered a big one; it was considerably cheaper and was much better tasting than two smaller fish.) This restaurant is so famous for its fresh fish meals and reasonable prices that people will drive from Cahuita and Limón for a repast. It can even serve a chilled bottle of white wine.

The beaches, food and people on the southeastern Caribbean coast of Costa Rica are marvellous.

Adventures of a Tilley Hat

If you have a Tilley Hat—mine was a gift from a golfing friend—then you will have to arrange for a trip where it is appropriate to wear it. After all, one doesn't usually wear a tuxedo to a smash-up derby, or a corsage to an open air rock concert, or running shoes to a ballroom dance, so why would one wear a Tilley Hat in downtown Kelowna, BC Canada?

Nope, it has got to be worn to protect an already red nose from a blazing tropical sun. It has to be worn while drifting down a jungle river where huge ripples form after silvery fish leap into the air. It has to be worn as one sits high up in a Mangrove tree, resting on a small branch that is so strong it barely bends under one's shifting weight. It has to be worn while looking at underwater creatures curious about a dugout canoe. It has to be worn while slogging through mud near a rusty narrow gauge railway abandoned among trees, vines and hordes of mosquitos. And it has to be worn while surfing in a canoe.

Have you ever surfed Caribbean waves at 30 km/hr or more in a 10-metre dugout canoe? If not, rev up your outboard and get going fast enough to catch a wave from behind. As you come at it from the side and the prow of the canoe passes over the top and hangs suspended in the air, quickly turn to your left and let the nose gently fall down and down until you and the boat are tilted waaay forward and skimming down the front of the wave. If you do it just right, the stern and idling motor stay behind the crest while wind blows faster and faster in your face. Gradually the boat will gain even more speed and slip down the slope until the motor is completely past the crest and once again pumping cooling water. Then, whenever a coral reef or a sandy shore gets too close, turn sideways, cruise up the slope, slip gently through the now foaming crest, turn, and look for another wave. Put your Tilley back on, rev up your motor, and chase another one.

Jorge and John are up a tree.

Have you ever eaten coconut sponge? No!? When you get the chance, grab an old grey weather-beaten coconut that is lying on a sandy beach. It should have at least 10 cm of green sprout growing out of one end. Take your trusty machete, sharpened on a flat stone or whetstone, and try to cut that coconut in half lengthwise. After a couple of whacks, leaving your machete jammed in the fibrous shell, pull on each end of the machete and bend it like a bow. Poouff, the shell rips apart, the coconut splits open and there, inside, is clean white and very tasty coconut sponge. A delicious secret treasure!

In "Old Bones", a detective story that takes place in France, Inspector Joly expresses disbelief by snorting "And oysters grow on trees." Strangely enough, they do. At least they do in some freshwater Costa Rican rivers that flow into the Caribbean. Near the shore, where salt water mingles with fresh and Mangrove trees grow, many of the branches that dip into the water are covered with thin-shelled oysters. Below the waterline, the bark of those branches can be completely hidden beneath hundreds of these barnacle-like bivalves. Unfortunately, due to insecticides and fertilizers from onshore banana plantations seeping into nearby rivers, most of these oysters are now dead or very sick.

Perhaps in a few years Inspector Joly will be right and oysters will no longer grow on trees.

To swim in a secluded Caribbean cove, under a warm midday tropical sun, in light blue waters above brightly coloured sand shaded by coconut trees, is the dream of many. Ours too. And we did. Schools of tiny fingerlings flipped their tails and were gone. A barracuda escaped to the left as we fled to the right. Liz and I rescued a young sick seagull who was drowning because it couldn't keep its head above water. It was so easy to imagine ourselves as explorers in uncharted waters, as Mr. and Mrs. Robinsen Carusoe (a shipwrecked Scandinavian singer) stranded on a deserted island. But imagination failed us when we walked ashore between plastic bottles and aluminum cans. Why can't people—locals and tourists alike—carry out what they take in?

Oh the colours, sights and animals that my bird-shat-upon hat has seen. If you have one, don't lock it up in a chrome and glass shopping mall. Hike it into a pine forest, help it climb a mountain, carry it into a green jungle, let it rest on top of a Mayan pyramid, sail it across ocean waters.

Take your Tilley on an adventure. You'll have fun too.

This large, beautiful topiary garden is a gathering place for many of the local people of Zarcero, two hours northwest of Alajuela.

Central Pacific Coast

After heading west from San José and Alajuela then down, down, down a narrow winding strip of blacktop with no shoulders to San Mateo, you will be near the central Pacific coast. (La

Radial in Alajuela is a good garage for brake work.) There are some great beaches, both commercialized and deserted.

But before you get there, you'll cross Rio Tarcoles. Immediately pull off to the side of the road, park, then walk back along a large concrete bridge with your binoculars. Being on the edge of the Caraca Biological Reserve, you'll probably see things we never saw, and vice versa. If you're as lucky as most, you'll see several crocodiles sunning themselves in the shallow river on both sides of the bridge. You might mistake some as tires, or you might see one or more crocs curled up inside semi-submerged tires. You'll probably see a few fish and several colourful birds, large and small. Why would that reddish-brown bird with no tail feathers have feet bigger than its body?

Driving on, you'll come to Playa Jacó (Ha-koh beach). It's long, shallow, grey sand beach is great for dunking in the waves. As with all large beaches, we were warned about riptides and sideways currents, especially at high tide, so we never went into water which was more than waist-deep. Never, that is, unless we fell into a few holes, which sounds much worse than it was.

Jacó has many hotels, hospedajes, and at least one spacious tenting campground at its northern end. A Québec family had lived there in a Chevy camper van for two months, with electricity and access to water. They had hoped to be able to sell their van for sufficient profit to pay for their vacation and flight back to Canadá. Unfortunately they didn't, and they were just starting to pack up for their return drive when we arrived.

We parked on a dead end street, next to that campground and across from Hotel El Jardin and its highly rated restaurant. We had stopped next to a telephone pole, which unexpectedly gave us excellent reception on our short wave radio, even when it was inside our motorhome. By connecting a wire between the telephone ground wire and our roof ladder, which is connected to aluminum siding and window frames, we created an antenna that was miles long. What a pleasure it was to hear Radio Canada International so clearly.

Two Days Short of a Month

Two kilometres from Panamá, two days before we have to leave Costa Rica, two frustrated people are wondering how it happened.

Two days ago, after a few relaxing days with sunsets in Bird of Paradise colours and yet another sand-free morning swim, Liz and I left quiet Playa Bejuco. This is a private beach area. However, all beaches are public 50 m from the high water mark, so we parked unobtrusively off to the side of the road. Unobtrusively? Not really. It is impossible to hide a 7 m motorhome behind a couple of palm tree trunks on the edge of a very wide beach. But the owners of several beach houses didn't mind us; in fact, I think they enjoyed our company and the diversion we provided.

(Here we heard about a man from the United States of America who paid US $25,000 for a beachside lot. [American, yes, and so is anybody who lives in the Americas: North, Central and South. It is well to remember that, and that Central Americans were here long before thirteen colonies formed a USA.] All paper and legal work was done quickly and inexpensively. But when he came to build on his land which was two lots over from where we were parked, it was registered in the name of the town clerk who registered the deed. Oops, sorry!)

Interesting stories, friendly people, great sandy beaches notwithstanding, we had much more to see before our visa expired.

From Playa Bejuco we travelled the coast dirt road to Domical, then up, up, slowly up and up to San Isidro. We enjoyed an hour's shopping in four, that's right, four well-stocked grocery stores. We wandered around the area and finally found a lilliputian post office only a block and a half from where we set up, a mere hour after it closed. Liz cooked up another fabulous supper, washed dishes, won again at Boggle, and we finally climbed into bed.

The night was cool, refreshingly cool up here high above those faraway beaches below. At 5 a.m. we had to put the quilt over us.

At 6:13 we laughed at a would-be sneak thief as he jumped out of his skin. Both truck horns blared a warning from only a foot away as he tried to open the motorcycle storage compartment. We have a horn switch beside our bed.

It was a good start to another day of adventure.

To leave something unseen for our return through Costa Rica, we left the PanAmerican Highway at Paso Real and travelled eastward instead of westward, leaving the rest of Route 2 for our return. We rode the ridges and looked down into several valleys. Scenery was beautiful on both sides of the highway and well worth all those curves and 'lost' hours.

Eventually we got to Agua Buena and its internationally recognized Biological Gardens, only to find out that we had to park on the side of a narrow, almost shoulderless highway. For ¢1.000 each we thought that they should at least provide some parking spaces. They didn't, so we didn't go in.

Bougainvillaea are everywhere in a variety of brilliant colours.

Suddenly, we had a few hours free. There was no sense in stopping where we planned to overnight, so what was to be done? We decided to swim and camp at Playa Cacao, next day we'd go to Golfito and shop in 50 duty-free stores at the end of town.

The dirt road to Playa Cacao was under construction and impassable. We didn't feel like hiring a water taxi for just a couple of hours of beach time and scratched Playa Cacao from our list of activities. Oh well.

So we drove to the Puerto Libre (Free Port) to see what kind of prices there were. They advertise duty free but it really isn't, although the prices are reduced. We arrived in mid afternoon, when the lineup to get in was 50 metres long and 3-4 people wide. Costa Ricans might be willing to wait an hour or more under a blazing tropical sun to get great bargains, but Liz and I aren't. Besides, we only wanted to look, not buy; there would be even cheaper prices in the gigantic, truly duty-free complex in Colón, Panamá. So why should we pay to park while we stood in line and, eventually, to browse about? We didn't.

OK, now what?

We checked the books and map. Righto! We were off to Playa Zancudo, allegedly the best swimming beach in Costa Rica and close by mangrove forests in the delta of Rio Conte. The map was wrong, the road was paved. The map was right, we had to cross a river on a motorless cable ferry. The ferry was big enough, but we couldn't get on because the steep ramps would have caused our rear overhang to sink below water and scrape the bottom of the river. We didn't even try.

Quite a day so far. We had struck out in everything we tried. Well not quite. I climbed up on our roof with my machete and got some green platanos (they're like bananas but bigger and great for frying) and golden coconuts from trees on the side of the public highway. We also managed to buy pop from a delivery truck, at half store price. Whoopee!

What else is there to do? Nothing. Right. So it was off to the border crossing on an unexpectedly excellent high speed road. We magically appeared at 4 p.m., which was too late to clear customs for both countries before their supper hour but too early for ours.

I decided that I might as well get the lay of the land, so to speak. Maybe we could get by without hiring a guide. I drove to the Panamá border, inadvertently bypassing the Costa Rica customs. Upon our return to Costa Rica, we had great fun trying to explain that we hadn't yet left Costa Rica, that we hadn't been in Panamá, and that we planned on leaving next day, not now. Eventually we were allowed back in the country.

There certainly wasn't any place at the border crossings where we could stay overnight, so we drove back a couple of kilometres to a Texaco 24 hour gas station and got permission to stay there for the night. I should mention the station also sells lots of diesel every hour to tens of noisy trucks and buses.

So here we sit, in a dusty, smelly, noisy gas station, having lost the need for two days of travel and sight seeing, anticipating a sleepless night, and expecting to be in Panamá two days sooner than necessary.

If I could have seen the future, we would have camped and swum in Playa Bejuco for two more days. But I can't, and we didn't. We're here. Oops, sorry Liz!

A Letter to Tico Times

Note 1: Tico Times is an English language USA-style newspaper. It is a great source of locally scheduled events and activities.

Note 2: This letter was written as we zipped through Costa Rica "en transito". It was started in Grecia, continued near Cañas, and was finished in Liberia, a very nice, very clean, very friendly town.

It was printed in Liberia while we enjoyed a tasty lunch at "Restaurante Beppe Italiano". During our meal the owners let us string our electrical cord from one of two outlets, over a sidewalk and to our motorhome on the street so we could use our 110V AC printer. We mailed the letter as we left for Nicaragua.

Dear Editor;

It is amazing how one little mistake can lead to so much trouble.

My wife and I drove from Canadá to Panama in our motorhome, passing through both Costa Rican frontiers on the PanAmerican highway. Entering this beautiful country we were informed that we could stay up to three months but, if we left and returned within 90 days with our vehicle, we would have to transit through the country in three days. Our vehicle permit was so annotated.

(I was surprised because in Nicaragua we had met several people living in Costa Rica who, in order to avoid paying import duties on their vehicles, drove out of the country and were planning to stay out for at least three days before returning.)

That "out of country for 90 days" regulation costs Costa Rica a lot of Colones, most of which are not spent in hotels and restaurants but in gasoline stations, brake shops, auto-parts stores, mercados and supermercados and for works of local artisans, often in remote places not usually visited by tourists.

A Canadian couple we met in Liberia hadn't understood the regulation and after previously rushing through to Panamá for a family celebration, they were disappointed to learn that they could not now visit Costa Rica. Talking with the Canadian Consulate, other Canadians with vehicles have also been unable to revisit Costa Rica. Pity! That regulation short-changes both Costa Ricans and visitors.

We returned to your country on the Caribbean coast, via Sixaola from Chiriquí Grande, a memorable adventure. Sixaola is a very small customs detachment. When we presented our passports and papers—including the original vehicle permit—Sixaola customs informed us that it was unable to give us a new tourist card. It didn't have the authority (even though the necessary computer, printer and forms were in evidence).

Instead, we received a transit visa, or some such similar thing. We also had to have a representative from the Civil Policia accompany our vehicle to Limón, for which privilege we had to pay ¢4.500. That just about used up the Colones we had budgeted to buy a model oxcart in Grecia-Sarchí.

Upon our arrival in Puerto Limón, while I was finding a place to park that suited customs personnel, the policeman presented our 'transit visa' to someone and re-processing began. I never got an opportunity to explain the situation as I understood it. Three and a half hours later we discovered that (1) a second custodian was required to accompany us to the Nicaraguan border, for another ¢13-17.000 and (2) we would get our papers, which had been prepared by an import-export agency without consultation with us, after we paid an additional ¢10.000.

At that point I was confused. All I wanted was a free tourist permit for my motorhome. What the he-- was going on? We didn't have that many colones, Balboas, dollars, or whatever.

The requirement for a custodian (I'm 1.9 m tall but he was much bigger and it wasn't all muscle) was eventually cancelled when, in broken español, I finally made his superior understand that there was no second bed in our motorhome, that there is only one room with an over-the-cab bed, that in the privacy of our home my wife and I sleep with only a thin sheet over us because of the heat, that we had almost no food because we planned to buy much cheaper supplies in Nicaragua, and that our drinking water came from a Panamanian gas station.

Later, I was arguing about payment with the agency's representative and his boss in the middle of a sidewalk when they asked someone who spoke English to translate. That was when I learned that yet another transit visa paper had been prepared.

This good Samaritan—he never did give his name—took me back to Customs and explained to several people what had happened, and that I didn't need a transit visa but only tourist papers. I overheard him say something like "El turista pago, pago, sempre pago" in a voice heavy with frustration. (My not being able to speak español is very frustrating for both myself and those I have to talk with, but I think he said "The tourist pays, pays, always pays.")

Eventually, with the help of a bilingual employee, I was told to come back next day. They didn't know what could be done because the paperwork couldn't be cancelled even though it wasn't needed. I stated I wasn't going to pay, period!

Then I discovered that my custodian had taken his money and returned to Sixaola, that I couldn't legally drive my vehicle, that if the police asked for papers I didn't have I could end up in jail and have my motorhome confiscated, that I couldn't park on Customs property, and that parking overnight in downtown Limón is not the smartest thing for a tourist to do.

That night I was so angry about the mistake, the confusion, the danger, and the need to pay for someone else's error that I got the names and addresses of several local newspapers, radio stations and TV stations. I already had a number for a Canadian international short-wave radio program. I was going to go public about idiotic bureaucracy not being able to, or not being willing to, correct its own mistakes.

Next morning I phoned the Canadian Consulate and spoke of my intentions. They told me that it might help but that they certainly couldn't endorse the idea. They also mentioned that I could get a lawyer, but it would cost more than the custom charges.

Back at customs, I got to speak again with another person who spoke English, and he arranged for a meeting with his superior. I also talked several times with the agency representative who rightly wanted some money for his work, but I told him that I wasn't going to pay because it was a customs mistake and they could pay. By now I was fuming.

When I walked into the administrator's office, I spoke quietly. Really I did, although clenched teeth and pulsing veins might have given away my true feelings. I gently put some newspapers and magazines on a desk, in plain view of everyone.

I started out by stating that I didn't want to embarrass anybody, that it was a custom's mistake, that I wasn't going to pay, that I would live in my motorhome until this was resolved, that I needed water and electricity at least once a week, and since I couldn't move my vehicle, I probably needed permission from the city to park over a sewer, and . . .

At that point it was suggested that I calm down so that the two customs administrators could have discussions and make some phone calls. Eventually, with input from several people, I was told that the agency had magnanimously agreed to forgive their charges, the paperwork could now go ahead, and I had to wait only a few minutes. Liz visibly relaxed; we weren't going to be handcuffed and dragged off to jail after all.

We waited. The last signatures were collected. I got my papers, and we were free to travel by ourselves to Nicaragua within three days.

This has been a long story, and one I hope doesn't happen too often to too many people. I'm no longer mad, but I am still frustrated because of a small mistake that lead to so many unnecessary problem and expense.

The real hero of this incident was the 'man-off-the-street' who listened to both sides of a story – one in español, one in English – and took time to help a tourist.

¡Muchas gracias! el Señor Desconocido.

Many thanks Mr. Unknown.

C275

Panama

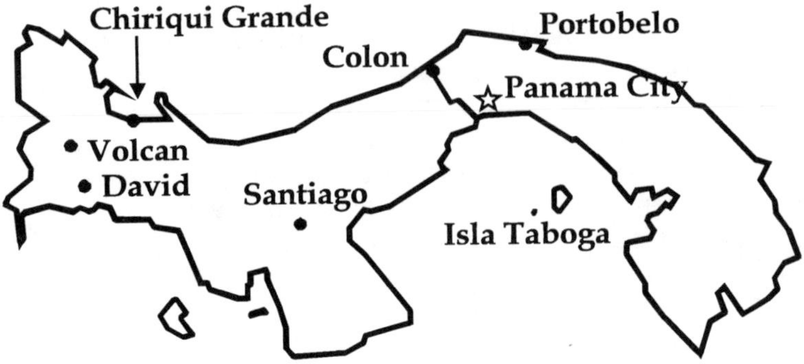

Chiriqui Grande
Colon
Portobelo
Panama City
Volcan
David
Santiago
Isla Taboga

FEDERAL RESERVE NOTE
THE UNITED STATES OF AMERICA
THIS NOTE IS LEGAL TENDER FOR ALL DEBTS, PUBLIC AND PRIVATE
G 20923778 T
WASHINGTON, D.C.
G
G 20923778 T
ONE DOLLAR

Panamá

Border Crossing: Costa Rica to Panamá

Paso Canoas is a simple border crossing. The only problem is that the number of people passing through is so large that waiting in line can consume hours. En route to the border we managed to pass two buses, but unfortunately there was one already there ahead of us.

In Costa Rica there are two processing lines, one for entering and one for exiting. Both are fed from one long line outside of an office, so it pays to check to see where the delay is. There was no charge to leave the country and they didn't care about any paperwork for our motorhome and motorcycle. All they did was stamp our Passport and send us on our way.

Panamá was almost as easy. First we had to go to the Tourist Office to get road maps, brochures and our 30 day tourist cards (US$ 5.00 each). Then we walked around a corner to Immigration to get our passports stamped (no charge), then next door to Customs (Aduana) to get paperwork for each vehicle. As always, we checked them very carefully! There is no charge for this, and I ignored hints about money. Finally we had to back track a few steps to Transito where they entered information in a note book, and where they did not charge for this seemingly unnecessary service.

Putting a tape recorder in plain view—ostensibly so I could record the conversation as background material for my book—really cut down on requests for money. Imagine that!

Once all that was done, we drove a few metres, stopped, and paid the required U$ 3.00 to have the wheels and undercarriage of our motorhome fumigated. We closed our windows because they did a thorough job. Then it was off down the highway where, 4 km later, highway police stopped us and checked all our papers. Then and only then were we free to speed along a concrete highway.

Fuel and Propane

The following values have been used to calculate equivalent prices in Canada. The exchange rate was US$ 1.00 = Can$ 1.42 and 1 US gallon = 3.76 Litres. As of March 1995 representative prices were:

	Panamá	Canada
Regular	U$ 1.68/USgal	Can$ 0.63/L
Premium	U$ 1.79/USgal	Can$ 0.68/L
Propane	U$ 1.41/USgal	Can$ 0.53/L

Gasoline in Costa Rica was cheaper than here, I should have filled up at that Texaco station immediately prior to crossing the border.

Regular gasoline and diesel are available in Chiriquí Grande at prices only moderately higher than in David (Da-veed).

Propane can be bought in David, a town close to the border with Costa Rica. We stayed on the PanAmerican Highway rather than venturing into the centre of David. Very shortly after driving around an initial highway curve and before seeing the Kentucky Fried Chicken franchise on the left, we blundered upon the propane plant on our right. Being Sunday, it was closed. However, we did get propane there on our return trip.

Heading towards our ultimate destination, the Panamá Canal, we bought propane just past Divisa (and the Los Santos - Chitré turnoff) en route to Aguadulce.

Credomatic - ISTMO

In Panamá, you can use both VISA and Master Card at Banco de ISTMO. There is no charge for that service; Costa Rica charged US$ 5.00 per transaction and Nicaragua's Club Credomatic charged 5% of the amount requested.

Bypassing David on the PanAmerican (also called TransAmerica) Highway, we drove past a Kentucky Fried Chicken franchise on our left and immediately turned right at the next major intersection. ISTMO was to our left, on the corner, next to an excellent supermarket.

There is also an ISTMO on the main street in Santiago and, of course, several in Panamá City.

First Impressions of Panamá

The Paso Canoas border crossing took 2 1/2 hours, but at least an hour was due to our making coffee, chatting and preparing for money changers while waiting for lunch hour to pass.

The concrete highway is well marked and in excellent condition, although it is only two lanes wide with no shoulders and deep drop-offs in a few places. Being concrete with joints between sections, the highway reminded me of riding a train on non-welded tracks—clickety-click, thumpity thump—and became quite annoying.

There could have been more distance-to-go signs, but we soon realized more signs were not needed because there was nothing ahead. We were reminded of our long-ago drive on the TransCanada Highway from Stephensville to Saint John, Newfoundland: boring. I felt as if I were driving near Moose Jaw, Saskatchewan in late August. Grass was brown, lonely trees with dusty leaves could be seen everywhere, the climate was hot and dry, roads and fields were flat, and cruise control had no problem holding at 75-80 km/h. But it wasn't Saskatchewan; there were fewer villages and towns. Ho hum.

Liz and I both expressed the feeling that our tour of Panamá might merely consist of driving straight through to Panamá City, over the Bridge of Americas, and back to Nicaragua in a couple of weeks. Why wasn't that bridge closer to the border?

There was a constant, high wind blowing from cloud-covered mountain peaks on our left to the unseen beaches on our right. For a short time I thought my front wheels needed alignment—the steering wheel was canted counter-clockwise at 20-30 degrees—because our motorhome kept drifting to the right. With farms of electricity-producing windmills in this area, this country would never be short of power.

This country looks prosperous, not third world. Roadside billboards are common, at least as far as David. Roads and towns are clean with very little visible litter or garbage.

Gas is measured in US gallons, food is dispensed by pounds. Mercado prices for vegetables and fruit seem less than in Costa Rica. Oops, not so. Panamanian money is always the same as that of the USA; one Balboa (B.1.00) equals US $1.00.

Random Thoughts about Panamá

Liz and I are tiring of travelling. Nothing seems as exciting as it was even a couple of months ago.

If you leave the PanAmerican highway, south to Playa Las Lajas or a short distance north of San Felix, you might see many tall, leafy Cashew trees with hundreds of bright red or yellow fruit, each with a pale green thumb-like nut affixed below. We were told not to eat the nut; it is poisonous until double-roasted. But do eat the fruit or squeeze it for its juice; it is deliciously tart with a refreshingly unique flavour. Take fruit from public trees that are between roads and private fences. If you can climb on top of your motor home, there'll be lots of fruit available where most people can't reach.

In Panamá City, some local bus tours are made using buses with only one windowed side; the other side is open and accessible from sidewalks. When the bus is moving chains are strung between seats to keep passengers from falling out. Each seat also has a liquor cupboard in front of it. Tourists can have a drink or three as they listen to music and colourful descriptions from their tour guide. Party time on wheels, a great idea!

Now having driven in every capital city in every country in Central America and Panamá, I believe that downtown Guatemala City is the worst.

In Chiriquí Grande we talked to crew members of a coastal tanker that was loading Alaskan crude oil to transport to Texas. That's like taking coal to Newcastle, fridges to Eskimos, or sand to a beach. Crude is unloaded at the Pacific side and piped overland to Chiriquí Grande because supertankers are too wide to use the Panamá Canal. There is some speculation about building a similar pipeline, and even a railroad for shipborne containers, across Honduras or Nicaragua because of potential problems in Panamá.

JOY dishwasher soap can be used in saltwater and still produce suds. One sailor uses saltwater to wash and rinse dishes, then gives them a final rinse in fresh water. On a sailboat, fresh water is always in short supply, and there are few refilling stations offshore.

We've driven over the Bridge of the Americas. It's too bad we couldn't fly back to Canada and avoid the long drive back.

Beaches of Panamá

The beaches of Panamá were disappointing because there are so few good ones. We saw none on the Caribbean side, and only two worth stopping at on the Pacific side.

We did visit several beaches, including the supposedly beautiful Playa Coronado, but we didn't stop for more than a few disappointing minutes at each. Playa Uverito near Playa Las Tablas was filthy. Another beach was contaminated and swimming was prohibited.

Contrary to our map's indication of asphalt, we drove 60 km of extremely dusty and rocky dirt road to the black sand of Playa Santa Catalina in Golfo De Montijo. Our rig shook so much that our family portrait crashed down and sent glass everywhere. The dust was so fine and so thick that by the time we reached the beach I could write my name and other four letter words on any flat surface or window.

While returning from the tiny fishing port of Santa Catalina, we had two flats and only one spare. In a hamlet 8 km off the road, I managed to buy a patched 15" inner tube for one of my 16.5" tubeless tires. It worked, for a while. But when the tube went flat in the middle of nowhere, I had to dismount our motorcycle then drive the last 15 km to Santiago where I finally got the tire repaired. I was balanced precariously high up on a wheel lashed to my motorcycle seat, and I got some mighty curious looks from those I passed.

Once back on blacktop, I stopped and shook clouds of dust out of the motor's air filter. We must be suckers for punishment, this was worse than the trip to Languín.

Although some Panamian buses are colourfully decorated, they come in a distant second to those in El Salvador.

I suggest you do NOT go to a Panamanian beach on Sundays or Mondays. As one Costa Rican acquaintance said, Sunday is the day that most Panamanians go to a beach and they really know how to litter. On weekends, expect thousands of people, noise, dust and maybe one stabbing or shooting. When a beach, any Panamanian beach, is deserted at dusk, it will be buried in plastic bags, plastic plates, plastic bottles, pieces of paper, and piles of uneaten foodstuffs. Those hired to clean the beaches on Monday need all day to do so.

However, during other days of the week, except festival days, the beaches are clean. Playa Santa Clara—only a couple of hours from Panamá City—has a beautiful white sandy beach bracketed by two rivers which are kilometres apart. At low tide, fresh or slightly salted water can be seen forming unusual patterns as it seeps out of the sand. At high tide, as is the case in all Pacific beaches, one has to be careful about riptides and currents.

Playa Las Lajas is another reasonable beach, and it is only a short distance from San Felix, 100 km from Costa Rica's border. We turned left past the Beach Club and parked near one of the several public palapas. The fine, dry sand is very soft and we had to choose our way carefully so as not to sink down to our axles. I helped push out a half ton truck and a small car that were stuck.

There are two reasonable public beaches on the Island of Taboga. The one to the right of the dock looks like it belongs to Hotel Taboga but it doesn't; at high tide that beach quickly disappears. The water is c-c-cold. The island can be reached by boats from Pier (Muelle) 18, located in the Balboa area of Panamá City. Pier 18 is also Pier 17 and Pier 19. A round trip costs US $10.00 per person.

If you can get a ride on a small boat or yacht transitting through the Panamá Canal, you might enjoy the fresh water of Gatun Lake. Diving and swimming from moored boats is not recommended, but when humidity is high and the temperature is 32°C or higher (90+°F) who cares?

On the Caribbean side, everyone says the San Blas Islands and Isla Grande are truly unique, with great beaches and water so clear that it seems you are swimming in air. It is necessary to travel on a dirt road, leave your rig behind and take a small boat to the islands. We didn't go because of time constraints, and have complained about our missing it ever since.

However, Portobelo was definitely worth driving to, but en route we should have ignored littered Playa Maria Chiquita. Although there is almost no beach at Portobelo, clean water is truly blue green only a few metres from shore. We rented a cayuco and paddled and swam in the middle of the bay and on the far side between two sailboats.

Line Handling in the Panama Canal

As much as we wanted to drive our motorhome through the Panamá Canal, we couldn't arrange it. Driving through the Canal is possible. We arrived two days too late to see an amphibious vessel—allegedly a stainless steel milk truck converted to motorhome and boat—pass through the locks during its around-the-world adventure.

But Liz and I did sail through the canal.

Friday dusk found us camped on Perico Island, one of three islands at the end of the Amador Causeway in Panamá City. Pat came by, knocked, and was invited in for a coffee. Eighteen years ago he had driven a beat up half-ton from USA and stayed in Panamá; some of his stories made us realize how easy we have had it during our trip. A Panamá Canal Pilot, Pat will be retiring soon, wants to drive back to USA, and was wondering what problems we had. We answered there was nothing that elimination of bureaucracy wouldn't cure.

When Pat heard that we were considering paying $45.00 each for a two hour boat trip through the Mira Flores Locks, he suggested we apply to work as line handlers instead. Great idea! But, uh, what's a line handler?

We learned that every vessel passing through the Canal must have a canal pilot and four persons (two at the bow, two at the stern) to throw or catch lines or ropes which are used to stabilize a boat/ship in the middle of the Canal locks. This prevents it from crashing into the sides of the locks or other vessels. When these locks fill with water at millions of gallons per minute, there are some very tricky currents. Small boats with small crews, such as fishing boats, yachts and sailing craft usually have to hire extra people as line handlers, at $40.00+ per transit.

Next morning we stopped in at the Balboa Yacht Club, struck up a conversation with the first person we met—a bearded 'old man of the sea'—and within minutes we were novice line handlers. His Captain and Mate had been negotiating with two 'boat bums' whom they obviously did not like and we were a godsend to them, ignorant landlubbers notwithstanding.

Their 10 m Ketch, painted black like Canada's original Bluenose, was battered from a storm and a near accident. It was going to pass through only the Mira Flores locks, then put up in San Pedro for repairs. It was scheduled to leave at 6:30 am. We could return by bus.

A quick meeting with the Club manager (Commodore? Admiral?) and it was arranged that we could park our motorhome in his parking lot overnight, and leave it there until our return next afternoon.

But first we had to drive to NOVEY's—an excellent hardware store, on par with any in North America—to buy some garden gloves. (Once there I just had to buy other bits and pieces that satisfied my craving for more "man's stuff".) Gloves were essential. Lines can be wet and dirty, and nylon rope zipping through bare fingers quickly leaves a stinging scar.

Then we drove to a sports store because I needed a new pair of runners. I had been putting off buying new shoes because, hey, sure, the soles of mine were cracked and flopping about, but they were OK for strolling on beaches or driving a motorcycle. Besides, my needing size 12s in countries where most men are shorter than my five foot five inch wife didn't make the task any easier either.

Although we had got lost going there, getting back to the yacht club was a breeze.

At about 8 p.m. one of the three crewmen came by, knocked, and asked if we could give their sailboat engine an electrical boost. A three-way electrical switch had been left in a wrong position for two days and both of their deep cycle batteries were completely discharged. Although taken aback, I said sure and disconnected one of my larger RV batteries. We picked up battery, cables, a crescent wrench and a flashlight, then staggered down 23 steps, along a 100 m wharf and into a launch which took us out to their darkened, unlit, black sailboat. Fortunately, the skipper could signal us with one of their own flashlights.

Five minutes work and their diesel engine was quietly turning over. (I wonder how many motorhomes have jump-started a sailboat?) Initial charging current from their generator was off the meter, which maxed out at 60 Amps, but it soon dropped. I picked up my battery, etc., hailed another launch, and left them happily enjoying their lights.

Early to bed, early to rise, coffee and egg salad sandwiches (the other 60% of my marriage always plans ahead), down to a darkened wharf, then to find a man to drive a launch to Fancy Free. As we climbed aboard at 6 am, we were informed that sailing time had been delayed at least an hour. Oh well, who likes to sleep in anyway? We, that's who.

But being early was OK because we had to familiarize ourselves with a sailboat, and we had to mark a new 600 foot line in four equal lengths. (It seems to me that too many Americans still refuse to recognise international metric standards of measure. But it is understandable. Twenty-five years after Canadá went metric, I still think in both units and prefer the British-American system.) Measurement was a little tricky on a short boat whose deck was cluttered with plastic cans of diesel, containers of water, a couple of bags, numerous short pieces of rope/line/hawser and a damaged, loosely tied Jib.

Canal pilot Jaiminéz arrived at 7:15, the diesel engine was started, mooring lines were dropped, and we and the three bachelor crewmen were on our way. Jaiminéz told us that we would tie up alongside a tug, and therefore we didn't need four long lines. That was great news because I think we would have had 2-150, 1-180 and 1-120 lengths.

We motored under the Bridge of Americas and then we were there, in the Panamá Canal, watching those mammoth locks slowly open. We seemed to be riding on a water-logged twig as Fancy Free moved slowly between towering concrete walls and next to our designated tug. Now I think I know how Pinocchio and Jonah felt as, in psychological slow motion, they watched whales open their mouths and swallow them whole. As we secured ourselves to our tug, those rusty but original gates closed, and we began to rise slowly.

Twenty-nine feet in eight minutes is slow enough that it is difficult to watch the water level rising, but certainly fast enough to be noticed when you look away for a few seconds then suddenly realize that those walls have indeed become lower. 59,000,000 gallons of fresh water from manmade lakes fed through one 80 ft diameter tube creates significant turbulence; it felt good to be snugged up to a tug.

Rising up from the depths, waiting for the locks to fill then open.

As the water level reached dry concrete, two locks at the other end ponderously opened and, temporarily released from our tug, we both eased into another canyon of concrete. We secured to the same tug again, directly below the Mira Flores Lookout. Yesterday, Liz and I had stood there and watched ships and boats float by below us. That was interesting, but being in the Canal, waving to other tourists from a sailboat as we inexorably rose up from the depths of eighty years of history, now that was really exciting. Those watching didn't know we were poor working line-handlers rather than filthy-rich tourists, and we didn't tell them.

Faraway, another pair of gates swung open. We untied for the last time and moved aside as the tug churned up water in a hurry to go somewhere. Then we gracefully moved up the canal almost to the second set of locks, turned into our destination, and hove to.

Our journey, slow though it was, was over. Sadness co-existed with excitement. Disappointment lurked beneath our desire to have seen more, to have sailed all of the canal.

But what the heck. We had reached and surpassed our goal. Fourteen months and eight countries after leaving Canadá —plus one transmission, a new fridge, a rebuilt storage compartment, one battery, a dozen flats, two tires, a roll of duct tape, and thousands of litres of gas later—we drove over the Panamá Canal. Not only that, but we sailed in it!

That's not too bad for a unilingual couple in their early fifties who had never owned a motorhome before. Not bad at all.

Portobelo

We had crossed the Bridge of Americas, visited and transitted through Mira Flores Locks, so now what? Should we visit some museums and parks in Panamá City?

Not likely! Early on Liz and I decided that we really didn't like large cities with numerous unnamed streets and avenues that didn't meet at right angles. To keep our sanity we would rather miss a few tourist spots than fight traffic and one-way streets in crowded cities. So we opted to visit Portobelo on the Caribbean side.

It's easy to know when you are on the right highway, just follow the hundreds of signs advertising stores in the duty-free zone of Colón. They begin at least 30 km from that city.

After leaving the main highway for Portobelo we saw a few beaches but, even after months of living in Central America, they seemed awfully littered and unkempt. Portobelo is a small town without much to see or do, but there are a couple of ruins to visit and a beautifully clear bay to swim in.

The best fort is the first one, which is also a great spot for dry camping or picnicking. We drove out onto a tiny but flat spit of land and were surrounded on three sides by water, no more than a metre from our trailer. To walk past our chairs we had to walk on rocks or get our feet wet. Looking out from our dining table, we had the impression we were living in a house boat: water, water everywhere, and all of it Caribbean blue.

One of several, narrow, safe but noisy, wood-planked bridges en route to Playa Maria Chiquita and Portobelo.

Although it is hard to believe, one local claimed that there is still ancient gold buried nearby. He claimed to have found some old coins, which he took to a bank and received US $8,000; later he read that they were worth closer to US $35,000. Supposedly there was also some modern gold from a bank robbery stashed in a nearby culvert, but it was discovered and disappeared before the police got there.

In the afternoon we arranged to rent a cayuco, a hollowed-out log canoe, from two young teens for U$5.00. Next morning and most of the day, Liz and I paddled across the bay, walked the cayuco over a sand bar, and slowly worked our way up a river for several kilometres. For a while we were in virgin jungle, with nothing but brown water drifting between meandering banks covered with brush, vines and some flowers. Occasionally birds flew overhead or unexpectedly burst out from behind leaves.

Once, when close to a left bank, we heard a tremendous splash and huge ripples moved outwards from a maze of tree roots. Crocodile! Well maybe. We never did see it, but surely no bird or fish could make that much noise. It amazes me how, in 1995, we could tip over, disappear, and no one would ever find our remains. I suppose eventually the boat would drift into the bay and people would realize we were gone. Ah well, we are born to die, and I'd rather do it on vacation than in a stress-filled office.

That's our motorhome, as seen from a rented cayuco.

A young man and his dog drifted downstream in a really tiny cayuco—now that would have been a super souvenir to carry on our roof —and they reminded us that even in a jungle river one is never truly alone.

Eventually we decided we'd paddled enough, so we stopped and settled back on our pillows. Slowly, ever so slowly, under a hot afternoon sun in a cloudless sky, with only occasional bird songs or a flutter of hidden wings, we drifted back down the muddy river. Lazy? You betcha. Sometimes the prow would catch on a clump of weeds or a submerged log so we let the cayuco spin around and continue drifting backwards until the prow swung around again.

But all good things must come to an end, and we had to paddle out into the delta, get out and walk across yet another part of the sandbar, then paddle out into the middle of the turquoise bay. We had worked so hard that it was absolutely essential we throw out an anchor — a stone tied to lots of 50# fish line — and slip below those cool blue-green ripples highlighted with flashing diamonds. Having brought inner tubes, we floated much more than we swam. We watched in awe as a school of fish literally flew over the water, soaring tens of metres before relaunching themselves from the water, again and again and again. Eventually we had to head to shore, but we stopped for awhile to watch a Manta Ray undulate by just above the sandy bottom.

While we were gone a mother and two married daughters had adopted our lawn chairs while their children played in nearby shallow waters. Hey, no problem. We'd left the chairs out in the open in the minuscule space in front of our motorhome, hadn't we? They thanked us and gave them back.

Next day, the boys came back for their cayuco and we packed up and drove away. Well, not quite.

As I backed off our miniature peninsula and turned onto the grassy field behind, Liz warned "Don't go too far, it looks soft.". As I eased backwards, methought to meself "Sure sure Love. Grass is grass. Sshee..". I changed thoughts in midstream, converting "..eesh" to "..eet", as all four rear wheels sank down until the differential, the axle, the rear bumper and much of the truck frame came to rest on that lovely carpet of green grass. It seems that I had backed onto a rivulet and the soil was sopping wet beneath the grass. Liz was right again, darn it!

It took over an hour of digging and stuffing anything available — boards, branches, stones, gravel, shells — under the wheels in sufficient quantity so I could drive forward onto harder ground. Jacks on 8x10 boards just pushed the boards deeper under the grass without raising the trailer one little bit. My hands were scratched, bloody, black and muddy. So were my clothes.

Not once did my Love say "I told you so", so she lived another day. Nothing is more frustrating that being absolutely and totally wrong and the only one to blame is yourself!

Ah well, I'm learning to take good with bad, and vice versa.

Transitting the Panamá Canal

While camped at Portobelo, our motorhome was noticed by a group of sightseeing US tourists, who came over for a brief visit. One of the men has an old converted school bus and would like to take his family on a trip such as ours, so he asked a lot of questions. And now, with our encouragement, he probably will.

During our conversations, we mentioned how we had become line-handlers and how much we had enjoyed our transit through the Mira Flores Locks. "Would you like to do it again?" we were asked. Instantly we replied "Of course, when and where?". Two days later we were aboard a clean, organized, 43 ft sloop christened Small Change and guaranteed food, beer and lodging in the captain's cabin for two days and two nights.

Unbelievable!! We started our trip in Mexico by riding on the front of a locomotive throbbing its way through La Barranca del Cobre, and now we were going to finish by silently sailing easterly—yes, easterly—through the Panamá Canal, from the Atlantic to the Pacific! Unbelievable.

Due to previous problems with a Canadian motorhome, we could not park in Colón's Panamá Yacht Club. So we drove back to Panamá City and once again parked at the Balboa Yacht Club, then returned by bus to Colón and the enchanting Small Change.

Next morning, we crew hauled in our wobbly gangplank, untied and sailed out to waiting area 'F', anchoring next to a Green Peace boat. Promptly at 9 am, our pilot and a young trainee came aboard, we hauled anchor, and we were on our way.

Traffic in the locks can go two ways at once, although I think they usually use those side-by-side locks in the same direction. Being on an ocean-capable racing sail boat passing close by a towering 1500 passenger cruise ship certainly does put one's outlook into perspective. Humbling first comes to mind, then appreciation for the skills of men and women who sail little fibreglass bubbles from continent to continent, trusting only upon their skills and the probability of reasonable weather.

Our schedule called for us and a smaller boat to tie up alongside a larger steel-hulled ketch, then we three would drive into the locks as a single unit. Two ropes from the Chinese-red ketch and two from us would be necessary to keep us in the middle as turbulent water lifted and lowered us tens of feet. Plans change, the smallest boat tied up next to a tug. Which was just as well because otherwise it might have been crushed against concrete walls.

My job was to catch a light line thrown from atop the locks, tie our 1" stern line to it, ensure that that line played out cleanly as it was hauled to the top then, after it was looped over a stanchion, pull in the slack and help position both boats in the middle of the lock. Simple, especially since I could use a hand winch.

As I started to wind the rope counter-clockwise I realized that wouldn't work, so I had to unwind and rewind in the other direction. Meanwhile both boats were starting to drift so I quickly spun the winch handle and the rope jammed.

Jammed! No one had seen this happen before, how did I do it? Meanwhile, we were still drifting sideways. Tugging on the rope wouldn't release the jam, and the winch only turned one way. I left it, pulled on the rope to get rid of all slack and tied it to a cleat. The rope was too long, we were way off centre, but we stopped drifting.

Somehow, by unwinding the rope and tugging it, our pilot pulled the jam loose. Once again I wound the rope around the winch and started winding. Jammed! Oh no, not again. But I stopped quickly enough to be able to free the rope. This time the owner-captain at the helm saw the problem. The lines we were using were flexible anchor rope, not the usual stiffer hawsers, and in this type of winch they just wrapped themselves around the spindle. Solution? Simple. Use one hand to wind the winch and the other to guide the rope.

As the water level and boats rise it is necessary to constantly bring in the lines. I worked my line and slowly managed to winch both boats closer to the middle and away from the walls. The bow crewman had to work extra hard because he didn't have a winch. Whenever I managed to bring our stern closer to the middle, he would wait until the boats twisted or yawed in the turbulence and then pull in a bit more of his now slack rope.

Eventually I felt much better about my being a landlubber klutz.

The second set of gates went much easier (it's surprising how even a little experience helps), the last gate opened, both boats untied from the locks and each other, and we motored into the canal side-by-side. Use of "sails only" power is prohibited in the Canal. When our captain saw the red ketch unfurl its foresail, so did we, and the race was on. A big steel-hulled ketch with a big diesel is no match for a smaller, lighter sloop with a much smaller engine. Minutes later it was obvious that we had more speed—6.2 to 5.9 knots—and thereafter we maintained lead position.

Small Change had a newly installed GPS (Global Positioning Satellites) navigation system that could tell us where we were within 15 m. There is always some error. For example, I really don't think our hull was ever 38 m above water level. I had tested a similar system several years ago. During our transit, I managed to figure out many of its capabilities and showed their navigator a few new techniques.

Not that we needed a GPS to sail through Gatun Lake and Gillard Gut. Both are well marked by lights and buoys.

Building the Panamá Canal was a great engineering and logistical triumph. Americans completed what the French started but couldn't do, because they had 20 more years of technological advancement. And they discovered how Malaria spread. Even today it would be an undertaking worthy of international applause, just as is our massive Canadian James Bay hydroelectric project. But all that energy, all that concrete, all those deaths, all the sweat and tears and joys can only be appreciated in one's imagination.

I found it very hard to visualize that the land where the Canal goes was once level swamp land. Now the Canal is surrounded by hills, hills made by men and horses and mules and trains and earth-movers and dredges digging millions of cubic metres of rock and earth out of a gigantic trench and dumping it off to one side. Much of downtown Panamá City is built on Canal soil. I could see those hills but I couldn't live their history.

Because of our late start, we had to stop and overnight in Gatun Lake. We anchored outside of the marked channel fairly close to a weedy shore. Several massive shadows rumbled in the dark of night, the most surprising ship being a trans-Pacific car carrier that look like a huge gigantic shoe box. Honest!

A light breeze kept mosquitos and noseeums away but wasn't brisk enough to keep us from sweating. Crewpersons are not allowed to swim in Gatun Lake because of potential limb-severing bites from crocodiles. We hadn't seen any, it was hot, the lake looked cool so, one by one, we all jumped in for a quick swim. Liz and I had several minutes by ourselves.

Try to imagine a couple in their fifties who have rarely been outside of Canadá and the United States, who couldn't speak Spanish, who are almost broke, who had never owned a motorhome before, who never owned a sailboat, and who were splashing about in the Panamá Canal under the Southern Cross while hoping that those stories about crocodiles weren't true. If you ever wondered why we started this trip, there's your answer. We didn't know what was going to happen, but we knew it would be different!

Next morning, once again we were scheduled to sail through the last two sets of locks as a threesome. As always in the Canal, timing was critical. When the third small boat tried to join up with us as we motored along at 5 knots, a crewman failed to secure a bow line in time, there was a moment of great concern as it's bow swung wide. Suddenly it was behind us, stern to stern. I don't know how long they had to wait before they could enter the locks again.

But we were in the locks and securely centred almost immediately. (Time has a different and slower meaning on sailboats.) Water levels dropped and rope had to be played out instead of pulled in. That is really very easy to do and requires very little strength. Liz performed her bow duties admirably, not once having to ask for assistance. Now she and I were both truly qualified line handlers.

OK. Just where are your alleged certificates or diplomas?

As we sailed under power out of the locks and past the San Pedro Yacht Club, we saw our first boat, Fancy Free, tied up and forlornly awaiting its turn at dry dock. Unfortunately, we saw none of its friendly crew.

Into the Mira Flores Locks, down 81 ft in two stages, and then we were motoring east towards the Pacific. Our captain was a little concerned about his tall racing mast hitting the Bridge of Americas, but we cleared it by a mere 60 m. Then into Balboa Yacht Club moorage (they never did answer radio calls so we moored where we wanted), into a launch, onto a floating wharf, up a few stairs, past customs, and finally Liz and I were back in our home on wheels.

Behind were new friends and many, many memories. Panamá started off as a boring drive, but ended up by providing a once-in-a-lifetime experience.

We sailed the Panamá Canal.

Hotel Bambito

You really should take the drive to Volcan and Cerro Punta, then stop at Hotel Bambito for lunch or supper. Liz and I think it is the prettiest place in Panamá.

And it's cool. As we climbed away from the PanAmerican Highway and rumbled up that narrow, steep and curving asphalt secondary road to Volcan, hot, dry and windy quickly changed to cool and breezy. Nighttime temperatures were in the low sixties so Liz and I slipped under a quilt for an hour or so just as the sky began to lighten above the mountain peaks.

We were lucky. Our torn and worn guide book was slightly out of date, else we would never have discovered Hotel Bambito.

According to our book, Volcan has a small, secluded swimming hole—spring fed by clear and very cold subterranean water—that can only be reached by walking to the end of an unpaved road. It is a secret place where lovers meet. Because Liz and I are only in our 29th year of honeymoon we just had to go.

Big mistake! That secret place is a city park with baseball, softball and soccer fields, restaurants, two small swimming pools, and a large swimming hole on the other side of an earthen dam. On weekends, hundreds of people drive in through both the entrance and exit gates and along a one-way paved street. This makes for some interesting situations because most cars park on both edges of that narrow paved road.

But the drive to Volcan was worth the time and effort, especially after three weeks of monotonous driving on Panamá's flat roads at the end of a dry season. This elevated land appears to be a greengrocer belt of Panamá, a veritable mirage in dusty Panamá only a few kilometres from humid, hot and dusty Pacific beaches. Within minutes of turning off that long, monotonous ribbon of concrete PanAmerican highway, flat, dull, dry, brown lands changed to green grass, flowering shrubs, and cultivated hillsides filled with potatoes, tomatoes, cabbages, lettuce, carrots, celery, strawberries, and oranges. En route to Cerro Punta, grassy fields provided lunch for offspring of Kentucky Derby winners.

By the way, if black Fransesa berries (they look like huge black raspberries) are being sold on the roadside by an orange coloured footbridge when you drive by, stop and buy some before the locals get them all. They are delicious.

As we rounded yet another curve we were amazed to see beautifully landscaped lawns surrounding a luxurious hotel in the middle of nowhere. There was no town, no village, nary a house. There was only this massive hotel resting in shadows cast by towering valley walls.

We often wondered what the rich folks do; now we know. They enjoy good meals at a fair price (at least during off-season) and they scramble around tennis courts, sweat in saunas, soak in hot tubs and swim in indoor pools. After walking on landscaped lawns between terraced lakes complete with geese and ducks, beneath high lookouts amid leafy trees, some fall asleep listening to sounds of a manmade waterfall.

So what did we two poor gypsies do? We parked overnight in the hotel's paved parking lot and did what the rich folks do. It was a relaxing change, and worth every centavo of the much reduced rate we were offered.

Yes, even mistakes can turn out all right. Volcan was a disappointment. But the road to it was a refreshing change from the monotonous lowlands, and it took us to fabulous Hotel Bambito.

Young enterpreneurs will sell anything.

Chiriquí Grande

Chiriquí Grande on the Caribbean has one major attraction: it is possible to travel by ferry to Almirante, then by road to Costa Rica.

That 92 km of asphalt from the PanAmerican highway to Chiriquí Grande was an interesting drive. One third passed through brown, desert-dry level ranch land. The second third was a cool, twisting climb up to 1100 m and past a dam near the Continental Divide. The last third was a downhill road damaged by massive runoffs that quickly levelled off and wandered through damp green tropical jungle. The changes were instantaneous.

Such massive, such gigantic rhubarb probably exists nowhere else except on this highway. Hu-mung-us!

While climbing I began to wonder if my spark plugs were fouling because our 7.5L engine didn't seem to have much power. But when we quickly passed two trucks labouring in bull low, I stopped worrying. How easy it is to get tricked into thinking a steep grade is only a gradual incline.

If you can get used to the litter this is a quaint little community. This was one of the poorest and dirtiest villages we've seen in Panamá. Many of the beach-front houses are built on stilts over the ocean and two or more small creeks that empty into the bay. Elevated outhouses drop their business directly into those waters.

Nevertheless, an excellent photo opportunity exists after walking to the end of town and up a small hill. It still amazes me how distance can change the look of a place for the better.

Once in Chiriquí, it took Liz and me some time to determine when a ferry (un trasbordador) would leave for Almirante. Only after talking with several piple (oops, I'm phonetically acclimatizing to español, I mean people) did we realize that the freshly painted schedule over the locked door of the unused office was incorrect. There is only one large ferry on Monday and Tuesday, not two as indicated. The smaller ferry can squeeze in 8 - 10 trucks, the larger, 15-20. The ferry schedule posted at the PanAmerican highway turnoff was also wrong but, on 20/20 hindsight, it was being repainted. It might be correct next time we drive by.

Another sign indicated U$ 65.00 for our 4500 kilogram vehicle, plus U$ 4.00 per person. Quite reasonable for a 5 hour, 55 km ocean trip where few motorhomes have gone before. It was even better after I convinced them we weighed only 3.8 tons and paid U$ 45.00. I love to barter.

From Almirante we could get a small tour boat to Boca Del Toro for a day trip.

Both ferries are always full, and it is necessary to wait in line on the highway if you want to get aboard. Security is good, and a person takes licence plate numbers to ensure that no one tries to jump the line. At 3 Pm we were third for next day's 1:30 Pm departure. Overnight nine more trucks formed up behind us.

At the wharf—a narrow unpaved street which abruptly stops at a weathered concrete wall with two tie-down posts—we saw a huge dugout canoe carrying unplaned lumber from a saw mill located somewhere in distant hills. That canoe must have been 13 m long, 1.6 m deep, and 1.3 m wide; what a tree that was! I wonder if those superb boat makers were able to carve a second, smaller fishing boat from the unwanted wooden core? And maybe even a third, two-man cayuco?

Chiriquí Grande is not in the province of Chiriquí, as I would have expected. It is a great place to get caught up on one's letter writing while waiting for a ferry to a most unusual international border crossing.

Sailing the Caribbean in a Class C

Sailing the Caribbean was more fun than sailing through the Panamá Canal because we did it in our motorhome.

Liz and I gambled, and we won.

Although we had asked several people in various parts of Panamá, we never could determine if we could get our 7m motorhome on the ferry at Chiriquí Grande. Nor did we find out if we could then drive to Costa Rica. So we left Volcan, drove to David, said the heck with it, and drove over 100 km and parked in a lineup for next afternoon's ferry. Once we realized that tractor trailers were able to get on we knew we could too.

A good night's sleep; a breakfast of eggs, bacon, mangoes, papaya, sandia (watermelon) and honey-dew melon; some conversation; some typing on the computer; all these helped to pass the hours, but we finally decided it was time for a walk. When we got back, an unhappy and frustrated man with a portable radio told us to drive immediately to the ferry. It was an hour ahead of departure time and the two trucks in front of us were still silent, but we did as commanded.

Guiltily, we zoomed down to the end of a narrow dusty road that acted as a wharf, then stopped and waited and waited while foot passengers got on first and a ferry crewman determined how much to charge us. Three trucks lined up behind us. Waiting gave us time to realize that we couldn't drive onto the ferry. High tide and an empty boat produced a steep ramp that guaranteed we would drag our rear bumper and rip off the black and grey water drain pipe.

Once more a frustrated crewman sighed deeply and asked us to back up and park off to one side so other trucks could drive on first. In a Congo Line, all four of us backed up. Then I parked off to one side, close to the water, coming to rest at a 20^0 list. That almost emptied our freshly made pot of stew, but Liz caught it as it started to slide, stubbing two toes during her rescue mission.

Two fully loaded trucks went by, the ferry's bow dipped lower, we got the sign and we cautiously drove onto the steel deck. Immediately arms began waving, hand signals were given, and rapid Spanish was spoken. Neither Liz nor I had any idea of where they wanted us to park. Forward, back, turn left, turn right, now left, backup, right, forward, alto, stop. Finally we understood, and proceeded to jam our rig behind one truck and immediately next to the starboard gunwale. When finish- ed, we were 4 cm from the railing—the driver's mirror could have dropped unimpeded into the water—and our motorcycle was even closer to the truck ahead of us. There was room for only a suitcase and a couple of boxes behind us.

The truck on the right was transporting (& selling)watermelons.

During the next hour, fourteen other vehicles were driven on, shunted forward, back, forward, sideways, right turn, backward, left turn, forward, etc., etc. until all were within centimetres of each other. One truck had soapy water poured over its front wheels so that crewmen could push it sideways on the now slippery steel deck. A short truck, a last minute arrival, had to drive on backwards so that he could swing his front end into a wedge shaped area, which just happened to be available close to us. The boat crew couldn't completely raise the loading ramp, the truck's bumper was in it's way.

Obviously foot passengers got on first because they could not have taken their luggage with them once the trucks were crammed aboard.

We were trapped inside, and had to escape the wet heat. Although Liz and I were prepared to climb out the driver's window, we discovered that, by exhaling, we could squeeze out the side door and between two trucks. From there we could walk on the bumper of the last truck, climb up onto a two foot high ledge to gain access to our roof ladder and scramble onto our roof. We had tied one lawn chair to the ladder and stored one tire and one tube on the roof.

We spent almost four hours up there alternating between lounging in a chair or curled up inside a blown up tire tube, with hats to keep off the sun, with a 12 knot breeze to keep away bugs and perspiration, with cool beer and juicy watermelon to ward off dehydration, and an unimpeded, magnificent view of sky and water.

We were floating above and sailing in the Caribbean in our Class C. A "C" asea. "Ah sí."

As the sun shone over our shoulders, shadows on the deep gun-metal blue waters were encased in a misty halo.

Depending where we were—in deep water, in a shallow bay, beside sandbars or close to mangrove trees—these Caribbean waters constantly changing from blue to turquoise to lime-green to invisibility above a ghostly white bottom.

Occasionally a momentary breeze would fling thousands of glittering diamonds across the surface. Or large fish would explode from the deeps—sometimes lunging completely out of water, sometimes merely splashing about—and cast out a few more rhinestones.

We always sailed within sight of land, but sometimes we had to look hard to see those distant hills turned cloudy blue.

Being at the front on the ferry, high above gunwales of steel and with smaller trucks hidden beneath the edge of our trailer roof, we needed very little imagination to pretend we were sailing alone in Laguna de Chiriquí. Are there still pirates out there?

We spent the last couple of hours weaving our way between high islands covered in banana plantations, low islands with houses built on stilts (one or two were restaurants, serving cool? cervezas) and thousands of mangrove swamps where no land was visible beneath the trees.

Even out here in seemingly virgin jungle and bayous, women and children were seen often. Or at least their houses or laundry were. Sometimes fishermen in cayucos would suddenly appear from a tiny passage, or be seen paddling beside mangroves or checking their nets. Once or twice a power boat would zoom by with four or five people returning our wave. Slightly more often, a large fibreglass boat with two big outboards lumbered by loaded down with several families, groceries, barrels of water or gasoline, and dogs or goats.

Many seaside houses were nothing but a thatched roof above a wooden floor; there were no walls. Houses built on land, higher than storm-driven waves, were usually more substantial. A few had walls made from planed wood covered with sun bleached paint, but always the roofs were thatched palm.

At last, at long last that nonetheless seemed too soon, we rounded the final bend (again!) and Almirante slowly revealed itself. Tendrils of smoke appeared, gradually followed by buildings, trucks, houses, TV antennae, cars, people and litter.

We docked, several trucks unloaded and then we were free to leave our magical sailing-carpet behind. It took several attempts to unwedge ourselves from beside the gunwales, much to the consternation of one deckhand, but finally we drove down the steel ramp onto an asphalt street. It quickly disappeared into rutted dirt and water-filled potholes and just as quickly reappeared as a smooth highway that went all the way to Costa Rica.

"Take care." is said all too often. We prefer "Take a risk, it's more fun." We did, and we sailed the Caribbean in our motorhome. You could too.

Final Impressions of Panamá

Once we had driven over the Panamá Canal, which had been our destination and goal for all those months, mild depression set in.

After fourteen months of travelling, Liz and I were bored with coconut trees, banana plantations, piles of rocks masquerading as archaeological wonders, mediocre beaches, crowded cities and littered towns. We were tired of driving thousands of kilometres, tired of dusty roads, and tired of fixing innumerable flats. We were tired of being stared at, tired of attempts of mordida and bribery, tired of having to struggle to be understood, tired of poverty, tired of people. We were tired of being broke. We were tired of a hot tropical sun, tired of sweating, tired of having only limited water for showers.

We were vacationed out.

But even with all that, we still enjoyed being line handlers aboard two boats sailing the Panamá Canal, and we certainly enjoyed the magical ferry ride in the Caribbean.

Panamanians are friendly people, always willing to talk and ready to help.

And hey, we did have some fun.

Just before Lent, Panamanians celebrate the joy of living. One of their harmless activities is for children to throw water on passersby, whether they were walking or driving. Of course the water isn't cold, but it is still a shock to experience a litre of water entering an open window of a vehicle doing 50 km/hr.

My first attempt at friendly revenge was thwarted when I tried to throw a potful of water through a closed window. With my hair soaked and water dripping off my nose and ears, I did not need to hear resounding laughter from my beloved.

My second try was more successful. We had driven by a bridge near Río Piedras and seven kids had soaked us good. We had seen them and almost closed both cab windows in time. A couple of kilometres later, I stopped, went back to a cupboard, got out four balloons, and filled them with chilly water from our fridge. Then I asked Liz to drive back while I hid on the rear bumper, with one arm through the ladder for safety and the other holding those balloons.

As she drove onto the bridge those water-hurling creatures rushed at her again, and she stopped. At the same time I leapt off the bumper, ran around to the front of the rig and started throwing water balloons. The squeals of surprise and the amazed looks would have been enough reward, even if one of my watery missiles hadn't found a fleeing target. Out of ammunition, I ran towards the biggest fellow and tried to grab his five gallon pail. I wasn't fast enough and I got drenched, but at least I had the satisfaction of throwing his empty pail into the river (after making sure that it was tied to the bridge). Quickly I retreated back to our motorhome, jumped inside, and we sped away.

That'll teach those kids not to ambush a 50+ Canadian who is still a child at heart. When they stop laughing, that is.

Border Crossing: Panamá to Costa Rica

Leaving Almirante and the ferry Palanga behind was like saying good bye to an old friend, and the thought of having to drive to Sixaola wasn't all that exciting either. After all, we would have only three days in Costa Rica and it would take at least two full days to drive across the country. What a pity we couldn't stopover at Manzanillo again.

As we drove up and down and around hills covered in leafy trees, dark vines growing overhead on electrical wires, tall thick grass, lush elephant ear plants, and row-upon-row of banana plantations, the light overcast and occasional misty rain mirrored our grey emotions.

A banana commuter train—eight rows of wood benches in each of five, narrow-gauge cars covered by a green roof supported by cast iron forgings—rattled by. It reminded us of a city park bandstand. It momentarily aroused our desire to go for a ride, but what would we see in this mist and rain?

Having covered 50 km in a little over an hour, darkness of night was ready to crush down upon us as we drove into Changuinola. As we rounded a highway curve, mirrored glass windows of a Catholic church displayed a large empty parking lot, so we pulled in and set up for the night.

The stew pot was placed on our rusty diffuser (and fabulous toast maker) which evenly spread the tiny blue flame peeking out of the rear propane burner, and Liz and I went for a short walk. Neither she nor I enjoy stew that hasn't simmered for at least one, flavour-enhancing day.

Behind the church we discovered a neat little subdivision, almost out in the middle of nowhere. For some undetermined reason, we both thought it looked like a company town. We saw only one car and two rusting truck frames in front of a couple of dozen, single-level concrete houses. Under a carport, next to a purple flowerbed, a father was fixing a tricycle as his little daughter looked on; suburbia of the late 1950's!

After a supper of hot thick tasty stew, bolillos (delicious handmade buns), fruit and yogurt, we went for another walk. I found one dark narrow path, beside a broken down building, beneath a huge tree whose roots had raised up chunks of sidewalk, and Liz reluctantly agreed to follow. I would never consider walking such a path in Canada or the USA, but here there was no sense of danger; it was just another locale to explore. At the far end were a pair of shiny railroad tracks and a Mom and Pop corner grocery store.

The Chinese owners, or at least their children, spoke excellent English but they did let us practice español. After fourteen months of travel, Liz and I would find ourselves speaking español to others while they would speak to us in English and, after parting company, we were never sure who spoke which language when.

From them we learned that it cost twenty-five cents for a 2 to 2 1/2 hour train ride through steep walled valleys and high above rushing rivers back to Almirante. The train would return to Changuinola at 4 pm, plus or minus an hour, depending how many stops it had to make. All we had to do was be right in front of their store at 5:30 am.

Tempting it was, but 5:30 came and went and still we slept on. After we finally got out of bed, showered, dressed and broke fast we headed north to the border. How surprised we were to discover that this town was much larger than we thought. We had parked in a subdivision that was separated from the main city by a banana plantation.

Downtown was large, with several stores on a busy main street-highway. Liz spied a large fabric store and I had to stop so quickly that I think we left tire marks on the black top. Four skirts and a blouse later I was allowed to drive on. On to an ESSO station where I filled up with premium gasoline and a lot of potable water, potable, that is, after adding a capful of chlorine bleach. I also talked with some friendly truck drivers and got instructions about which road to take to the border.

The instructions were clear, but I still took a wrong turn and quickly realized that I'd goofed. Back to the highway we went then on to Guabito on the Panamá side of the Sixaola River.

Guabito is a very small, one-street town. The only problem is that the one street is a dead end, lined with shops and a few curious people. Where is the road that goes to the bridge? For that matter where is the highway bridge? All I see is a dilapidated and unused railway trestle.

Oh. You mean that's it? But there is no way to get to it. Oh. You mean I have to drive along the tracks. But there's no ... Oh. You mean that dusty ramp up the side of the track bed is the road. Oh. Ok.

And so we drove back and left the highway before driving past those few duty-free stores, swayed up a bumpy ramp, straddled rusty train tracks, and bumped along railroad ties until we reached the bridge. Here the ties were, usually, covered by huge

This is part of the Caribbean road from Panamá to Costa Rica.

planks held down by six-inch spikes. Unfortunately several boards were broken or had pieces missing and an unnerving number of spear-like nails towered above the ties. Fortunately they did not puncture our tires. Why I don't know, but I'm not one to look a gift horse in the mouth so I'll never know. Further on, tens of wooden ties were replaced by short pieces of steel track loosely bolted on the bridge. What a clanging racket we made as we inched forward.

Although no one was on the bridge at the same time as we were, it was reassuring to see holes torn into heavy mesh protective screening in which those on foot could hide as vehicles lumbered past, almost scraping the steel supports holding the screens.

But it was not reassuring to look down and see muddy water through a hole where one piece of track was missing and to realize we had to drive over empty space. Even though knowing that Panamanian and Costa Rican vehicles did it every day was intellectually reassuring, it was emotionally frightening. But we did it. We had to.

Finally we escaped off the bridge and rocked to a halt in front of a customs building perched on a wider than usual piece of trackbed. No other vehicles were on the tracks. Liz and I disembarked and walked into a building where a young woman stamped our passports. Even now Liz and I aren't sure, but we think that was Panamanian customs.

Next we wobble-walked the rails for a few metres, crossed to the other side of the tracks, and entered a much larger building where we tried to get a tourist card or transit visa for Costa Rica.

The man there did not seem to know what to do with us. Apparently we were only the second motorhome to cross here in the last few years.

A long time went by. I had to go outside and move our rig off the tracks and ahead a couple of hundred metres where a dirt road was wide enough for a bus to pass, followed by a couple of trucks. Still we waited for our papers. Finally they were prepared but we had to wait for a policeman from the local constabulary. ¿Pourqué? Why?

It seems that we needed a special pass because we were returning to Costa Rica within 90 days of leaving it. He said he didn't have the authority to issue that pass, but we could get one in Puerto Limón. However, we couldn't go there on our own; we needed to be accompanied by a police officer who would make sure we didn't go somewhere else. (As if we would!!?) Of course, I had to pay for his time.

Eventually the policeman showed up. He took whatever papers were ready and we drove off and down to a dusty, rocky road. En route we stopped so he could visit his mother and drop off his laundry.

Eventually we came to blacktop and increased speed to 70 km/hr. Only once did we have to slow down and swerve around a broken down truck, but a now familiar presence of a tree bough in the middle of the road gave lots of warning.

En route to Puerto Limón we drove into Cahuita to buy a piece of delicious chocolate cake for each of us and, of course, a cup of coffee for me.

Being here again was like being back among old friends. Maybe if the policeman hadn't been with us we just might have gone back to Manzanillo for another visit after all.

We still might.

Index

Note. The letters in front of the page numbers are the first letter of a section; for example, **N** for **N**icaragua.

C

D

E

F

G

H

I

J

N

O

P

Q

R

S

THE END

(until we go back, and we will)

NOTES